An Outline of the Law of Evidence

by

SIR RUPERT CROSS, F.B.A., D.C.L.,

Solicitor; formerly Vinerian Professor of English Law in the University of Oxford

and

NANCY WILKINS

of Gray's Inn, and of the Midland Circuit, Barrister

FIFTH EDITION

LONDON
BUTTERWORTHS
1980

ENGLAND:	BUTTERWORTH & CO. (PUBLISHERS) LTD. LONDON: 88 KINGSWAY, WC2B 6AB
AUSTRALIA:	BUTTERWORTHS PTY. LTD. SYDNEY: 586 PACIFIC HIGHWAY, CHATSWOOD, NSW 2067 Also at MELBOURNE, BRISBANE, ADELAIDE and PERTH
CANADA:	BUTTERWORTH & CO. (CANADA) LTD. TORONTO: 2265 MIDLAND AVENUE, SCARBOROUGH, M1P 4S1
NEW ZEALAND:	BUTTERWORTHS OF NEW ZEALAND LTD. WELLINGTON: 77–85 CUSTOMHOUSE QUAY
SOUTH AFRICA:	BUTTERWORTH & CO. (SOUTH AFRICA) (PTY.) LTD. DURBAN: 152–154 GALE STREET
USA:	BUTTERWORTH (PUBLISHERS) INC. BOSTON: 10 TOWER OFFICE PARK, WOBURN, MASS. 01801

First Edition	*May* 1964
Second Edition	*February* 1968
Third Edition	*June* 1971
Reprinted	*March* 1973
Fourth Edition	*May* 1975
Fifth Edition	*July* 1980
Reprinted	*August* 1981
Reprinted	*June* 1985

ISBN Casebound: 0 406 57067 1
Limp: 0 406 57068 X

Printed in Great Britain by
Antony Rowe Ltd., Chippenham

Preface to Fifth Edition

The accounts of the following matters have been fairly drastically altered in this edition: refreshing memory (art. 22); legal professional privilege (art. 33); confessions (art. 46); public policy (art. 68); issue estoppel, or, more accurately, its absence in criminal cases (art. 71;) similar facts (art. 76); and discretion (pp. 305–307).

Owing to more pressing practical demands on the time of the junior author, this edition is entirely the work of her senior. He is dismayed at the increase in length. Attempts to console himself with such reflections as that it may have been partly due to the resetting of the type, and was certainly due to some extent to the need for clarification at various points have proved abortive. [This sort of thing has got to stop, and whoever has control of the sixth edition must see that it does.]

It is hoped that this edition contains a reasonably accurate account of the law as it stood at the date of its preface.

21st *March*, 1980 RUPERT CROSS

Extract from Preface to First Edition

This book had its genesis in the junior author's disappointment, when working for Bar Finals, on discovering that there was no book on evidence with a format similar to that of Cross and Jones' *Introduction to Criminal Law.* This led us to think that there is a need among some bar students for a concise account of the law of evidence, shorn of all frills in the form of references to academic literature or decisions from other jurisdictions, and written in the form of article and explanation.

Although the bar student has been uppermost in our minds, there are two other classes of reader for whom we hope that the book may be of some use. In the first place, we have been told that many candidates for police promotion examinations would welcome a book on evidence somewhat fuller than those normally used by police students. Candidates for these examinations will naturally have evidence in criminal cases as their main interest. They need not be alarmed because this book is not confined to criminal evidence; the principles are basically the same, and can only be deduced from civil as well as criminal cases. Those, therefore, whose main interest is in criminal evidence will still find it necessary to study most of the material in this book and we have accordingly taken pains, wherever it seem appropriate, to include illustrations that should be familiar to police officers. For their benefit we have also set out, in Chapter 17, the Judges' Rules, together with a brief commentary.

Secondly, we believe that many university students will find a book in this form useful, either as an introduction or as a convenient means of revision.

Although many of the passages in this book are substantially the same as those in Cross, *Evidence,* and Cross and Jones, *Introduction to Criminal Law,* it is in no sense a precis of those works. The present book is differently arranged, in many instances it puts points in a wholly different way, and it refers to cases that will not be found in the other books.

Dr. Cross did the bulk of the writing in the first place, but we have anxiously conned each sentence together, so that, for one brief moment of time at least, what we have said was comprehensible alike to an ageing academic and a very newly fledged barrister.

RUPERT CROSS

1st *February*, 1964 NANCY WILKINS

Contents

Table of Statutes

References in this Table to *Stats* are to Halsbury's Statutes of England (Third Edition) showing the volume and page at which the annotated text of the Act will be found.

PAGE

Road Traffic Act 1972—*contd*
s. 203 113
Road Traffic Regulation Act 1967 (28 *Stats* 517)
s. 78A 113, 115
Sexual Offences Act 1956 (8 *Stats* 415) 156
s. 2–4 113
12 (3) 315
15 (5) 315
22, 23 113
28 (5) 315
39 . . . . . . 65, 66, 67
Sexual Offences (Amendment) Act 1976 (46 *Stats* 321)
s. 2 270
(1) 91

PAGE

Statutory Declarations Act 1835 (12 *Stats* 804) 158
Supreme Court of Judicature (Consolidation) Act 1925 (25 *Stats* 708)
s. 102 23
Theft Act 1968 (8 *Stats* 782) . 70, 71
s. 1 24
25 32
(3) 33
27 (3) 274
(4) 158
30 (2) 69, 70, 71
(3) 69, 71
31 (1) 100
Witnesses Act 1806 (12 *Stats* 802) 99

List of Cases

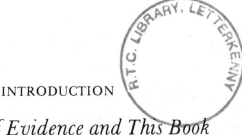

INTRODUCTION

The Law of Evidence and This Book

THE law of evidence determines how facts may be proved in a court of law, and what facts may not be proved there.

In almost every case, the plaintiff or prosecutor has to prove a great variety of facts. The law of evidence tells him how he may do this. Cast in its simplest terms, the answer is "by calling witnesses who have perceived the facts in question"; but, even if this were the full answer, there would inevitably be a good deal of law about who may be called as a witness, and the kinds of question which can be addressed to witnesses. The suggested answer would, however, be incomplete, because facts do not always have to be proved by witnesses who have directly perceived them. In certain cases, facts may be proved by the statements of persons who are not called as witnesses (hearsay); it is true that these statements are usually narrated to the court by witnesses, but the statements, and not the witnesses' testimony with regard to them, are the means of proof. The court may make use of documents and other things produced to it as exhibits for a variety of purposes. Finally, it may be necessary to prove one fact by proving some other fact. A murder is seldom proved by the testimony of an eye witness, but by inference from a large number of evidentiary facts which point to its commission by a particular person, such as motive, concealment of vital information and the purchase of the lethal weapon.

Certain facts may not be proved. An obvious instance is provided by state secrets; their disclosure may be essential to a party's success, but the national security is even more important than the due administration of justice. Sometimes a fact may not be proved for a particular purpose. Everyone knows that the prosecution cannot begin a criminal trial by referring to the accused's previous convictions and inviting the court to infer that he must be guilty of the offence charged because he has such a bad record.

The rules of evidence which prohibit certain facts from being proved are called "exclusionary rules". They play a very important part in the law of evidence, so much so, that it is sometimes said that the major portion of that law is devoted to the determination of what is not evidence. Other exclusionary rules prohibit certain ways of proving certain facts. An example is the rule against hearsay, according to which a statement other than one made by a person while giving oral evidence in the proceedings is inadmissible as evidence of any fact stated. Hearsay is a recognised means of proof, but is only so when permitted under an exception to the rule excluding it.

The two major functions of the law of evidence mentioned in the foregoing paragraphs account for the arrangement of this book. Part I is concerned with proof (how facts may be proved), and Part II is concerned with admissibility (what facts may not be proved owing to exclusionary rules). Part I is primarily concerned with the five main means of proof, testimony (the statements of witnesses), hearsay (the statements of non-witnesses), documents and things which may be produced to the court as exhibits, and, finally, facts as evidence of other facts. Part II deals with the exclusionary rules which prohibit the proof of certain facts. Sometimes the prohibition is absolute, and sometimes it is only against the proof of a fact for a particular purpose.

It is important for the student to realise that the second function of the law of evidence is to determine what facts may not be proved. It is not concerned with the question of what facts may be proved. All that the law of evidence has to say on this subject is that the evidence must be relevant to an issue before the court; it is in no way concerned with the definition of the issues in any case. Those have to be ascertained by reference to the law governing the case. Thus, it is primarily the law of murder which decides what may be proved in a murder case: roughly speaking, anything that tends to establish that the accused killed the deceased and did so with malice aforethought.

Some knowledge of the major branches of the law is assumed in the following pages. This is not asking very much because it is customary to study contract, tort, crime and real property before embarking on the law of evidence. A certain amount of difficulty is, however, caused by the law of procedure because this is not always studied before the law of evidence. Several procedural matters are mentioned in this book, and it will therefore be convenient to make a few elementary observations on the subject at this stage.

Procedure

It is proposed to outline the main procedural stages of a typical trial, dealing first with civil actions begun by writ, and then with criminal cases.

1. Civil cases

(a) **Pre-trial procedure.** Before the trial, pleadings are exchanged between the parties. These are intended to clarify the issues. The plaintiff serves the defendant with a "statement of claim", setting out the facts upon which he relies and the relief which he claims. The defendant counters with his "defence", a document which he serves upon the plaintiff. Generally speaking, facts which are not denied in the defence are deemed to be admitted. The defence may consist of a bare denial of the whole or large parts of the statement of claim, but it may also allege other facts upon which the defendant proposes to rely. Further pleadings may be necessary, but, in many cases, the issues are sufficiently clarified by the statement of claim and defence. A perusal of these documents will often show what facts have to be proved.

After the pleadings are closed, lists of documents are exchanged between the parties. These lists enumerate the documents, relevant to the case, which each party has in his possession. The object of exchanging lists of documents is to prevent one party being surprised by the production of a document at the trial. The lists may refer to documents, and yet claim privilege from producing them; an example is provided by documents in respect of which professional privilege can be claimed because they are communications between one of the parties and his legal adviser. Subject to possible claims of privilege, the documents mentioned in the lists are produced for inspection by the opposite party, and copies may be taken. The whole process of the exchange of lists of documents and inspection is called "discovery". From time to time, it may be necessary for the parties to resort to the court for an order to produce a document for inspection. This might happen when a claim to privilege is disputed, and several of the leading cases on the subject of privilege were decided on applications of this nature. Applications to the court for orders in connection with the pleadings and discovery are called "interlocutory" applications.

Another matter which must be dealt with by the parties before trial is the summoning of witnesses. If a party wishes to call a witness at the trial and knows that the person is willing to attend, it will usually be sufficient for him to notify the witness of the probable date of the trial, but, in order to ensure a witness's attendance, it is common practice to serve him with a *subpoena ad testificandum.* If a witness is duly served with a subpoena and given "conduct money", i.e. sufficient money to cover his expenses of getting to the court, he must attend. Failure to do so may lead to his imprisonment, or a fine, or an action for damages in respect of the loss sustained by the party at whose instance the subpoena was served. Subpoenas are issued out of the central office of the Royal Courts of Justice or out of a district registry or county court. They are in the form of royal commands to attend court. If all that is required is that a witness should produce a document known to be in his possession, he is served with a *subpoena duces tecum.* The same person may be served with both a *subpoena ad testificandum* and a *subpoena duces tecum.*

(b) The opening and the right to begin. In the vast majority of cases, the plaintiff "opens" because he usually has the right to begin calling evidence, i.e. his witnesses are called first. The party who opens gives a brief account of the issues and of what he hopes to prove. The opening speech should not contain any reference to disputed matters of which its maker is not going to call evidence, and, if the admissibility of an item of evidence is likely to be disputed, no reference should be made to it until the stage of the trial at which it is sought to introduce the evidence.

Subject to the judge's discretion to direct the contrary, if the case is of such a nature that the plaintiff would win on every issue unless the defendant were to adduce some evidence, the defendant has the right to open his case and begin calling witnesses. In *Mercer* v. *Whall*[1], the plaintiff claimed damages from his employer for wrongful dismissal. The defendant's pleading admitted that he had terminated the plaintiff's employment earlier than was permitted by the contract of service, but alleged that he was justified in doing so. It was

[1] (1845), 5 Q.B. 447. See also R.S.C. Ord. 35, r. 7.

held, nonetheless, that the plaintiff ought to begin calling evidence because the amount of damages claimed by him was not agreed. Had the damages not been in issue, the defendant would have had the right to begin.

(c) **The taking of evidence.** Assuming that the case is one in which the plaintiff has the right to begin, he calls his witnesses successively, and they are examined, cross-examined and re-examined in accordance with rules discussed in Chapter 4. In addition to calling witnesses, the plaintiff may sometimes read evidence to the court. This happens when an order has been made before trial for the taking of a particular witness's evidence on a different occasion because, for example, the witness was going abroad. Leave may also have been given for the use of an affidavit in evidence.

When the plaintiff has finished calling or reading his evidence, his case is said to be "closed". What happens then depends on the course adopted by the defendant.

(d) **Submission of no case to answer.** One thing that the defendant may do is to submit that there is no case to answer. This means that he is asking the judge to dismiss the action without calling on him or his witnesses to give evidence. The judge must ask himself whether there is enough evidence to justify a reasonable man in finding for the plaintiff on the case as it stands. If the answer is in the negative, the judge should accept the submission and dismiss the action; but, if he thinks that there is sufficient evidence to warrant a finding for the plaintiff unless that evidence is contradicted by the defendant's evidence, the judge should disallow the submission.

The procedure to be adopted by the judge when a submission of no case to answer is made varies slightly according to whether he is sitting alone or with a jury, a rare contingency in civil cases nowadays.

If he is sitting alone, he must put the defendant to his election whether to call evidence. This means that the judge will insist on the defendant undertaking to call no witnesses before ruling on the submission. If the judge rules against the submission, the defendant will have a further opportunity of addressing him on the credibility of the plaintiff's evidence before he comes to his final decision, but the defendant may not call any witnesses or give evidence himself.

If the judge is sitting with a jury, he has a discretion whether to put the defendant to his election. If he does put the defendant to his election, and the defendant elects to call no evidence, the judge will dismiss the action if he rules in favour of the submission, and sum up to the jury after hearing counsel's speeches in the event of his ruling against the submission. If the defendant is not put to his election, he has an opportunity of calling evidence in the event of the judge ruling against the submission, and the case will proceed in the ordinary way[2].

(e) **Advocate's speeches.** The defendant may call no witnesses, either because he has been put to his election on a submission of no case to answer, or else because he has no witnesses to call or deems it imprudent to call those that he has. When the defendant announces that he is calling no evidence, the plaintiff's advocate sums up his client's case and addresses the judge on its merits. The defendant's advocate then addresses the judge on the demerits of the plaintiff's case, and the points in favour of his client. The judge then gives judgment or sums the case up to the jury if there is one. The advocate's right to the last word is regarded as a valuable asset, so the defendant may gain something by not calling witnesses.

If the defendant calls witnesses, his advocate opens his case pointing out what he hopes to prove etc., and calls his witnesses, who are examined by him, cross-examined by the plaintiff and re-examined by the defendant. The defendant then sums up his case and addresses the judge or jury on its merits. The plaintiff's advocate then makes his closing speech; he has the last word when the defendant calls evidence.

In exceptional cases, the plaintiff may be allowed to call evidence in rebuttal after the close of the defendant's case and before the closing speeches are made.

In the very rare case in which the defendant has the right to begin calling evidence, the foregoing procedure is reversed.

2. Criminal cases

It is only necessary to mention the principal differences between the procedure at a criminal trial and in a civil case.

(a) **Pre-trial procedure.** In the first place, there is no equivalent to the pleadings and discovery. If the case is tried

---

[2] In matrimonial causes the judge has a discretion with regard to putting the party making a submission of no case to his election, although there is no jury.

summarily, there is nothing which can be properly described as pre-trial procedure. Unless he is in custody, the accused will have been served with a summons, and statements may have been taken from him by the police. Witnesses may also have been served with summonses to attend court.

If the case is tried on indictment, there will have been the proceedings before the magistrates, or a committal without consideration of evidence under s. 1 of the Criminal Justice Act 1967. In the first of these events the witnesses for the prosecution will have given their evidence and it will have been taken down in their depositions; in the second event they will have signed statements in accordance with the provisions of s. 2 of the Act of 1967. The depositions or statements will be available at the trial, but the witnesses will give their evidence there all over again, unless they were only conditionally ordered to attend the trial and were not, in the end, required to do so. When a witness is conditionally ordered to attend, he is told that he need not attend the trial unless subsequently served with a notice requiring him to do so. Witnesses are conditionally ordered to attend when there is no real dispute about their evidence. In exceptional cases, when the prosecution have discovered further evidence between the committal proceedings and the trial, the accused may be served with a notice of the prosecution's intention to call additional evidence.

(b) The right to begin. In every criminal case in which there is a plea of not guilty, the prosecutor has in practice the right to begin calling evidence[3].

(c) The submission. The accused, or his advocate, may submit that there is no case to answer at the end of the prosecution's case and, if he does so, the judge will never put him to his election whether to call evidence. If the judge rules in favour of the submission, and there is a jury, he will direct the jury to acquit. If the judge rules against the submission, the case will proceed in the ordinary way, the accused calling his evidence if any.

(d) The advocates' speeches. There are important differences between civil and criminal cases so far as the order of the advocates' closing speeches is concerned.

---

[3] Now that formal admissions (see article 16) and agreed statements of fact (see article 45) are permitted, it is possible to construct hypothetical criminal cases in which the accused would have the right to begin.

At a trial on indictment, whether or not he calls any evidence, the accused or his advocate has the right to make his closing speech after that made on behalf of the prosecution[4].

There are analogous provisions concerning the advocates' speeches, though of a somewhat more elaborate nature, in rules 13 and 14 of the Magistrates' Courts Rules 1968.

Law reform

Much of the law of evidence was brought into existence to meet the requirements of a past age. It was right that there should be rigid exclusionary rules when the parties were not allowed to testify and when almost every common law trial took place before a jury, many of whose members might be illiterate, but it is not so clear that there is need for all the elaborate rules of evidence at the present day.

In 1964 the Lord Chancellor referred the question of reforming the law of evidence in civil cases to the Law Reform Committee, and he referred the question of the reform of the law of evidence in criminal cases to the Criminal Law Revision Committee. The two committees were requested to keep in touch with each other, but the Law Reform Committee found it possible to do its work more quickly. It produced four reports, the 13th on hearsay, the 15th on the rule in *Hollington* v. *Hewthorn & Co., Ltd.,* the 16th on privilege, and the 18th on opinion. The first three of these reports were adopted by Parliament in the Civil Evidence Act 1968 and the fourth in the Civil Evidence Act 1972.

The 9th report of the Criminal Law Revision Committee, published in 1966, made some procedural recommendations which were adopted in ss. 9–11 of the Criminal Justice Act 1967; but its main report, the 11th, on evidence (general), published in 1972, gave rise to considerable controversy. None of its numerous recommendations has yet been adopted, and the student must face up to the unfortunate truth that the innovations of the Civil Evidence Acts of 1968 and 1972, unaccompanied by any corresponding changes in the law of evidence relating to criminal cases, have greatly complicated the law. A brief summary of the 11th report is given in Chapter 15.

A Royal Commission is currently considering matters concerning criminal procedure and the police. When it

---

[4] Criminal Procedure (Right of Reply) Act 1964.

appears, their report will no doubt contain recommendations with regard to several subjects mentioned in this book.

Evidence in civil and criminal cases

There will probably always be some distinction between the two, but the general rule is that the law of evidence is the same for both civil and criminal cases, although there are important differences apart from the anomalous ones created by the Civil Evidence Act 1968. Attention is drawn to all the more important differences in the course of this book, and they are enumerated in Chapter 15. The most important difference of all is the difference in practice, for the law of evidence is taken much more seriously in criminal than in civil cases. This is because all rules of evidence may be waived in the latter, and the vast majority of civil cases are tried without a jury. When, in the course of opening the debate on the Civil Evidence Bill in the House of Lords in 1968, the Lord Chancellor expressed the opinion that there would be no law of evidence in 20 years time, he may only have had civil cases in mind.

We realise that it is possible that this book may be used by those who are exclusively or mainly interested in evidence in criminal cases. It is necessary for such students to know quite a lot about evidence in civil cases because, as we have said, the law is basically the same in the two types of case; but for the convenience of students mainly interested in criminal cases, we append a list of articles which can be omitted by them:

Article 24	Article 72	Article 83
Article 33	Article 73	
Articles 39–41	Article 81	

Studying the law of evidence

In conclusion, a point may be made with regard to the study of the law of evidence. It is more highly integrated than most legal subjects. It cannot be studied in isolated compartments. The law of contract is often studied profitably without much attention being paid to such matters as form, duress and agency, but it is not possible to omit portions of the law of evidence from consideration because each rule is closely related to the others.

"One may be expert in many branches of torts, and yet know nothing of conspiracy. But he who does not understand the hearsay rule knows no evidence."[5]

[5] Professor Julius Stone, 55 Law Quarterly Review, 66.

The close integration of the different rules of evidence is reflected in our treatment of the subject. For example, we have found it necessary to refer to the rule against hearsay on several occasions before it is treated in detail in Chapter 6. There is also a good deal of necessary cross-reference at a number of points.

PART 1

Proof

SUMMARY OF PART I

CHAPTER 1

Items and Classifications of Evidence; Functions of Judge and Jury

ART. 1.—The principal items of judicial evidence

The principal items of judicial evidence are the testimony, admissible hearsay statements, documents, things and facts which a court will accept as evidence of the facts in issue.

Explanation: *Facts in issue.*—Facts in issue are all those facts which the plaintiff in a civil action, or the prosecutor in criminal proceedings must prove in order to succeed, together with any further facts that the defendant or accused must prove in order to establish a defence. In civil cases they are ascertained by reference to the substantive law and the pleadings; in criminal cases they are ascertained by reference first to the definition of the crime charged, and secondly to the points raised by the defence.

Suppose the plaintiff is claiming damages for personal injuries which he alleges were caused by the negligent driving of a motor car by the defendant. The question whether the defendant owed a duty of care to the plaintiff is the concern of the law of tort; the respects in which the plaintiff contends that the duty was broken are to be gathered from the particulars of negligence set out in his statement of claim; and, if negligence is denied in the defendant's defence, the law of evidence indicates how the plaintiff may substantiate, or the defendant contradict, the allegations of negligence. If negligence is not denied in the defence, and there is no plea of contributory negligence, the only issue between the parties will most probably concern the amount of damages to which the plaintiff is entitled; thus the sphere of the law of evidence may be restricted to one issue by the pleadings in a given case. But most cases involve more than one issue. Even the simplest claims for damages for assault or breach of contract normally give rise to disputes about the amount of damages to be awarded as well as the questions whether the defendant inflicted the blows, or made the agreement, as the plaintiff contends; while further issues may be raised by the defendant by means of such pleas as those of self-defence, and contractual incapacity.

To take an example from a criminal case, the definition of murder shows that the killing of the deceased by the accused and the existence of malice aforethought must be among the facts in issue whenever there is a plea of not guilty. Such questions as the presence of provocation and the availability of a plea of self-defence are only in issue if they are raised by the defence or suggested by the evidence for the prosecution, while insanity has to be proved by the accused. In a criminal case, there is no exchange of pleadings before trial, and the substantial issues usually only emerge as the evidence is called; but, when the proceedings are on indictment, the prosecution's case at least is made plain by the depositions or written statements on which the committal was founded, and, at any criminal trial, the general nature of the issues is often indicated in the opening of the case for the prosecution.

Evidence.—The evidence of a fact is that which tends to induce a belief in the fact's existence. Judicial evidence is that which a court is prepared to consider, or to allow the jury to consider, before deciding whether one of the facts in issue is proved. The principal items of judicial evidence are those enumerated in the article, and something must now be said about each of them.

(1) *Testimony*

Testimony is the statement of a witness in court. It is usually on oath or affirmation, but may be unsworn in a few exceptional cases. It may be defined as an assertion made by a witness in court offered as evidence of the truth of that which is asserted. The court is asked to assume that the witness is speaking the truth, and many of the rules governing the examination and cross-examination of witnesses are designed to show whether that assumption would be justified. Testimony is the basic item of judicial evidence because the court can usually only be made aware of the other items through the medium of a witness.

A witness must generally have had personal knowledge of the facts to which he deposes. He must have perceived them with one of his five senses. The only exception is the expert who is allowed to state inferences which he draws from facts perceived by him. His evidence is then said to be "evidence of opinion", and his opinion may to some extent be based upon facts of which he was informed by others. A doctor may tell the court that, in his opinion, A died of a certain illness before midnight on 1st January. His opinion concerning the time of death may be based on inferences drawn from his examination of A's corpse on 2nd January, and his opinion about the cause of death may be based in part on what he has read in medical text books about post mortem symptoms of the illness in question.

(2) *Admissible hearsay statements*

The rule against hearsay has already been formulated as follows: "a statement other than one made by a person while giving oral evidence in the proceedings is inadmissible as evidence of any fact stated."[1] A "hearsay statement" may be defined as "a statement other than one made by a person while giving oral evidence in the proceedings tendered as evidence of any fact stated". No litigant is entitled to have a hearsay statement received in evidence as of right; the relevant statutory or common law conditions of admissibility must have been fulfilled, or cause must be shown for the exercise by the court of its statutory discretion in favour of the reception of the statement. An "admissible hearsay statement" may therefore be defined as "a statement other than one made by a person while giving oral evidence in the proceedings which the court will accept as evidence of any fact stated".

If W were to say in the course of his evidence given in court on 1st June "I cannot remember what happened on 1st January, but, on 1st February I signed a document stating exactly what I had seen happen on 1st January and handed it to Smith", for aught that appears so far, the document is

---

[1] The full statement of the rule requires the insertion of the words "or matter of opinion" between the words "fact" and "stated". See Article 38.

inadmissible as a hearsay statement because, in spite of the etymological ineptitude, the rule against hearsay applies to written as well as oral statements. But, if the party calling W had served his opponent with notice of his desire to give the signed statement in evidence, the court might, in a civil case, give him leave to give the evidence under s. 2 (2) of the Civil Evidence Act 1968; if, unknown to the party calling him, W had suffered from an illness which impaired his memory, the court might exercise its discretion in favour of the reception of the signed statement although no such notice as is mentioned above had been served. If W had died before the trial, the court would be obliged, on proof of service of the prescribed notice, to admit the statement in evidence under the Act of 1968.

If the case were a criminal one, W's signed statement would have been inadmissible as evidence of the facts stated in any of the events mentioned in the last paragraph because the ambit of the admissibiliy of hearsay statements is far narrower in criminal than in civil proceedings. However, if W were dead, and the trial was for his murder, his signed statement would be admissible at common law provided it concerned the cause of his death and was made when he was under a settled hopeless expectation of dying.

The word "hearsay" is used to mean a hearsay statement as defined above in the technical sense of a statement tendered as evidence of the facts stated, but it is also used in a non-technical sense to mean any statement of another person narrated by a witness in court without regard to the purpose for which the court is informed of its contents. A witness's evidence at a trial for sedition of the words he heard the accused utter would be hearsay in the non-technical sense of the term. It would not be hearsay in the technical sense because the prosecution would not be inviting the court to assume that the words were true. The distinction between the two senses of the word hearsay is often expressed as one between original and hearsay evidence. A witness is said to give hearsay evidence when he narrates the statements of others as evidence of the truth of their contents. Original evidence consists of statements of others narrated by a witness because, true or false, the fact that they were made is in issue or relevant to an issue.

(3) *Documents*

Documents may be produced to the court for a variety of purposes. Their contents may be received as original evidence or under an exception to the rule against hearsay. An example of the former use of documentary evidence is provided by the production in affiliation proceedings of affectionate letters written by the alleged putative father to the applicant. The expressions of endearment possess probative value independent of their truth or falsity because they are the kind of thing a man would say to a woman with whom he was having an affair.

(4) *Things*

Things are sometimes produced to the court for inspection, as when bloodstained clothing or an axe is produced as an exhibit. Such evidence is often described as "real" evidence. It is of great value as far as it goes, because the court has direct access to it without having to rely on the descriptive powers of a witness, but there is very little real evidence in most cases.

(5) *Relevant facts*

Facts in issue often have to be inferred from other facts. These other facts are described as facts "relevant to the issue" or "evidential facts", and they may be proved by testimony, admissible hearsay, documents, things or other evidential facts.

On a charge of murder by poisoning, the following would be admissible as evidence of guilt: A's testimony that the accused bought poison from him; the receipt of B (since deceased), acknowledging payment of a fee for instructing the accused in the use of poisons (admissible under the common law exception to the rule against hearsay discussed in Article 48); a letter written to the accused informing him of the extent to which he would benefit in consequence of the deceased's death (original evidence because, true or false, the contents of the document tend to prove motive); and poison found in the possession of the accused.

ART. 2.—**The principal classifications of judicial evidence**

Evidence may be classified:

(1) into direct and circumstantial evidence, according to whether it consists of testimony as to the perception of a fact in issue or of evidential facts; (2) into primary and secondary evidence according to whether or not it suggests the existence of better evidence; (3) into insufficient, *prima facie* and conclusive evidence according to its weight.

Explanation:

(1) *Direct and circumstantial evidence*

Evidence is said to be "direct" when it consists of testimony concerning the perception of facts in issue and "circumstantial" when it consists of evidential facts. Arguments about the respective merits of the two types of evidence are liable to appear somewhat futile because reliance has to be placed on each of them in practically every case. It is seldom possible to call a witness to depose to the existence of every fact in issue. The weakness of circumstantial evidence is that it is subject to two infirmities. Not only may the witness who swears to the evidential fact be lying or mistaken, but, even if he is speaking the truth, the inference from that fact to the fact in issue may happen to be incorrect in that particular case. After all, inferences are nothing but the application of generalisations, and there is always the odd situation in which the generalisation does not hold good. People who surreptitiously possess themselves of poison are frequently up to no good, but there is always the possibility that the particular purchaser was merely seeking to acquire scientific knowledge. Although, in legal parlance, circumstantial evidence does not mean a detailed account of what happened (as it formerly did in popular speech), the phrase retains an important element of its original meaning when used by lawyers because circumstantial evidence derives its main force from the fact that it usually consists of a number of items pointing to the same conclusion. The accused's possession of poison may not be of much significance, but additional facts, such as his animosity towards the deceased, benefits to be derived by him from the death of the deceased and his efforts to conceal his possession of the poison may give it a very damning complexion.

> "It has been said that circumstantial evidence is to be considered as a chain, and each piece of evidence as a link in the chain, but that is not so, for then, if any one link break, the chain would fall. It is more like the case of a rope comprised of several cords. One strand of the cord might be insufficient to sustain the weight, but three stranded together may be quite of sufficient strength. Thus it may be in circumstantial evidence—there may be a combination of circumstances, no one of which would raise a reasonable conviction or more than a mere suspicion; but the three

taken together may create a conclusion of guilt with as much certainty as human affairs can require or admit of."[2]

The classification of evidence as direct or circumstantial does not cover all the principal items of judicial evidence. Admissible hearsay concerning a fact in issue is not usually included in direct evidence or circumstantial evidence. An all-embracing classification on similar lines is that into "testimonial", "circumstantial" and "real" evidence. "Testimonial" evidence comprises the assertion of a human being, whether by a witness, or by someone whose statement is narrated by a witness under an exception to the rule against hearsay, offered as evidence of its truth. "Circumstantial" evidence consists of evidential facts and "real" evidence consists of things. But English books on evidence make little use of this classification, although they abound in references to the distinction between direct and circumstantial evidence.

(2) *Primary and secondary evidence*

"Primary" evidence is that which does not, by its nature, suggest the existence of better evidence. "Secondary" evidence is that which does suggest the existence of better evidence. When it is sought to acquaint the court with the contents of a document, the original is primary and a copy is secondary evidence. The distinction is now mainly important in relation to documents which must generally be proved by primary evidence, but there was once thought to be a rule according to which secondary evidence was always excluded when primary evidence was available.

The best evidence rule.—This rule was called the "best evidence" rule because it required the production of the best evidence of which the nature of the case would admit. Testimony concerning the condition of a thing was inadmissible if the thing itself could be produced[3] and circumstantial evidence was inadmissible if direct evidence was available[4]. Decisions to this effect are, however, no longer law[5], and the best evidence rule may generally be treated as a counsel of prudence to adduce the best available evidence rather than a

---

[2] *Per* POLLOCK, C.B., *R.* v. *Exall* (1866), 4F. & F. 922, at p. 929.

[3] *Chenie* v. *Watson* (1797), Peake Add. Cas. 123.

[4] *Williams* v. *East India Co.* (1802), 3 East 192.

[5] *R.* v. *Francis* (1874), L.R. 2 C.C.R. 128; *Dowling* v. *Dowling* (1860), 10 I.C.L.R. 236.

rule of law excluding inferior evidence when superior evidence can be adduced. It is still possible to point to cases in which evidence was excluded altogether because it was not the best evidence, but these cases do not suggest that there is now anything in the nature of a best evidence rule as a fixed rule of law. They simply indicate that the secondary nature of the evidence tendered may sometimes render it so unreliable that it ought not to be admitted. In *R.* v. *Quinn and Bloom*[6], for instance, a film purporting to be a reconstruction of the strip-tease act in respect of which the accused were charged with keeping a disorderly house was held to be inadmissible, and it was said not to be the best evidence. The risk of the slightest alteration in emphasis was enough to render the film of relatively little value as a piece of evidence.

(3) *Insufficient, prima facie and conclusive evidence*

The evidence in support of a fact is said to be "insufficient" when it is so weak that no reasonable man could properly decide the issue in favour of the person adducing it. The fact that an issue was decided on insufficient evidence is a ground for allowing an appeal as a matter of law, and it is when the evidence is insufficient that a judge will rule that there is no case to answer, either of his own motion or else on the appropriate submission being made to him, in accordance with the procedure outlined in the introducion.

The evidence in support of a fact is said to be "prima facie" when it is such as to necessitate a finding that the fact is proved if the evidence is uncontradicted.

Evidence is said to be "conclusive" when the situation is such as to oblige the court to find a particular fact without giving the other party an opportunity of calling witnesses to prove the contrary. The fact that a boy is under fourteen is sometimes said to be conclusive evidence of his incapacity to commit rape. This is, however, merely a cumbrous way of saying that it is a rule of law that boys under fourteen cannot be convicted of this crime.

ART. 3.—Facts must generally be proved by evidence

Sufficient evidence must generally be adduced of all the facts ·n which a party relies, whether in issue or relevant to the ·ue. This means that there is no case to answer when a

---

·2] 2 Q.B. 245; [1961] 3 All E.R. 88.

plaintiff or prosecutor has failed to adduce evidence of a fact in issue, and that judges and jurors are generally precluded from acting on their knowledge of particular facts.

Explanation: A fact is said to be "proved" when the tribunal of fact (the judge if sitting alone, the magistrates, or the jury when there is one) is satisfied of that fact's existence to the requisite degree of conviction.

The effect of the general rule mentioned in the article is that if no sufficient evidence of a fact in issue is forthcoming in the form of testimony, admissible hearsay, documents, things or relevant facts, the case may be dismissed although the fact in question was not seriously disputed, and although the necessary evidence could readily have been produced. For instance, to the great surprise of the accused, prosecutions for motoring offences are sometimes dismissed because the prosecutor has failed to ask any of his witnesses whether the car about which they testified was being driven by the accused[7]; the court is not obliged to allow the prosecution to reopen its case when there is a submission that there is no case to answer, although it has a discretion to do so.

The procedure known as taking judicial notice of a fact, discussed in Chapter 3, forms an exception to the general rule, for, under that procedure, the judge or the jurors may make use of their knowledge of certain facts although they have not been proved by any of the principal items of judicial evidence.

ART. 4—Functions of judge and jury

The general rule is that questions of law are determined by the judge and questions of fact are determined by the jury; but there are exceptions under which certain questions of fact are determined by the judge, and the judge exercises considerable control over the jury.

Explanation: The four principal exceptions to the rule that questions of fact are decided by the jury are facts upon which the admissibility of certain items of evidence depends, foreign law, questions of reasonableness and facts affecting sentence proved after conviction in a criminal case. Nothing need be said about the last exception, but the others must be briefly discussed.

---

[7] *Middleton* v. *Rowlett*, [1954] 2 All E.R. 277.

(1) *Facts affecting the admissibility of evidence*

Hearsay is often only admissible if the maker of the statement which the witness wishes to repeat is dead; a child can only give sworn evidence if he appreciates the solemnity of the occasion and the special obligation to tell the truth imposed by the taking of an oath; a confession of guilt by the accused in a criminal case can only be received if it was voluntary. All these and similar matters are determined by the judge who can make the jury withdraw, but only when this is required in the interests of justice. It has been held that the competency of a child to give sworn evidence must be determined in the presence of the jury[8]. To enable him to determine these questions of fact, the judge may hear evidence on a special form of oath called the "voir dire". An example of a case in which the judge would almost certainly require the jury to withdraw is provided by a criminal trial at which the voluntariness of a confession is disputed. It would often be impossible to determine this question without reference to the terms of the confession, and it would be fatal to a fair trial if the confession was read out in the presence of the jury and then held to be inadmissible by the judge.

(2) *Foreign law*

So far as the courts of England and Wales are concerned, the law of other countries, including Scotland, Eire since 1921, and the Commonwealth countries, is a matter of fact to be determined on the evidence adduced in a particular case. Thus, if the validity of a foreign ceremony of marriage is among the facts in issue, proof of the ceremony will generally not be sufficient for it must be shown to have constituted a valid marriage according to the law of the place of celebration.

The evidence of foreign law is generally given by one or more expert witnesses, and the question of proof of foreign law is further discussed in Chapter 16.

Until 1920, the evidence relating to the relevant foreign law was submitted to the jury. Section 15 of the Administration of Justice Act 1920 provides that, where, for the purposes of disposing of any action or any other matter which is being tried by a judge with a jury in any court of England or Wales, it is cessary to ascertain the law of any other country which is licable to the facts of the case, any question as to the effect

---

Reynolds, [1950] 1. K.B. 606; [1950] 1 All E.R. 335.

of the evidence given with respect to the law shall, instead of being submitted to the jury, be decided by the judge alone. Section 15 of the Administration of Justice Act 1920 has been repealed so far as the High Court is concerned, by the Judicature Act 1925, but a similar provision is contained in s. 102 of that Statute, and there is a corresponding enactment in the County Courts Act 1959.

(3) *Reasonableness*

The reasonableness of such matters as a particular belief or course of conduct is essentially a question of fact, and, as such, it normally has to be determined by the jury, but, in certain cases, it must be decided by the judge. In actions for malicious prosecution or false imprisonment, the question whether the defendant had reasonable and probable cause for initiating the criminal proceedings or arresting the plaintiff must be answered by the judge[9]. It is also the duty of the judge to determine whether the terms of a covenant in restraint of trade are reasonably necessary for the protection of the covenantee[10].

Ordinary meaning of words, value judgments and questions of degree.—On the authority of some old civil cases[11], it is sometimes said that the ordinary meaning of words is a question of law for the judge but, in *Brutus* v. *Cozens*[12] a case turning on the meaning of the words "insulting behaviour" in s.5 of the Public Order Act 1936, the House of Lords held that the words were used in their ordinary sense and that this was a question of fact. Lord Reid recognised that the power of magistrates (and hence that of a jury when there is one) to determine such questions is subject to appellate control in the sense that their decision would be set aside if it were unreasonable because it could not reasonably have been reached by any tribunal acquainted with the ordinary use of language. On this basis the meaning of ordinary words is a question of fact for the jury in accordance with the general rule and, as is the case with other questions of fact, the jury are liable to be controlled by the judge by means of his summing-up.

It is sometimes said that the decision of the Court of Appeal

---

[9] *Herniman* v. *Smith,* [1938] A.C. 305.

[10] *Dowden and Pook, Ltd.* v. *Pook,* [1904] 1 K.B. 45.

[11] *E.J. Neilson* v. *Harford* (1841), 8 M. & W. 806, at p. 823.

[12] [1973] A.C. 854; [1972] 2 All E.R. 1297.

(Criminal Division) in *R.* v. *Feely*[13], a decision on the meaning of the word "dishonestly" in s. 1 of the Theft Act 1968, goes further and holds that no judicial control over the jury's deliberations with regard to the ordinary meaning of statutory words is permissible, but it is unlikely that the Court meant to do more than give effect to the rule, since reiterated by the House of Lords[14], that, although a judge may withdraw a criminal case from the jury and direct an acquittal, he has not got a converse power to direct a verdict of guilty if the jury finds certain facts.

In *R.* v. *Feely* the Court of Appeal said that, when deciding whether a particular appropriation was dishonest, jurors can reasonably be expected to apply the current standards of "ordinary decent folk". Such remarks draw attention to the point that the general rule with regard to the functions of the judge and jury is not fully stated by saying that questions of law are to be decided by the judge, questions of fact by the jury. Allowance must be made for the jury's duty to make value judgments in certain cases– "was the accused acting dishonestly"? "was he grossly negligent"? This last question is also one of degree, like the question, to be determined by the jury when there is one, whether the conduct of someone charged with an attempt was sufficiently proximate to the crime alleged to have been attempted[15].

Judicial control of the jury.—There are various ways in which the judge exercises control over the jury. In the first place, the law with regard to presumptions, discussed in Chapter 3, restricts the jury's power of finding certain facts, because it enables the judge to dictate how those facts must be found. Secondly, the judge is restricting the powers of the jury whenever he rules that there is no case to answer, or holds that there is insufficient evidence on a particular issue with the result that that issue is not left to the jury to consider. At a trial for murder, for instance, there may be some slight evidence that the accused was acting in self-defence, but the judge may consider it insufficient to justify him in directing the jury on the subject. Thirdly, the Court of Appeal (Criminal Division) may

---

[13] [1973] Q.B. 530; [1973]1 All E.R. 341.

[14] *Director of Public Prosecutions* v. *Stonehouse,* [1978] A.C. 55; [1977] 2 All E.R. 909.

[15] *R.* v. *Cook* [1963], 48 Cr. App. Rep. 98.

allow an appeal by the accused and set aside the jury's verdict on the ground that it is unsafe or unsatisfactory[16], and a similar power is vested in the Court of Appeal (Civil Division) so far as civil cases are concerned. Finally, the judge frequently exercises a considerable influence over the jury by means of his summing-up. He may not direct a verdict of guilty, but there is no reason why he should not indicate to the jury what his opinion is with regard to issues of fact to be decided by them, and, in a proper case, the judge may express his views in the strongest terms.

[16] Criminal Appeal Act 1968, s. 2 (1).

CHAPTER 2

The Burden and Standard of Proof

ART. 5.—The burden of proof—general rules

1. The burden of proof must be distinguished from the burden of adducing evidence.

2. The incidence of the burden of proof (i.e. the question which party bears it) is dependent on the substantive law. At the trial of a civil action, it is borne by the plaintiff on the facts pleaded by him and not admitted by the defendant. At a criminal trial, it is borne by the prosecution on every issue except that of insanity and issues on which the burden of proof is cast on the accused by statute.

3. The burden of adducing evidence is generally borne by the party bearing the burden of proof, but, in criminal cases, the accused bears the burden of adducing evidence in support of many of the defences that would be open to him on the strength of his plea of not guilty.

Explanation: Discussions of the burden of proof are concerned with the proof of particular issues. Most cases raise several issues, and in some instances the burden of proving one of them is on one of the parties while the burden of proving another is on his opponent. To appreciate this, it is only necessary to consider a civil action for negligence in which there is an allegation of contributory negligence; the plaintiff bears the burden of proving the defendant's negligence, and the defendant bears the burden of proving the plaintiff's contributory negligence.

Although we speak of one party "bearing" the burden of proof, or the burden of adducing evidence, it must be remembered that he may be able to rely on those parts of his adversary's evidence which are favourable to him. It is not unknown for one party's evidence to be virtually sufficient to establish the other's case.

(1) *The burden of adducing evidence and the burden of proof*

It is important to distinguish between the two burdens—the burden of adducing evidence, and the burden of proof. The burden of adducing evidence makes itself felt at an early stage, and is one of producing sufficient evidence to justify the judge in leaving the issue to the jury or, where there is no jury, to allow the hearing to continue. This may be regarded as the first hurdle—the plaintiff or prosecutor must produce a sufficient quantity of evidence to prevent the judge from withdrawing the issue from the jury, either of his own motion or else on a submission that there is no case to answer. The moment of decision is usually at the close of the case for the plaintiff or prosecutor. If he surmounts this first hurdle, the plaintiff or prosecutor may yet fail at the second.

The second hurdle is the burden of proof. This burden is the one borne by the party who will lose on the issue if, after reviewing all the evidence, the jury or other tribunal of fact entertains the appropriate degree of doubt. In a murder case, for example, the prosecution must lose if the jury entertains a reasonable doubt whether the accused killed the deceased, while the plaintiff will lose a civil action for negligence if the judge or jury is not satisfied on the balance of probabilities that the defendant was negligent. The prosecutor and the plaintiff thus bear "the risk of non-persuasion". The burden of proof is crucial when all the evidence is in. It makes itself felt at a later stage than the burden of adducing evidence.

Although the distinction between the two burdens is generally recognised, there is no agreed terminology. The burden which has just been described as the "burden of proof" is sometimes spoken of as the "legal burden", the "burden of proof on the pleadings", the "persuasive burden" or the "probative burden". The burden of adducing evidence is sometimes spoken of as the "evidential burden"; it is a mistake to call it the "evidential burden of proof" because nothing is proved by its discharge, the issue simply has to be left to the jury[1].

(2) *Incidence of the burden of proof*

It follows from what has been said about it that the burden of proof is the determining factor when the tribunal of fact is in doubt. When there is a jury, it is essential that they should be properly directed on the question of which of the two parties bears the burden of proof. The question is usually not a particularly difficult one, for a fundamental requirement of any judicial system is that the person who desires the court to take action must prove his case to its satisfaction. This means that, as a matter of common sense, the burden of proving all facts essential to their claims normally rests upon the plaintiff in a civil suit or the prosecutor in criminal proceedings.

The rule is sometimes expressed in terms of such maxims as "he who affirms must prove", but this must not be taken to mean that the burden of proof cannot lie upon a party who makes a negative allegation. There are numerous instances in which the plaintiff or prosecutor assumes the burden of proving a negative. Absence of consent must be established by the Crown on a charge of rape or assault[2], and the leading civil case of *Abrath* v. *North Eastern Rail. Co.*[3] decided that the burden of proving absence of reasonable and probable cause in an action for malicious prosecution is borne by the plaintiff. In these cases the phrase "burden of proof" includes the burden of disproof.

Woolmington v. *Director of Public Prosecutions*[4] establishes the rule that, subject to an exception at common law in the case of insanity and to various statutory provisions, the Crown bears the burden of proof on every issue in a criminal case. Woolmington was charged with the murder of his wife by shooting. He admitted that she was killed by a bullet fired from a rifle he was handling, but stated that he pressed the trigger involuntarily while endeavouring to induce her to return to live with him by threatening to shoot himself. Woolmington was convicted after a summing-up which contained the following sentence:

---

[1] *Jayasena* v. *R.*, [1970] A.C. 618; [1970] 1 All E.R. 219.
[2] *R.* v. *Horn* (1912), 7 Cr. App. Rep. 200.
[3] (1883), 11 Q.B.D. 440, affirmed (1886), II App. Cas. 247.
[4] [1935] A.C. 462.

"If the Crown satisfy you that this woman died at the prisoner's hands, then he has to show that there are circumstances to be found in the evidence which has been given from the witness box in this case which alleviate the crime, so that it is only manslaughter, or which excuse the homicide altogether by showing that it was a pure accident."

An appeal to the Court of Criminal Appeal was dismissed, but a further appeal to the House of Lords succeeded, and Woolmington was acquitted. The following important sentences are taken from the speech of Lord SANKEY:

"If it is proved that the conscious act of the prisoner killed a man and nothing else appears in the case, there is evidence upon which the jury may, not must, find him guilty of murder. It is difficult to conceive so bare and meagre a case, but that does not mean that the onus is not still on the prosecution . . . . Throughout the web of the English criminal law one golden thread is always to be seen, that it is the duty of the prosecution to prove the prisoner's guilt . . . . If at the end of and on the whole of the case, there is a reasonable doubt, created by the evidence given by either the prosecution or the prisoner, as to whether the prisoner killed the deceased with a malicious intention, the prosecution has not made out the case and the prisoner is entitled to an acquittal."

The error of the trial judge lay in the suggestion that, on proof of the fact that the deceased met her death at the hands of the accused, the burden of negativing malice aforethought, by proving accident, shifted to the accused, whereas the Crown, in reality, bore the burden of proving malice aforethought from the beginning to the end of the case. The burden of proof does not shift in the course of a trial. This means that it is never possible to say that a party who starts with the burden of proof on a particular issue, be it affirmative or negative, has discharged that burden with the result that the opposite party has the burden of proving the negative or affirmative of the issue.

(3) *Incidence of the burden of adducing evidence*

As a general rule, the burden of adducing evidence is borne by the party who bears the burden of proof. Such party will lose if he fails to adduce sufficient evidence to warrant a finding on the particular issue in his favour if no further evidence were called on the point. When sufficient evidence to warrant a finding has been given, there is a sense in which a burden shifts to the other party, because he runs a risk of losing on the issue if he adduces no evidence. It is not certain that he will lose, even if all the evidence adduced by his opponent is believed, because the tribunal of fact may not consider it to be of sufficient cogency to discharge the burden of proof. The evidence may have been such that the tribunal of fact could legitimately draw from it "an inference one way or the other, or, equally legitimately, refuse to draw any inference at all"[5]. In such a case, the party against whom the evidence has been given is sometimes said to bear a "provisional" or "tactical" burden.

There are few, if any, civil cases where, at common law, the party who bears the burden of proof on a particular issue does not also bear the burden of adducing evidence with regard to that issue. This is because, in civil cases, special defences such as self-defence, infancy or privilege are raised on the pleadings by pleas in confession and avoidance. The defendant contends that, even if the plaintiff's allegations are true, he is in a position to prove further matter which relieves him from liability, and, as is nearly always the case with matters alleged in a pleading, the defendant bears the burden of proof with regard to these further matters.

There are no pleas in confession and avoidance in a criminal case; the plea of not guilty puts everything in issue. The prosecution must then adduce sufficient evidence of the accused's guilt, otherwise there will be no case to answer and the judge may direct an acquittal; but this only means that the prosecution must adduce sufficient evidence of the *actus reus* and *mens rea* mentioned in the definition of the crime charged. It is not necessary to negative every defence that might conceivably be available to the accused.

> "It would be quite unreasonable to allow the defence to submit, at the end of the prosecution's case, that the Crown had not proved affirmatively and beyond reasonable doubt that the accused was at the time of the crime sober, or not sleep-walking or not in a trance or blackout."[6]

---

[5] *Smithwick* v. *National Coal Board,* [1950] 2 K.B. 335, at p. 352, *per* DENNING, L.J.

[6] *Per* DEVLIN, J., in *Hill* v. *Baxter,* [1958] 1 Q.B. 277, at p. 284; [1958] 1 All E.R. 193, at p. 196.

Accordingly it is incumbent on the accused to adduce sufficient evidence to raise a number of defences although the burden of disproving them finally rests on the Crown. For example, in the case of murder, it is incumbent on the prosecution to dispel all reasonable doubt on the question of provocation, otherwise a verdict of manslaughter must be returned; but this duty of the prosecution only arises if the accused has adduced sufficient evidence to raise the issue whether he was in fact provoked; very exceptionally, the prosecution's evidence contains sufficient indication of the existence of provocation to warrant the judge's leaving the issue to the jury. If neither of these things happen the judge need not allude to provocation in his summing up[7]. Similarly, at a trial for murder the prosecution must negative self-defence[8] or duress[9] beyond reasonable doubt, but only if there is sufficient evidence in the case to raise the issue.

ART. 6.—The burden of proof—exceptional cases

There are three exceptions to the general rule that the prosecution bears the burden of proof on every issue in a criminal case: (1) insanity; (2) express statutory provision; (3) cases to which the principle of statutory construction laid down by the Court of Appeal in *R.* v. *Edwards*[10] applies.

Explanation:

(1) *Insanity*

It was recognised by Lord SANKEY in *Woolmington* v. *Director of Public Prosecutions* that the burden of proving insanity as a defence to a criminal charge is borne by the accused. This exception to what is now the general common law rule is traceable to *M'Naghten's* case[11] where it was said that everyone is presumed sane until the contrary is proved, and nothing more

---

[7] *Mancini* v. *Director of Public Prosecutions*, [1942] A.C. 1; [1941] 3 All E.R. 272.

[8] *R.* v. *Lobell*, [1957] 1 Q.B. 547; [1957] 1 All E.R. 734.

[9] *R.* v. *Gill*, [1963] 2 All E.R. 688.

[10] [1975] Q.B. 27; [1974] 2 All E.R. 1085.

[11] (1843), 10 Cl. & F. 200.

need be said about it beyond mentioning that in *R.* v. *Podola*[12] it was held that where the preliminary issue of the accused's fitness to plead is raised by the defence, the burden of proving unfitness to plead is borne by the accused.

(2) *Statutes affecting the burden of proof*

A typical statutory provision affecting the burden of proof in criminal cases is s.2 of the Prevention of Corruption Act 1916, according to which on a charge under the Prevention of Corruption Act 1906 a consideration shall be deemed to be given corruptly unless the contrary is proved. In *R.* v. *Evans-Jones and Jenkins*[13] this was held to mean that, if the jury were in doubt whether to accept the accused's explanation of a gift to a public officer, it was their duty to convict. This construction was also adopted by the Court of Criminal Appeal in *R.* v. *Carr-Briant*[14] where, however, the conviction was quashed because the jury had been wrongly directed with regard to the standard of proof. HUMPHREYS, J., stated the judgment of the Court in the following terms:

> "In any case where, either by statute or at common law, some matter is 'presumed' unless the contrary is 'proved', the jury should be directed that it is for them to decide whether the contrary is proved, that the burden of proof is less than that required at the hands of the prosecution in proving a case beyond reasonable doubt, and that the burden may be discharged by evidence satisfying the jury of the probability of that which the accused is called upon to establish."

The object of such a provision is to prevent a successful submission that there is no case to answer because the prosecution has failed to adduce sufficient evidence of the presence of *mens rea* or, in some cases, of the absence of lawful excuse. The accused is the person who knows most about these matters, and he should be obliged to give his explanation to the court; but this object can be achieved in a less draconian way than that of placing the burden of disproving *mens rea* or proving lawful excuse on the accused if no more than the burden of adducing evidence is placed on him. This is the technique adopted in s.25 of the Theft Act 1968. It is an offence

---

[12] [1960] 1 Q.B. 325; [1959] 3 All E.R. 418.
[13] (1923) 17 Cr. App. Rep. 121.
[14] [1943] K.B. 607; [1943] 2 All E.R. 156.

under the section for a person to have with him any article for use in the course of or in connection with any burglary, theft or cheat when not at his place of abode. Section 25(3) provides that proof that the accused had with him any such article "shall be evidence that he had it with him for such use." The effect is that, if the prosecution can satisfy the jury that the accused had the article with him, the jury must find that he had it with him for the specified uses, unless there is evidence to the contrary; if, however, there is evidence to the contrary, the burden of proving the improper purpose is borne by the prosecution.

The vast majority of statutes placing a burden on the accused are, however, worded like that with which *R.* v. *Carr-Briant* was concerned and s. 81 of the Magistrates' Courts Act 1952 provides that, where the defendant to an information or complaint relies for his defence on any exception, proviso, excuse or qualification, the burden of proving it shall be on him. It has been held that the section means what it says so that the accused bears the burden of proving that he comes within the exception, proviso, excuse or qualification upon which he relies, and not merely the burden of adducing evidence to that effect[15].

(3) *R. v. Edwards*

Section 81 of the Magistrates' Courts Act 1952 is confined to summary proceedings, but the principle enunciated by the Court of Appeal in *R.* v. *Edwards*[16] will produce similar results at trials on indictment. Edwards was charged on indictment with selling by retail intoxicating liquor without holding a justices' licence authorising the sale, contrary to s. 160 (1) of the Licensing Act 1964. The prosecution proved that he had sold intoxicating liquor but adduced no evidence showing that he had not got a licence, nonetheless Edwards was convicted. His appeal was dismissed after a number of authorities had been reviewed by LAWTON, L.J., who said:

> "In our judgment this line of authority establishes that over the centuries the common law, as a result of experience and the need to ensure that justice is done both to the community and to defendants has evolved an exception to

[15] *Gatland* v. *Metropolitan Police Commissioner,* [1968] 2 Q.B. 279; [1968] 2 All E.R. 100; *Nimmo* v. *Alexander Cowan, Ltd.,* [1968] A.C. 107; [1967] 3 All E.R. 187.

[16] [1975] Q.B. 27, at pp. 39–40; [1974] 2 All E.R. 1085, at p. 1095.

the fundamental rule of our criminal law that the prosecution must prove every element of the offence charged. This exception, like so much else in the common law, was hammered out on the anvil of pleading. It is limited to offences arising under enactments which prohibit the doing of an act save in specified circumstances or by persons of specified classes or with specified qualifications or with the licence or permission of specified authorities. Whenever the prosecution seeks to rely on this exception, the court must construe the enactment under which the charge was laid. If the true construction is that the enactment prohibits the doing of acts, subject to provisoes, exceptions, and the like, then the prosecution can rely on the exception."

It had formerly been thought that the principle was confined to cases in which the accused had peculiar means of knowledge of the positive of a negative averment forming part of the prosecution's case[17]; but the question whether a licence had been granted to Edwards could hardly be said to have been peculiarly within his knowledge because the clerk to the licensing justices is required to keep a register of licences which the police could easily have inspected. It had also been thought that the burden cast upon the accused by the principle when it operated against him was merely that of adducing evidence[18]. Certainly the mere existence of peculiar means of knowledge with regard to a fact in issue cannot place the burden of proving it on the accused, otherwise he would bear the burden of disproving guilty knowledge or criminal intent in every case[19].

ART. 7.—The standard of proof—general rules

In a civil case, the standard of proof is proof on a preponderance of probability; proof beyond reasonable doubt is required of the prosecution in a criminal case. This means that the party with the burden of proof on a particular issue will lose on that issue if, at the end of the trial, the tribunal of fact does not consider that the appropriate standard of proof has been reached.

---

[17] *R.* v. *Turner* (1816), 5 M. & S. 206.
[18] But see *R.* v. *Ewens*, [1967] 1 Q.B. 322; [1966] 2 All E.R. 470.
[19] See also *R.* v. *Spurge*, [1961] 2 Q.B. 205; [1961] 2 All E.R. 688.

Explanation: One of the important differences between civil and criminal cases concerns the manner in which the judge should direct the jury (or himself when there is no jury) on the question whether the burden of proof has been discharged. In civil cases, the party who has this burden merely has to satisfy the tribunal of fact on a preponderance of probability, but, in a criminal case, the tribunal of fact must be satisfied beyond reasonable doubt. The distinction was clearly stated by DENNING, J., in *Miller* v. *Minister of Pensions*[20]. Speaking of the degree of cogency which the evidence must reach in a criminal case before the accused can be convicted he said:

> "That degree is well settled. It need not reach certainty, but it must carry a high degree of probability. Proof beyond a reasonable doubt does not mean proof beyond the shadow of a doubt. The law would fail to protect the community if it permitted fanciful possibilities to deflect the course of justice. If the evidence is so strong against a man as to leave only a remote possibility in his favour which can be dismissed with the sentence 'Of course it is possible but not in the least probable', the case is proved beyond reasonable doubt; but nothing short of that will suffice."

Speaking of the degree of cogency which evidence must reach in order to discharge the burden of proof in a civil case DENNING, J., said:

> "That degree is well settled. It must carry a reasonable degree of probability, not so high as is required in a criminal case. If the evidence is such that the tribunal can say: 'we think it more probable than not', the burden is discharged, but if the probabilities are equal it is not."

Difficulties have sometimes arisen when judges have sought to explain to juries what is meant by a reasonable doubt. This led Lord GODDARD to say in *R.* v. *Summers*[1] that juries should simply be told that they must see that the evidence satisfies them "so that they can feel sure when they return a verdict of guilty". Whilst retaining a preference for this form of words, Lord GODDARD recognised later that a direction telling the jury that they must be satisfied of the accused's guilt beyond reasonable doubt would also be perfectly proper[2]. It has since

---

[20] [1947] 2 All E.R. 372.

[1] [1952] 1 All E.R. 1059.

[2] *R.* v. *Hepworth and Fearnley*, [1955] 2 Q. B. 600; [1955] 2 All E.R. 918.

been held that there can be no ground for an appeal if the summing up makes it plain that the jury cannot convict unless they feel sure of the accused's guilt[3]. But "though the law requires no particular formula, judges are wise, as a general rule, to adopt one. The time-honoured formula is that the jury must be satisfied beyond reasonable doubt"[4]. The reason why such a high standard is required of the prosecution's evidence is the necessity of protecting the liberty of the subject. Every precaution must be taken against the risk of convicting an innocent man.

ART. 8.—**The standard of proof—special cases**

1. Proof on a preponderance of probability will suffice on issues on which the accused bears the burden of proof in a criminal case.

2. The same standard of proof will suffice when an issue in a civil case is whether one of the parties has committed a crime.

3. The law with regard to the standard of proof in matrimonial causes is not finally settled, although the most recent authority suggests that proof on a preponderance of probability will suffice.

4. A standard of proof between proof on a preponderance of probability and proof beyond reasonable doubt is said to be applicable to some cases, but the concept is too vague to be of much use.

Explanation:

(1) *Burden on accused*

In the exceptional situations in a criminal case in which the accused has the burden of proof on a particular issue, the standard is the civil one of proof on a preponderance of probability. This was finally settled in *R* v. *Carr-Briant*[5]. The accused was charged with an offence against the Prevention of Corruption Act 1906. By virtue of the Prevention of Corruption Act 1916, a person seeking a government contract who

---

[3] *R.* v. *Allan,* [1969] 1 All E.R. 91.

[4] *Per* Lord SCARMAN in *Ferguson* v. *R.*, [1979] 1 All E.R. 877, at pp. 881–2.

[5] [1943] K.B. 607; [1943] 2 All E.R. 156.

pays money to a public official is deemed to have done so corruptly unless the contrary is proved. The accused was seeking a government contract and had paid money to a public official. He was convicted after a summing up which suggested that it was incumbent on him to satisfy the jury beyond reasonable doubt that he had not acted corruptly. His conviction was quashed by the Court of Criminal Appeal because the jury had been misdirected with regard to the standard of proof. They should have been told to acquit if satisfied on the balance of probability that the accused was not acting corruptly. This lower standard of proof is all that is required when insanity[6], fitness to plead[7] and diminished responsibility[8] are pleaded. In the case of insanity and fitness to plead the accused bears the burden of proof under the common law, and the burden of proof of diminished responsibility is placed on him by s.2 (2) of the Homicide Act 1957.

If the issue of fitness to plead is raised by the prosecution the burden of proving unfitness must be satisfied beyond reasonable doubt[9].

(2) *Civil case in which crime is alleged*

It is easy to think of a number of civil cases in which the question whether one of the parties has committed a crime may be raised. A claims damages for a libel in which B referred to him as a bigamist, and B pleads justification; the insurer's defence to an action on a policy of fire insurance is that the assured was guilty of arson, or the plaintiff simply claims damages for a conspiracy to defraud. In *Hornal* v. *Neuberger Products, Ltd.,*[10] the Court of Appeal recognised that the earlier English cases conflicted and concluded, in apparently general terms, that proof on a preponderance of probability will suffice when the commission of a crime is alleged in a civil action. The plaintiff claimed damages for breach of warranty and fraud on the ground that the defendant had falsely stated that a machine sold by him to the plaintiff had been reconditioned. So far as the alleged breach of warranty was concerned, the trial judge held that the words were spoken by the defendant, but the claim failed because he considered that the parties did not

---

[6] *Sodeman* v. *R.*, [1936] 2 All E.R. 1138.
[7] *R.* v. *Podola*, [1960] 1 Q.B. 325; [1959] 3 All E.R. 418.
[8] *R.* v. *Dunbar*, [1958] 1 Q.B. 36; [1957] 2 All E.R. 737.
[9] *R.* v. *Podola, supra.*
[10] [1957] 1 Q.B. 247; [1956] 3 All E.R. 970.

intend them to have contractual effect. The judge proceeded to award damages for fraud, although he said that he was merely satisfied on the balance of probability, and not beyond reasonable doubt, that the statement was made. If the statement had in fact been made, the defendant would have been guilty of obtaining money by false pretences, for it was beyond dispute that he knew that the machine had not been reconditioned. The Court of Appeal dismissed the appeal mainly because:

> "It would bring the law into contempt if a judge were to say that on the issue of warranty he finds that the statement was made, and on the issue of fraud he finds that it was not made."[11]

Yet this would have been the result of holding that the claim for damages for fraud had to be established beyond reasonable doubt. Although there were several previous decisions which were not discussed by the Court of Appeal, and, in spite of the somewhat exceptional nature of its facts, *Hornal's* case may be taken to have settled the law for the time being.

(3) *Matrimonial causes*

In *Preston-Jones* v. *Preston-Jones*[12], husband petitioned for divorce on the ground of adultery. The only evidence in support of this allegation was the fact the the wife had given birth to a child three hundred and sixty days after the husband could have had such intercourse with her as could have resulted in the conception of the child. There was medical evidence to the effect that it was highly improbable that the child was the husband's and the House of Lords decided by a majority of four to one that the petitioner had established his case beyond reasonable doubt—the test applied by the trial judge. On the authority of this case, HODSON, L.J., subsequently concluded that

> "the courts of this country . . . have come down on the side of the view that . . . in divorce, as in crime the court has to be satisfied beyond reasonable doubt."[13]

In earlier cases the criminal standard was held appropriate in divorce[14] and summary matrimonial proceedings[15] on the

---

[11] At pp. 258,973, respectively.
[12] [1951] A.C. 391; [1951] 1 All E.R. 124.
[13] *Galler* v. *Galler,* [1954] P. 252, at p. 257; [1954] 1 All E.R. 536, at p.541.
[14] *Statham* v. *Statham,* [1929] P. 131.
[15] *D.B.* v. *W.B.,* [1935] P. 80.

ground of sodomy. There was also authority in favour of the criminal standard in nullity[16], in summary matrimonial proceedings in which adultery is alleged[17], and in a case in which connivance was in issue[18].

The requirement of a standard of proof in matrimonial causes, or at any rate in divorce and nullity, which is the same as that demanded of the prosecution in criminal cases can be justified by the sanctity of marriage, but the view taken in the above authorities has probably ceased to represent the law owing to the decision of the House of Lords and the remarks of Lord DENNING in *Blyth* v. *Blyth*[19] together with the provisions of the Divorce Reform Act 1969 (now Matrimonial Causes Act 1973, s. 1). In *Blyth* v. *Blyth* it was held by a majority of the House of Lords that it was only necessary for the petitioner in a divorce suit to disprove condonation on a balance of probability. Lord DENNING, with whom Lord PEARCE agreed, said that proof on a balance of probability would suffice in the case of the establishment of the grounds of divorce as well as the negation of the then bars to relief. The requirement of proof beyond reasonable doubt on any issue in a civil case is an anomaly, and, now that proof of adultery is only a guide line on the question whether the marriage has irretrievably broken down, it may well come to be held that proof on a balance of probability will suffice in divorce and hence, by analogy, in other matrimonial causes. In *Cleary* v. *Cleary*[20] SCARMAN L.J., said "In my judgment the Divorce Reform Act 1969 does put on the court the duty of satisfying itself on the balance of probability that the petitioner is in fact speaking the truth", but the authorities on the standard of proof were not under consideration.

(4) *A possible third standard*

There are statements suggesting that, in certain types of civil case, a standard higher than proof on a preponderance of probability and yet lower than proof beyond reasonable doubt is called for. Thus, it has been said that, where there is a claim for rectification, there must be "convincing proof"[1], and,

---

[16] *C. (otherwise H.)* v. *C.*, [1921] P. 399.

[17] *Ginesi* v. *Ginesi*, [1948] P. 179; [1948] 1 All E.R. 373.

[18] *Churchman* v. *Churchman*, [1945] P. 44.

[19] [1966] A.C. 643; [1966] 1 All E.R. 524; considered in *Bastable* v. *Bastable and Sanders*, [1968] 3 All E.R. 701.

[20] [1974] 1 All E.R. 498, at p. 501.

[1] *Joscelyne* v. *Nissen*, [1970] 2 Q.B. 86, at p. 98.

where the contention is that a couple who had cohabited after an apparently valid marriage ceremony are not married, the evidence must be "strong, distinct and satisfactory."[2] But the notion of a third standard of proof would be difficult to explain to a jury and too imprecise to be of much value to a judge sitting alone. The main point of remarks such as those which have been quoted is that there are claims which are more inherently improbable than others and those making them may be required to adduce weightier evidence to establish them on the balance of probabilities.

[2] *Piers* v. *Piers* (1849), 2 H.L. Cas. 331, at p. 380.

CHAPTER 3

Facts which need not be proved by Evidence

Art. 9.—**Introductory**

No evidence need be given of facts of which the court will take judical notice, of presumed facts or of facts which are formally admitted.

Explanation: In this chapter we are concerned with exceptions to the general rule, stated in article 3, that all facts must be proved by sufficient evidence. In the situations mentioned in the succeeding articles of the chapter, the court may find that a fact exists although there is no testimony or admissible hearsay on the subject, and although no relevant document, thing or evidential fact is produced or proved. This is indubitably so with regard to facts judicially noticed or formally admitted. There is usually some evidence of a presumed fact, but an artificial weight is added to that evidence by a rule of law with the result that the fact does not have to be proved exclusively by evidence, as do facts which are not presumed, judicially noticed or formally admitted.

Art. 10.—**Judicial notice**

The court will take judicial notice of the following:—notorious facts, facts ascertained after inquiries which it is proper for the judge to make, English law, E.C.C. law, the practice of Parliament, and matters of which judicial notice is permitted or required by statute.

Explanation: When a court takes judicial notice of a fact, as it may in civil and criminal cases alike, it declares that it will find that the fact exists, although the existence of the fact has not been established by evidence. If, for instance, the date of Christmas should be in issue, or relevant to the issue, it would not be necessary for the party who desired to establish that fact to call witnesses to swear that the birth of Our Lord is celebrated on the 25th of December, because this is a matter of which judicial notice will be taken.

(1) *Notorious facts*

Other matters of common knowledge of which judicial notice will be taken are that a fortnight is too short a period for human gestation[1], that the advancement of learning is among the purposes for which the university of Oxford exists[2], that criminals do not have happy lives[3] and that cats are kept for domestic purposes[4]. These are of course but examples, and no useful purpose would be served by producing a long list of facts of which judicial notice will be taken because they are notorious.

The facts must be of public notoriety, and hence they are usually general in nature, comprising such matters as the habits of all animals of a species, the ordinary meaning of English words[5], or the general practice of those who compile ordnance survey maps[6]. The taking of judicial notice of such matters does not preclude a party from adducing evidence to show that in the particular case, the habits of a certain animal deviated from those of its species or the general practice was not in fact followed.

The effect of the requirement that the facts of which judicial notice is taken should be of public notoriety is that judges and arbitrators cannot act on information acquired in their private capacity. Thus, in *Reynolds* v. *Llanelly Associated Tin Plate Co.,*

---

[1] *R.* v. *Luffe* (1807), 8 East 193.

[2] *Re Oxford Poor Rate Case* (1857), 8 E. & B. 184.

[3] *Burns* v. *Edman,* [1970] 2 Q.B. 541; [1970] 1 All E.R. 886.

[4] *Nye* v. *Niblett,* [1918] 1 K.B. 23.

[5] *Chapman* v. *Kirke,* [1948] 2 K.B. 450, at p. 454; [1948] 2 All E.R. 556, at p. 557.

[6] *Davey* v. *Harrow Corporation,* [1958] 1 Q.B. 60; [1957] 2 All E.R. 305.

Ltd.[7], the Court of Appeal held that the County Court judge had erred in taking into account a fact about a workman's earning prospects of which he must have had special information; he had done more than take into account the general conditions of the labour market prevailing in the neighbourhood. This case was cited in *Wetherhall* v. *Harrison*[8], a case in which a Divisional Court held that a distinction must be drawn between the use of their private knowledge by judges and arbitrators on the one hand and by justices and jurors on the other hand. The latter are not trained to exclude certain matters from their consideration and, in any event, as a cross section of the community they should pool their general knowledge. The issue before the justices had been whether a motorist whose roadside breath test had proved positive had simulated a fit at the police station in order to prevent a specimen of his blood from being taken. One of the justices was a doctor and he communicated his views about the possible effects of having blood taken on the accused to the other members of the Bench. They also drew on their wartime experience of the possible effect of innoculations on some people. The justices concluded that the accused had a reasonable excuse for not providing the specimen, and the Divisional Court held that their conduct had been proper because there had been no question of one of their number giving evidence to the others in private.

The courts act with considerable caution in expressly taking judicial notice of facts on the ground that they are notorious. In *Preston-Jones* v. *Preston-Jones*[9], for instance, the only fact of which the entire House of Lords would take judicial notice was that the duration of the normal period of gestation is about nine months. Only Lord MORTON OF HENRYTON was prepared to follow DENNING, L.J., in taking judicial notice of the fact that a child born to a woman 360 days after she last had intercourse with her husband could not be his child.

Tacit judicial notice of notorious facts.—In spite of the Courts' caution in expressly taking judicial notice of notorious facts, allowance must be made for the innumerable occasions on which tacit notice is taken of such facts. Whenever a judge imposes a particular sentence because an offence is rife, or admits evidence concerning the discovery of the instruments of

[7] [1948] 1 All E.R. 140.
[8] [1976] Q.B. 773; [1976] 1 All E.R. 241.
[9] [1951] A.C. 391; [1951] 1 All E.R. 124.

crime in the possession of the accused or of the fact that someone alleged to have been drunk spoke with slurred speech, he is tacitly taking judicial notice of the commonness of certain offences, the uses to which instruments are normally put and the manner of speech of drunken persons.

(2) *Facts judicially noticed after inquiry*

> "Judicial notice refers to facts which a judge can be called upon to receive and to act upon either from his general knowledge of them, or from inquiries to be made by himself for his own information from sources to which it is proper for him to refer."[10]

In the case of facts falling within the second category, the inquiries may simply take the form of listening to a witness in court, but they may also take several other forms. The court will act on information supplied by a Secretary of State concerning the sovereign status of a foreign government[11], the extent of territorial waters[12] and the existence of a state of war[13]. When it is obtained, such information cannot be questioned. It is not evidence, but "a statement by the Sovereign of this country through one of his ministers upon a matter which is peculiarly within his cognisance."[14] Courts frequently consult works of history for historical information when that is in issue, or relevant to the issue[15]. As a general rule, a court cannot treat a fact as proved on the basis of the evidence in a previous case[16]; but this does not apply to the proof of custom, for it has been recognised that a time must come when judicial notice may properly be taken of a custom[17].

Even when a judge hears witnesses on matters of which judicial notice will be taken, such as the course of nature, he is not receiving evidence in the strict sense[18]; he can use his own knowledge, obtained from books or any other source, things

[10] *Commonwealth Shipping Representative* v. *P. and O. Branch Services*, [1923] A.C. 191, at p. 212, *per* Lord SUMNER.

[11] *Duff Development Co., Ltd.* v. *Government of Kelantan*, [1924] A.C. 797.

[12] *The Fagernes*, [1927] P. 311.

[13] *R.* v. *Bottrill, Ex parte Kuechenmeister*, [1947] K.B. 41.

[14] *Per* Lord FINLAY, [1924] A.C., at p. 813.

[15] *Read* v. *Bishop of Lincoln*, [1892] A.C. 644.

[16] *Roper* v. *Taylor's Central Garages (Exeter), Ltd.*, [1951] 2 T.L.R. 284.

[17] *Brandao* v. *Barnett* (1846), 12 Cl. & F. 787.

[18] *McQuaker* v. *Goddard*, [1940] 1 K.B. 687; [1940] 1 All E.R. 471.

which he is not usually allowed to do. He can withdraw the issue from the jury, although there is a conflict of testimony, and his decision concerning the fact judicially noticed constitutes a precedent which is more than can be said for other findings of fact.

(3) *English Law, E.E.C. law and parliamentary practice*

A judge is said to take judicial notice of the English common law. This means that he never hears witnesses on the subject. The judge also takes notice of the contents of statutes without proof of their due passage through Parliament. He has always done this in the case of public general Acts of Parliament, and he is entitled to do so in the case of private Acts (passed since 1850) by virtue of s. 3 of the Interpretation Act 1978. He is empowered to take judicial notice of E.E.C. law by the European Communities Act 1972. The judge will also take notice of the practice of Parliament[19].

(4) *Statutory provisions*

Section 3 of the Interpretation Act 1978 is one among quite a number of statutory provisions authorising the taking of judicial notice of various matters. Some of the more important of such provisions [20] relate to the proof of the proper seals and signatures on court orders. We shall see later that the due execution of a document (i.e. the fact that it was signed or sealed by the person by whom it purports to be signed or sealed) must be proved before it is received in evidence. This would lead to endless trouble in the case of official documents in constant use in everyday litigation, and the statutes help by providing that judicial notice shall be taken of the signatures and seals of various persons when attached to specified documents. The effect of these provisions is that the judge will treat the document in question as being properly signed or sealed until it is challenged.

ART. 11.—**Meaning and classification of presumptions**

1. A presumption is an assumption which must be made until evidence to the contrary is adduced. The amount of evidence required in rebuttal varies in the case of different presumptions.

---

[19] *Stockdale* v. *Hansard* (1839), 9 Ad. & El. 1.

[20] Evidence Act 1845, s. 2; Bankruptcy Act 1914, s. 142.

2. Presumptions are often classified as presumptions of fact, irrebuttable presumptions of law and rebuttable presumptions of law. Rebuttable presumptions of law are the only true presumptions.

3. Conflicting presumptions cancel each other out and the issue has to be decided as if it were not affected by any presumption.

Explanation:

(1) *Meaning*

Presumptions that do not depend on the proof of basic facts.—The word "presumption" is sometimes employed as no more than a means of stating the effect of the relevant rules with regard to the incidence of the burden of proof and the burden of adducing evidence. No facts need be proved to bring the presumption into play. Typical examples of this use of the word are provided by the presumption of innocence, the presumption of sanity and the presumption that the accused was acting voluntarily in a criminal case. When it is said that an accused person is presumed to be innocent, all that is meant is that the prosecution is obliged to prove the case against him beyond reasonable doubt. Similarly, the presumption of sanity in a criminal case simply means that the accused bears the burdens of proof and of adducing evidence of his insanity. The presumption that he was acting voluntarily means that the accused bears the burden of adducing evidence to show that he did not act voluntarily owing, for example, to a sudden illness; it is not incumbent on the prosecution to raise the issue of the voluntary nature of the accused's conduct in the first instance, but once the issue has been raised by sufficient evidence, the burden of proving that the accused's acts were voluntary is borne by the prosecution. These examples show that the amount of evidence required to rebut a presumption varies. In a criminal case, the presumption of innocence must be rebutted by evidence proving the contrary beyond reasonable doubt, the presumption of sanity must be rebutted by proof on a preponderance of probability and the presumption of voluntary action must be rebutted by sufficient evidence to raise the issue whether the accused was acting *voluntarily*. There is a presumption against wrongdoing at a civil trial, but this simply means that the contrary must be proved on the balance of probabilities.

Presumptions that depend on proof of basic facts.—The word "presumption" is also used to mean an assumption of the existence of one fact (the presumed fact) which must be made in the absence of further evidence, when another fact (the basic fact) is proved, admitted or judicially noticed. In a civil case, for example, once the tribunal of fact is satisfied that a child was born in wedlock, it must assume that the child was legitimate unless evidence sufficient to prove the contrary on the balance of probability is adduced; again, once a person is proved to have been absent unheard of after due inquiry by those likely to hear of him for a period of seven years, his death must be presumed, at least until some evidence to the contrary is adduced.

The distinction between the types of presumption mentioned in the last two paragraphs turns on the presence or absence of basic facts. For the rest of this chapter we shall be mainly concerned with presumptions which are only brought into play when basic facts are proved, admitted or judicially noticed. It is important to appreciate that the presumption of a fact as a result of one of these presumptions is not necessarily the same thing as proof of that fact by circumstantial evidence. In some cases, a court might infer, as a matter of common sense, that someone who had been absent unheard of for seven years or more was dead, but it would not do so in every case. Nevertheless, death must be presumed, unless there is evidence to the contrary, although the tribunal of fact may think it is just as probable as not that the person in question is still alive.

Presumptions are to be found in every branch of the law, and no useful purpose would be served by an effort to compile a list. Four common presumptions, relevant to most branches of the law, are mentioned in the next four articles.

(2) *Classification*

It is customary to divide presumptions into presumptions of fact and presumptions of law. Presumptions of law are then subdivided into those which are irrebuttable and those which are rebuttable.

(a) *Presumptions of fact*

A presumption of fact is an assumption which may be made on proof of the basic fact; the court is under no obligation to make the assumption even if no evidence to the contrary is given. Presumptions of fact are nothing more than frequently recurring items of circumstantial evidence, and it is a pity that the term "presumption" was ever applied to them. They are sometimes said to be "provisional". Examples are the presumption of continuance, the presumption of intent and the presumption of guilty knowledge on a charge of receiving stolen goods.

Continuance.—The existence of a state of affairs in the past justifies an inference that it continued to exist down to the moment into which the court is inquiring. Evidence has been received of a person's theological opinions four years before the time at which their nature was in issue[1]. The fact that someone was alive at an antecedent date may justify an inference that he was alive at a subsequent date. This point is relied on so frequently that it is not uncommon for language to be used suggesting that the presumption of the continuance of life is the outcome of some special rule of law, but no decision suggests that this really is so. The more remote the basic fact, the less likely is the court to conclude that the presumed fact exists. Proof of the theological beliefs entertained by a man thirty years earlier would not support a reasonable inference concerning his beliefs at the time which the court was examining[2], while, quite apart from any presumption based on seven years absence, a court may well infer that a man has died after some time has elapsed since he was last heard of[3].

Intention.—The presumption that everyone intends the natural consequences of his acts is vital to the administration of the criminal law, for *mens rea* can often only be proved by inference. If A is proved to have shot at B or put poison in B's tea, there may be no further evidence that he did these things with the intention of killing B, but an inference of intention is justified in each instance. It is not obligatory[4] although, in the absence of further evidence, it is hard to believe that the inference would not be drawn.

Guilty knowledge.—Where the only evidence is that the defendant to a charge of handling was in possession of property soon after it had been stolen, a jury may infer guilty knowledge; they are entitled, but not bound to convict. The inference is warranted by the possession of recently stolen

---

[1] *A.-G.* v. *Bradlaugh* (1885), 14 Q.B.D. 667, at p. 711.

[2] *Ibid.*

[3] *Re Watkins, Watkins* v. *Watkins,* [1953] 2 All E.R. 1113.

[4] Criminal Justice Act 1967, s. 8.

goods together with the absence of an explanation of that possession. If an explanation is given, it may be so incredible as to worsen the accused's position, it may convince the jury of the accused's innocence or it may raise sufficient doubt in their minds to entitle the accused to an acquittal.

(b) *Irrebuttable presumptions of law*

Irrebuttable presumptions are not, strictly speaking, presumptions at all, but rules of law. For example, s. 50 of the Children and Young Persons Act 1933 (as amended by the Children and Young Persons Act 1963) says it shall be conclusively presumed that no child under ten can be guilty of any offence. These presumptions are sometimes said to be "conclusive".

(c) *Rebuttable presumptions of law*

A rebuttable presumption of law is an assumption which must be made in the absence of evidence to the contrary. Examples are given in the four following articles.

(3) *Conflicting presumptions*

The leading case on conflicting presumptions is *R.* v. *Willshire*[5]. Willshire had been convicted of bigamously marrying D during the life of his wife C. He married A in 1864, and, in 1868, he was convicted of bigamously marrying B in A's lifetime. The prosecution proved a formally valid marriage ceremony between the accused and C in 1879, together with a further marriage ceremony with D in 1880. Willshire was therefore guilty of the offence charged in the indictment if he was validly married to C, but his defence was that this was not the case because A, who was alive in 1868, was still alive in 1879. The conviction was quashed because the jury had not been properly directed with regard to the burden of proof. They had been told that the burden of proving that A was alive in 1879 was on the prisoner, whereas the proper way regarding the case was to say that the presumption that the 1879 marriage was valid conflicted with the presumption that A's life continued after 1868. These presumptions may be said to have cancelled each other out, with the result that the case should have been left to the jury without any direction concerning the burden of proof beyond one to the effect that it was for the prosecution to prove the guilt of the accused.

---

[5] (1881), 6 Q.B.D. 366.

The conflict in *R.* v. *Willshire* was between a rebuttable presumption of law and a presumption of fact. An example of a conflict between rebuttable presumptions of law is provided by *Monckton* v. *Tarr*[6]. A woman claimed workmen's compensation in 1930 on the footing that she was the widow of a deceased workman. She had gone through a ceremony of marriage with him in 1913, but the employers contended that this marriage was void because the deceased was, at the time, a married man, having gone through a ceremony of marriage with AJ in 1895. AJ was alive at the date of the proceedings, but the applicant contended that the 1895 ceremony was void because AJ was, at the time, a married woman, having gone through a ceremony of marriage with DC in 1882. DC deserted AJ in 1887, and there was no direct evidence that he was alive at the time of the 1895 ceremony.

The County Court judge refused to infer, on the footing of the factual presumption of continuance, that DC was alive when AJ married the deceased workman in 1895, and he accordingly dismissed the claim. His decision was affirmed by the Court of Appeal because the issue was simply one of fact – was DC alive at the time of the marriage of AJ to the deceased? There was a rebuttable presumption of law that the 1913 ceremony was valid, but this was upset by the presumption of the validity of the 1895 marriage. As ROMER, L. J., put it:

> "Those two presumptions, one being on one side and one on the other, being considered of equal weight . . . we get rid of presumptions altogether."

ART. 12.—The presumptions of legality and accuracy

1. Everything is presumed to have been done lawfully until some evidence to the contrary is adduced.

2. Instruments and methods generally known to produce accurate results are presumed to have done so until some evidence to the contrary is adduced.

Explanation:

(1) *The presumption of legality*

"The wheels of business will not go round unless it is assumed that that is in order which appears to be in order."[7]

---

[6] (1930), 23 B.W.C.C. 504, C.A.

[7] *Morris* v. *Kansen*, [1946] A.C. 459, at p. 475; [1946] 1 All E.R. 586, at p. 592.

Therefore, on a charge of assaulting a police officer, formal proof of his appointment is not essential; evidence that he acted as a police officer will suffice[8]; if a solicitor claims damages for words spoken of him in the way of his profession, it is unnecessary for him to produce any evidence of his admission as a solicitor provided there is evidence that he acted in that capacity[9]; and, if a marriage was celebrated in a chapel, the due consecration of the chapel need not be proved in order to establish the validity of the marriage[10].

The presumption of legality is often stated in terms of the Latin maxim *omnia praesumuntur rite esse acta.* It is important in practically every branch of the law, for it saves the expense of calling witnesses to prove a number of facts and prevents unmeritorious submissions of no case to answer; but it must be applied with caution in criminal cases[11] and, in any event, it is rebuttable by comparatively slight evidence—it need only be sufficient to raise a doubt in the mind of the tribunal of fact.

(2) *Presumption of accuracy*

This is also true of the presumption of accuracy; but, until sufficient evidence to rebut it is adduced, there is a presumption that instruments, such as stop watches and speedometers, were in order on the occasion under investigation. As a matter of law, it is unnecessary for the party relying on them to prove that they had recently been tested[12], although the opposite party may always challenge their accuracy. The answer to the question when such an instrument enters the category of those with regard to which the presumption of accuracy will be drawn depends on whether there is a sufficient body of common knowledge concerning the general accuracy of the instrument, this being one of those matters of which judicial notice is tacitly taken[13]. The same principle applies with regard to business methods such as systems of accountancy or record keeping.

---

[8] *R.* v. *Gordon* (1789), 1 Leach 515.
[9] *Berryman* v. *Wise* [1791], 4 T.R. 366.
[10] *R.* v. *Cresswell* (1876), 1 Q.B.D. 446.
[11] *Scott* v. *Baker*, [1969] 1 Q.B. 659; [1968] 2 All E.R. 993.
[12] *Nicholas* v. *Penny*, [1950] 2 K.B. 466; [1950] 2 All E.R. 89.
[13] See p. 43, *ante*.

ART. 13.—The presumption of legitimacy

Provided the spouses were not legally separated at the time of conception, there is a presumption that a child born or conceived in wedlock is legitimate until the contrary is proved on the balance of probabilities in a civil case.

Explanation: The basic facts of the presumption of legitimacy are the marriage of the child's mother and the birth or conception of the child during that marriage; the presumed fact is that the spouses had intercourse by which the child was begotten. It follows that proof that the mother committed adultery with any number of men will not suffice to rebut the presumption, for she may also have had intercourse with her husband[14]. A common way of rebutting the presumption is to show that the husband was abroad at the material time, but it is not essential to negative the bare possibility of access. The fact that the mother was living with another man as his wife for a considerable time before the birth of the child, or the improbability that the husband had access to his wife, and the conduct of the wife or her paramour with regard to the child may all be taken in account[15]. Proof of the husband's impotence is of course another method of rebutting the presumption.

The presumption applies where conception occurred before marriage[16] and where the marriage is terminated by death or divorce before the birth of the child[17].

In *Re Overbury, Sheppard* v. *Matthews*[18], the paternity of a woman who died intestate was in issue. Her mother's first husband died in January 1869. The mother married again in July of that year, and the intestate was born in September. It was held that she was the legitimate daughter of her mother's first husband, as there was no evidence adequate to rebut the presumption. There is no English authority indicating how the courts might resolve a case in which a widow marries so soon after the death of her first husband as to render it impossible to say during which union the child was conceived.

---

[14] *Gordon* v. *Gordon*, [1903] P. 141.

[15] *Morris* v. *Davies* (1837), 5 Cl. & F. 163.

[16] *The Poulett Peerage Case*, [1903] A.C. 395.

[17] *Maturin* v. *A.-G.*, [1938] 2 All E.R. 214; *Re Heath, Stacey* v. *Bird*, [1945] Ch. 417.

[18] [1955] Ch. 122; [1954] 3 All E.R. 308.

If, at the time of conception, the mother was separated from her husband by a decree of judicial separation or a separation order (but not by a separation agreement or in consequence of a maintenance order), there is a presumption that the child is illegitimate[19].

Rebutting the presumption

Section 26 of the Family Law Reform Act 1969 provides that "Any presumption of law as to the legitimacy or illegitimacy of any person may in any civil proceedings be rebutted by evidence which shows that it is more probable than not that that person is legitimate or illegitimate as the case may be and it shall not be necessary to prove that fact beyond reasonable doubt in order to rebut that presumption". The effect of the section is to overrule former decisions and dicta in civil cases according to which the presumption of legitimacy could only be rebutted by evidence tending to prove illegitimacy beyond reasonable doubt; there was no authority concerning the quantity of evidence necessary to rebut the presumption of illegitimacy.

Criminal cases

There is no doubt that the presumption applies in a criminal case. Thus, in *R.* v. *Hemmings,*[20] the girl with whom the accused was alleged to have committed incest was born to his wife while she was married to another man. The accused had admitted that the girl was his daughter but it was held that the admission did not rebut the presumption of the girl's legitimacy; for this purpose there must be evidence that the wife's husband did not have intercourse with her at the material time. Apart from this case there does not appear to be any authority on the operation of the presumption of legitimacy in a criminal case. Suppose a father was charged with incest with his daughter, and he disputed paternity of the girl. Should the jury be directed that they must find her to be legitimate if born during the accused's marriage to her mother unless satisfied beyond reasonable doubt that he did not have access to his wife at the material time? Or should the jury be directed that they must be satisfied of the daughter's illegitimacy on the balance of probabilities? Or should they be told that, sufficient evidence of illegitimacy having been adduced to raise the issue, it is for the Crown to

---

[19] *Ettenfield* v. *Ettenfield,* [1940] P. 96; [1940] 1 All E.R. 293.
[20] [1939] 1 All E.R. 417.

prove legitimacy beyond reasonable doubt in accordance with the ordinary principles prevailing at a criminal trial? The possibilities have been ranged in what we regard as the ascending order of likelihood.

ART. 14.—The presumption of marriage

1. Where there is evidence of a ceremony of marriage, the validity of the marriage will be presumed in the absence of evidence to the contrary.

2. Where a man and woman are proved to have lived together as man and wife, the law will presume, unless the contrary be clearly proved, that they were living together in consequence of a valid ceremony of marriage[1].

Explanation: The two aspects of the presumption of marriage mentioned in the article must be treated separately because the basic fact and the presumed fact are different in each case.

(1) *Presumption of validity of ceremony*

The basic fact of the presumption in its first aspect is the celebration of a marriage ceremony, and the presumed fact is the validity of that ceremony. The leading case is *Piers* v. *Piers*[2] in which a marriage celebrated in a private house was upheld, although there was no evidence that the requisite special licence was ever granted. There are dicta suggesting that the presumption can only be rebutted by proof of invalidity beyond reasonable doubt, but it is questionable whether they will be held to have survived legislation such as s. 26 of the Family Law Reform Act 1969 and the dicta in *Blyth* v. *Blyth*[3]. When the issue is whether one of the parties was married to someone else at the time of the ceremony, the presumption is usually stated in some such terms as the following—a marriage which is unexceptionable in point of form "remains a valid marriage until some evidence is adduced that the marriage was, in fact, a nullity."[4] In a criminal case, it is doubtful whether the accused is ever called on to rebut the presumption by anything more than sufficient evidence to raise the issue of the validity of the marriage.

---

[1] *Sastry Velaider Aronegary* v. *Sembecutty Vaigalie* (1881), 6 App. Cas. 364.
[2] (1849), 2 H.L. Cas. 331.
[3] See p. 39 *ante*.
[4] *Tweney* v. *Tweney*, [1946] P. 180, at p. 182.

(2) *Presumption of ceremony from cohabitation and repute*

The basic facts of the presumption in its second aspect are the cohabitation of the parties with the reputation of being husband and wife; the presumed fact is that, at some time, they went through a ceremony of marriage. An example is provided by *Re Taplin, Watson* v. *Tate*[5]. It was proved that a solicitor had lived with a woman as his wife in Rockhampton for nineteen years. The birth certificates of their children referred to a marriage in Victoria, a district in which the local law required marriages to be registered. No ceremony between the man and woman was registered in Victoria, but it was held that a valid marriage should be assumed, because the presumption could only be rebutted by evidence of the most cogent kind. In *Elliot* v. *Totnes Union*[6], a man contested a claim for maintenance of a child on the ground that he had never married its mother (since deceased). His evidence was disbelieved, and a marriage was presumed from cohabitation and repute, although no ceremony was shown to have taken place. It is usually said that the contrary must be clearly proved, but reliance cannot be placed on the presumption by the prosecution in order to prove a valid marriage ceremony on a charge of bigamy[7].

ART. 15.—The presumption of death

Where there is no acceptable affirmative evidence that a person was alive at some time during a continuous period of seven years or more, then if it can be proved first, that there are persons who would be likely to have heard of him over that period, secondly, that those persons have not heard of him, and thirdly, that all due inquiries have been made appropriate to the circumstances, that person will be presumed to have died at some time within that period[8].

Explanation: In the reported cases there are various formulations of the presumption of death. The formulation adopted in the article is among the most rigorous as well as the most recent. There are three basic facts—the fact that the person in question has not been heard of for a continuous period of seven years or more, the existence of people who

---

[5] [1937] 3 All E.R. 105.

[6] (1892), 57 J.P. 151.

[7] *Morris* v. *Miller* (1767), 4 Burr. 2057.

[8] *Chard* v. *Chard*, [1956] P. 259, at p. 272; [1955] 3 All E.R. 721, at p. 728.

would be likely to have heard of him, and due inquiry by those people. The presumption frequently does not apply because the second or third basic fact cannot be proved. When the presumption does not apply, the question whether someone was alive or dead at the material time has to be decided by inference. Thus, in *Chard* v. *Chard*, the case from which the formulation in the article is taken, the question was whether a marriage celebrated in 1933 should be annulled because the husband was then still married to his first wife. He had married her in 1909, and she was known to have been alive in 1917. She had not been heard of after that year, but there was every reason why she should not have been heard of by her husband, as he had been in prison for much of the time. The wife was nineteen in 1909, and SACHS, J., inferred that she was still alive in 1933. He therefore granted decrees of nullity relating to the ceremony of that year. There was no question of the presumption of death applying because it was not proved that the first wife had been unheard of by those likely to have heard of her, and there was no evidence that adequate inquiries had been made.

The clearest instance of the application of the presumption is provided by an action on a fully paid life insurance policy. If it is proved that the assured has been unheard of after due inquiry by those likely to have heard of him for a period of seven years or more, the court must presume his death and direct payment of the policy monies to those who would then be entitled to them. In such a case, it does not matter when the assured may be presumed to have died, but, in other cases, difficulty may be occasioned by the fact that there is no presumption as to the date of death.

Date of Death

In *Re Phené's Trusts,*[9] for instance, a testator died in January 1861, having bequeathed his residuary estate equally between his nephews and nieces. N, one of his nephews, was born in 1829, went to America in 1853, communicated with his family up to 1858, joined the American Navy, and was last heard of as a deserter in 1860. Advertisements for N were inserted in English and American newspapers in 1868, and the plaintiffs then obtained a grant of representation to his estate. Their claim to N's share of the testator's residue failed because the

[9] (1870), 5 Ch. App. 139.

court was not prepared to infer that N survived the testator. Although he might be presumed dead in 1869, the year in which the action was begun, there was no presumption as to the date of his death. The judgment in *Re Phené's Trusts* has been taken to mean that the continuous period of seven years or more giving rise to the presumption of death must always run backwards from the date of the trial[10]; but there is authority against this view. In *Chipchase* v. *Chipchase*[11], a woman who had married in 1915, and who had not heard of her husband since 1916, married again in 1928. She applied for a magistrates' maintenance order in 1939 against the man she married in 1928, and he disputed the validity of the marriage. The magistrates dismissed the application because there was no evidence that the woman's first husband was dead in 1928; but the case was remitted to them by the Divisional Court on the ground that the presumption of death applied as at 1928. If the Divisional Court acted correctly, this means that it is sufficient if there is a continuous period of seven years or more running back from whatever date may be crucial to the case.

Statutory provisions

Three statutory provisions, having a bearing on the presumption of death, are s. 184 of the Law of Property Act 1925, s. 57 of the Offences against the Person Act 1861, and s. 19 of the Matrimonial Causes Act 1973.

Section 184 of the Law of Property Act provides that, where two or more persons have died in circumstances rendering it uncertain which of them survived the other, such deaths shall (subject to any order of the court) for all purposes affecting the title to property, be presumed to have occurred in order of seniority, and accordingly the younger shall be deemed to have survived the elder. The section is not confined to deaths occurring in the same disaster. If A were to die in an air crash and B were to die under an operation on the same day in circumstances rendering it uncertain which of them survived the other, the younger would be presumed to have been the survivor for all purposes affecting the title to property[12]; had the section been in force at the time it would have ensured the

[10] *Lal Chand Mawari* v. *Mahant Ramrup Gir* (1925), 42 T.L.R. 159.
[11] [1939] P. 391; [1939] 3 All E.R. 895.
[12] *Hickman* v. *Peacey*, [1945] A.C. 304, at pp. 314–5.

success of the plaintiffs in *Re Phené's Trusts*. The section does not apply between husband and wife in the case of intestacy[13]. Therefore, if a husband and wife perish in a shipwreck, and are intestate, nothing will pass to the estate of either from the estate of the other, assuming there is no evidence of survivorship.

After defining the offence of bigamy, s. 57 of the Offences Against the Person Act 1861 provides that nothing in the section shall extend to any person marrying a second time whose husband or wife shall have been continually absent for the space of seven years last past, and shall not have been known by that person to have been living within that time. The proviso simply affords a defence to a charge of bigamy. It does not raise a presumption of the death of the first spouse before the second ceremony, and, notwithstanding the applicability of the proviso, that ceremony is void if the accused's first spouse was alive when it was celebrated. There does not appear to be any authority directly covering these points, but they are assumed in a number of cases[14] and, to some extent, by those responsible for what is now s. 19 of the Matrimonial Causes Act 1973. It has been held that the legal burden of proving that the accused knew that the first spouse was alive during the period of continuous absence is borne by the Crown[15].

Section 19 (1) of the Matrimonial Causes Act 1973 enables any married person who alleges that reasonable grounds exist for supposing that the other spouse is dead to petition for a decree dissolving the marriage and presuming the death of such spouse. Under s. 19 (3) the fact that for a period of seven years or upwards the other party to the marriage has been continually absent from the petitioner, and the petitioner has no reason to believe that the other party has been living within that time, shall be evidence that he or she is dead until the contrary is proved. The petitioner has to prove less in proceedings under the section than someone seeking to establish the common law presumption of death as formulated in the article. The petitioner simply has to prove that he has no reason to believe the other spouse to have been living for the

---

[13] Intestates' Estates Act 1952, s. 1 (4). See also Finance Act 1975, s. 22(9), as to double death duties.

[14] There was for example no reference to the proviso as something which could have raised a presumption of the validity of the 1895 ceremony in *Monckton* v. *Tarr* (1930) 23 B.W.C.C. 504, p. 50 *supra*.

[15] *R.* v. *Curgerwen* (1865), L.R. 1 C.C.R. 1, a decision which is hardly consistent with the passage from the judgment in *R.* v. *Edwards,* [1975] Q.B. 27, at pp. 39–40, cited on p. 33 *supra*.

past seven years. The fact that the other spouse would have been unlikely to have communicated with him is immaterial.

ART. 16.—**Formal admissions**

In civil cases facts may be admitted on the pleadings or in answer to a notice to admit facts. In criminal cases facts may be formally admitted at or before the proceedings.

Explanation: The formal judicial admissions, discussed in the article, must be distinguished from the informal extrajudicial admissions, admissible under an exception to the rule against hearsay, and discussed in Article 42. The formal admissions are for the purposes of the trial only and they do not constitute evidence. They are in the nature of a dispensation from proof. Informal admissions do constitute evidence, their weight varying according to the circumstances in which they were made and the manner in which they are explained away by the party against whom they are tendered.

Civil Cases

Allegations of fact contained in a pleading, such as the plaintiff's statement of claim in a running down action, are deemed to be admitted unless denied[16]. The whole or any part of the opponent's case may be admitted on the pleadings or otherwise in writing, and, before the trial, one party may serve the other with a notice to admit specific facts. These facts may be admitted for the purposes of the trial only[17], and failure to admit may involve the party on whom the notice is served in paying the costs of proving the facts mentioned in the notice.

The allegations in a divorce petition are not deemed admitted in the absence of a denial.

Criminal Cases

Section 10 of the Criminal Justice Act 1967 makes provision for formal admissions by the prosecution or defendant in criminal cases at or before the trial. If made before the trial the admission must be in writing and, if by a defendant who is an individual, it must have the approval of his counsel or solicitor.

---

[16] R.S.C. Ord. 18, r. 13.
[17] R.S.C. Ord. 27, r. 1.

CHAPTER 4

Testimony

ART. 17.—**The competence and compellability of witnesses generally**

All sane adults not subject to sovereign or diplomatic immunity are competent and compellable to give evidence, subject to the exceptions relating to the accused and his spouse, discussed in the next three articles.

Explanation: Testimony has already been defined as the assertion of a witness in court offered as evidence of the truth of that which is asserted. This chapter is concerned with who may be a witness, how witnesses give evidence, the types of question that can be put to witnesses and the extent to which they can refuse to answer them.

It is necessary to distinguish between the competence, compellability and privilege of witnesses. A witness is competent to give evidence if his testimony is admissible. He is compellable if he can be obliged to go into the witness box, the ultimate sanction being imprisonment for contempt of court if he refuses to do so. A witness who is unwilling to give evidence is obliged to attend court if a subpoena is served on him and the appropriate conduct money paid. When in the witness box the witness is generally guilty of contempt of court if he refuses to answer questions that are put to him, but he may claim to be privileged from answering certain questions on the grounds mentioned in Article 28.

The law concerning the competence and compellability of witnesses was greatly simplified by four nineteenth century statutes. The Evidence Act 1843 abolished "incapacity from crime or interest" (someone who had been convicted of an infamous crime or who had an interest in the outcome of the proceedings was formerly incompetent to testify); the Evidence Act 1851 rendered the parties to a civil action at common law competent and compellable to testify[1]; the Evidence (Amendment) Act 1853 contained a similar provision with regard to the spouses of the parties to a civil action; and the Criminal Evidence Act 1898 made the accused and his spouse competent witnesses for the defence in all criminal proceedings. The result is that all sane adults, not subject to sovereign or diplomatic immunity, are competent and compellable in all cases except that there are special rules concerning the accused and his spouse in criminal proceedings. In this context the term "witness" includes a party to the litigation. The plaintiff and defendant in a civil action can *subpoena* each other, although it is seldom thought desirable to resort to such procedure.

Mental incapacity

The mentally ill may give evidence if they appreciate the duty of telling the truth on oath. This is a matter which has to be decided by the judge on the *voirdire.* In 1851 it was said that he must ask himself two questions: does the proposed witness

---

[1] The parties were already competent in Chancery proceedings.

understand what he is saying? and does he understand the nature of an oath, i.e. the sanction which attaches to false swearing?[2]

Infancy

There are no fixed age limits governing competence to testify at common law. It used to be said that the judge had to be satisfied that the proposed witness appreciated the nature and consequences of an oath[3], and the context made it plain that the court had the divine sanction in mind. The Court of Appeal has recently adopted a more secular approach. The important thing is for the judge to be satisfied that the child appreciates the solemnity of the occasion and is sufficiently responsible to understand that the taking of an oath involves an obligation to tell the truth over and above the ordinary duty of doing so. It is unnecessary for the child to believe in anything in the nature of a divine sanction for the majority of the adult population probably does not believe in it[4]. It remains to be seen whether the new approach to children's evidence will affect the courts' attitude to a proposed witness who is mentally ill.

The common law still governs the competency of children in civil cases, but, in relation to criminal proceedings, it has been modified by what is now s. 38 of the Children and Young Persons Act 1933. A child of tender years may give unsworn evidence in any criminal proceedings if, in the opinion of the court, he is possessed of sufficient intelligence to justify the reception of the evidence, and understands the duty of speaking the truth.

Sovereign and diplomatic immunity

The sovereign, foreign sovereigns and those entitled to diplomatic privilege are competent, but not compellable, witnesses.

ART. 18.—The accused

The accused is a competent and compellable witness for the prosecution or the defence in the unimportant and wholly exceptional class of criminal case covered by the Evidence Act

[2] *R.* v. *Hill* (1851), 5 Cox C.C. 250
[3] *R.* v. *Brasier* (1779), 1 Leach 199.
[4] *R.* v. *Hayes*, [1977] 2 All E.R. 288.

1877. In all other criminal cases, the accused is an incompetent witness for the prosecution, but competent to give evidence on his own behalf and competent, though not compellable, for a co-accused. The issue of the accused's competency must be determined when he is called upon to testify. The prosecution may not comment on the accused's failure to give evidence and, if the judge does so in his summing up to the jury, he should make it plain that the accused has a right not to give evidence.

Explanation: The Evidence Act 1877 deals with cases of non-repair of bridges and highways. The proceedings are not really punitive in aim, and that is presumably why the accused is treated like the defendant in a civil case.

Dislike of facing an accused who is guilty, or who at least has something to hide, with the choice of incriminating himself out of his own mouth or committing perjury accounts for the fact that, at common law, he was an incompetent witness. He could not give sworn evidence on his own behalf or on behalf of the Crown, or a co-accused. He was, however, allowed to make an unsworn statement from the dock if he so desired, and this common law right has been preserved by s. 1 (h) of the Criminal Evidence Act 1898. The accused may not be cross-examined on the statement and, for this reason, as well as the fact that it is not on oath, the statement, though something which the jury should consider, is less weighty than sworn evidence[5]. The 1898 Act enables the accused to give sworn evidence for the defence in all criminal cases if he desires to do so.

Incompetence for the prosecution

Subject to the exception of cases falling within the Evidence Act 1877, the common law still governs the accused's capacity to be a witness for the prosecution, and he is therefore incompetent. This rule must be borne in mind whenever there is more than one defendant. If A, B and C are being jointly tried, A cannot be called by the prosecution, even though the only questions the prosecutor wishes to ask relate to the complicity of B and C[6].

---

[5] *R.* v. *Frost*; *R* v. *Hale* (1964), 48 Cr. App. Rep. 284.

[6] *R.* v. *Payne* (1872), L.R. 1 C.C.R. 349.

If one of several accused gives evidence on his own behalf, what he says for or against his co-accused, in-chief or in cross-examination, becomes evidence for all purposes and may be relied on by the prosecutor or co-accused as the case may be[7]. If the accused makes an unsworn statement from the dock it is wholly ineffective against a co-accused who cannot call evidence in rebuttal[8].

Competence for a co-accused

Even if he does not give evidence on his own behalf, one co-accused may be called by another, but he can only be obliged to testify in cases falling within the Evidence Act 1877. In all other cases, the accused is competent, but not compellable, for his co-accused.

Time for determining competency

One of several accused may have ceased to be an accused by the time a question of his competence or compellability in the particular proceedings is raised. This happens if the prosecution offers no evidence against him with the result that he is acquitted (a course which is sometimes adopted to enable the prosecution to call him as a witness against the remaining accused); or if the judge directs his acquittal at the end of the prosecution's case[9]. It also happens if the Attorney-General files a *nolle prosequi*; if the accused has pleaded guilty; or if an order for separate trials has been made. In these cases the former accused is a competent and compellable witness for the prosecution, or for the remaining accused[10]. But, if proceedings are pending against him, the judge has a discretion to prevent the prosecution from calling him, especially if he may be required to incriminate himself[11]; and, where he has pleaded guilty, it is generally desirable that he should have been sentenced before he is called on behalf of the prosecution[12].

Comment

Section 1 (b) of the 1898 Act provides that the prosecution

---

[7] *R.* v. *Rudd* (1948), 32 Cr. App. Rep. 138, at p. 140.

[8] *R.* v. *George* (1978), 68 Cr. App. Rep. 210.

[9] *R.* v. *Conti* (1973), 58 Cr. App. Rep. 387.

[10] *R.* v. *Richardson* (1967), 51 Cr. App. Rep. 381.

[11] *R.* v. *Turner and others* (1975), 61 Cr. App. Rep. 67 (judgment of LAWTON, L.J.).

[12] *R.* v. *Payne,* [1950] 1 All E.R. 102.

may not comment on the accused's failure to testify, but there is no statutory restriction on such comment by a co-accused[13]. The judge may draw the jury's attention to this fact, but his summing up should make it clear that the accused is not bound to give evidence, that he can sit back and see if the prosecution have proved their case, and that, while the jury have been deprived of the opportunity of hearing his story tested in cross-examination, the one thing they must not do is to assume that he is guilty because he has not gone into the witness box[14]. Comment in stronger terms is permissible when the accused's defence to a charge of murder is that he was unaware that his co-accused, with whom he had agreed to commit robbery, had got a gun; but, even then, the jury must not be left with the impression that the defence must fail as a matter of law if the accused does not give evidence[15]. The judge must also observe caution when commenting on the accused's failure to call a witness because this may be explicable on many grounds[16].

ART. 19.—**The competence and compellability of the accused's spouse when neither victim nor prosecutor**

1. As a general rule, the accused's spouse, when he or she is neither the victim of nor the prosecutor for the offence, is an incompetent witness for the prosecution. The exceptions are that he or she is (a) competent and compellable in cases falling within the Evidence Act 1877; (b) probably competent and compellable on charges of treason; (c) competent but not compellable in cases mentioned in the Schedule to the Criminal Evidence Act 1898 (as amended) and in cases mentioned in other enactments such as s. 39 of the Sexual Offences Act 1956.

2. As a general rule the accused's spouse, when neither victim nor prosecutor, is competent but not compellable as a witness for a co-accused, provided the accused consents. The exceptions are that, without the consent of the accused, his or her spouse is (a) competent and compellable in cases falling within the Evidence Act 1877; (b) probably competent and

---

[13] *R.* v. *Wickham* (1971), 55 Cr. App. Rep. 199.
[14] *R.* v. *Bathurst,* [1968] 2 Q.B. 99; [1968] 1 All E.R. 1175.
[15] *R.* v. *Sparrow,* [1973] 2 All E.R. 129.
[16] *R.* v. *Gallagher,* [1974] 3 All E.R. 118.

compellable on charges of treason, and (c) competent but not compellable in cases mentioned in the schedule to the Criminal Evidence Act 1898 (as amended) and in cases mentioned in enactments such as s. 39 of the Sexual Offences Act 1956.

3. As a general rule the accused's spouse, when neither victim nor prosecutor, is a competent, but not a compellable, witness for the accused. The exceptions are that he or she is competent and compellable (a) in cases covered by the Evidence Act 1877, and (b) probably in cases of treason.

4. The foregoing rules apply to a former spouse testifying to matters occurring during his or her marriage to the accused.

Explanation: The special cases of proceedings brought by one spouse against the other and of proceedings by third parties for offences committed by one spouse against or with reference to the other are dealt with in the next article.

(1) *The accused's spouse as a witness for the prosecution*

The general common law rule that the accused's spouse is an incompetent witness for the prosecution is based on the view that marital unity might be endangered if the law were otherwise. The rule has only been slightly eaten into by statute and, in the vast majority of criminal cases, the accused's spouse still cannot be called on behalf of the prosecution, however willing he or she may be to testify. Accordingly, if A, B and C are charged with theft from D, Mrs. B is an incompetent witness for the prosecution, and, if she does give evidence resulting in a conviction, the conviction will be quashed by the Court of Appeal unless that Court is able to hold that there has been no miscarriage of justice[17].

The common law rule applies even when the events to which the spouse is required to testify occurred before the marriage[18], and even if the marriage took place between committal and trial[19]. It continues to apply after the spouses have been separated by a decree of judicial separation even when the accused's spouse is only required to testify to matters occurring after the decree[20].

---

[17] *R.* v. *Boucher* (1952), 36 Cr. App. Rep. 152. See also *R.* v. *Deacon,* [1973] 2 All E.R. 1145 (wife incompetent for prosecution on charge against husband for murdering her brother).

[18] *Pedler* v. *Wellesley* (1829), 3 C. & P. 558.

[19] See for example *Hoskyn* v. *Metropolitan Police Commissioner,* [1978] 2 All E.R. 136, p. 70 infra.

[20] *Moss* v. *Moss,* [1963] 2 Q.B. 799; [1963] 2 All E.R. 829.

It is unnecessary to say anything about the first exception because proceedings falling within the Evidence Act 1877 are of no importance in the general criminal law.

Treason.—There is no decision on the question whether a spouse is a competent or compellable witness against the accused on a charge of treason, but there are dicta suggesting that this is the case[1].

Scheduled offences.—Section 4 (1) of the Criminal Evidence Act 1898 provides that the wife or husband of a person, charged with an offence under any enactment mentioned in the schedule, may be called as a witness, either for the prosecution or for the defence, and without the consent of the person charged. The section says that the wife or husband *may* be called as a witness, and it has been held that, in cases covered by the sub-section, competence does not imply compellability. Accordingly a wife who does not wish to testify against her husband in a case coming within the schedule cannot be obliged to do so[2].

Subsequent enactments have from time to time made additions to the schedule, and various later statutes, notably s. 39 of the Sexual Offences Act 1956, have expressly provided for the competence, but not the compellability, of the accused's spouse as a witness for the prosecution. The following is a summary of the present position.

The accused's spouse is a competent, but not a compellable, witness for the prosecution in the following cases:

1. Neglect to maintain, or desertion of a wife or family, contrary to s. 51 of the National Assistance Act 1948;
2. Offences against children mentioned in the Schedule to the Children and Young Persons Act 1933 (including murder, manslaughter, infanticide and offences involving bodily injury to a child or young person), child destruction and indecency with children;
3. Bigamy;
4. Offences in relation to national insurance;
5. Sexual offences other than buggery with someone above the age of seventeen, indecent assault on a man, and assault with intent to commit buggery.

---

[1] *Director of Public Prosecutions* v. *Bladey*, [1912] 2 K.B. 89, at p. 92.
[2] *Leach* v. *R.*, [1912] A.C. 305.

6. Taking or permitting to be taken indecent photographs of children contrary to s. 1 (a) of the Protection of Children Act 1978.

(2) *The accused's spouse as a witness for a co-accused*

At common law, if A and B were being jointly tried for any offence, Mrs. A was incompetent as a witness for B, whether or not she was willing to testify and whether or not her husband was willing that she should do so[3]. The effect of the Criminal Evidence Act 1898 is that the accused's spouse is always a competent witness for a co-accused with the consent of the accused. Such consent is unnecessary in the exceptional cases mentioned in the second clause of the article. Cases (a) and (c) are covered by the terms of the relevant statutes, and it may be assumed that the accused's spouse is compellable for the defence in treason if compellable for the prosecution.

(3) *The accused's spouse as a witness for the accused*

As a result of s. 1 of the Criminal Evidence Act 1898 the accused's spouse is always a competent witness for the accused. However such authority as there is supports the view that he or she is generally not compellable[4]. The 1877 Act expressly provides for compellability and compellability is assumed in treason if the spouse is compellable for the prosecution.

(4) *Former spouse testifying to matters occurring during the marriage*

At common law, a divorced spouse was as incompetent to testify to matters occurring during the marriage as one who had not been divorced[5]. This common law rule still applies in criminal cases subject to statutory modifications, mentioned in this and the next article, governing the competence of the present spouse of the accused. The words "husband" and "wife" when used in these provisions must be taken to include a former husband or wife testifying to matters occuring during the marriage. In *R.* v. *Algar*[6], Mr. Algar was charged with forgery of Mrs. Algar's signature on cheques drawn in 1947 and 1948. The bank on which the cheques were drawn was the victim of these offences because Mrs. Algar's account had to be reimbursed. In 1949 the Algars' marriage was annulled on the

---

[3] *R.* v. *Thompson* (1872), L.R. 1 C.C.R. 377

[4] *R.* v. *Acaster* (1912), 7 Cr. App. Rep. 187; *R.* v. *Boal*, [1965] 1 Q.B. 402; [1964] 3 All E.R. 269.

[5] *Monroe* v. *Twistleton* (1802), Peake Add. Cas. 219.

[6] [1954] 1 Q.B. 279; [1953] 2 All E.R. 1381.

ground that it had been rendered voidable by the husband's impotence. In 1953 Mrs. Algar was called as a witness at Mr. Algar's trial at which she was not the prosecutrix. He was convicted but his conviction was quashed by the Court of Criminal Appeal because she was incompetent. At the time there was no statute in force enabling the accused's spouse to testify for the Crown on charges of forgery in which he or she was neither the victim nor the prosecutor. Mrs. Algar would have been competent if the marriage had been void[7].

ART. 20—The competence and compellability of the accused's spouse when either victim or prosecutor

1. At common law the accused's spouse is a competent witness for the prosecution, the accused and a co-accused on charges of violence against himself or herself (including injury to his or her health or liberty) committed by the accused.

2. Under s. 30(2) of the Theft Act 1968 a person bringing proceedings against his or her spouse for any offence is a competent witness for the prosecution, and, under the Criminal Evidence Act 1898, he or she is competent for the accused or, with the consent of the accused, a co-accused.

3. Under s. 30(3) of the Theft Act 1968 when the proceedings are not brought by the accused's spouse, he or she is a competent, but not a compellable, witness for the prosecution and the defence on charges of any offence committed with reference to him or her or to property belonging to him or her.

Explanation:

(1) *Common law*

There was a long established exception to the general common law rule concerning the incompetency of the accused's spouse covering offences involving violence by one spouse against the other, and it is preserved by s. 4(2) of the Criminal Evidence Act 1898. It covers all cases in which one spouse is charged with assaulting the other or causing him or her bodily harm. It has been held to extend to the case of a husband charged with buggery of his wife[8]. A wife has been held competent to give evidence against her husband charged

[7] *Wells* v. *Fisher* (1831), 1 Mood. & R. 99.

[8] *R.* v. *Blanchard,* [1952] 1 All E.R. 114.

with attempting to cause her to take poison with intent to murder her, contrary to s. 14 of the Offences against the Person Act 1861[9], and there are old cases in which it was applied to charges of abduction against men who subsequently married the girls abducted[10]. The exception probably applies to all charges affecting the health, liberty or person of the accused's spouse and to attempts to commit such crimes.

On the principle that what is sauce for the goose is sauce for the gander[11], it is generally assumed that the accused's spouse would be competent for the accused and a co-accused in cases coming within the common law exception, although there is no direct authority on the point, a fact which is hardly surprising having regard to the nature of the exception.

The Court of Criminal Appeal held that the accused's spouse was compellable for the prosecution in cases covered by the common law exception[12], but this decision was overruled by a majority of the House of Lords in *Hoskyn* v. *Metropolitan Police Commissioner*[13]. Hoskyn was charged with causing grievous bodily harm with intent to the girl he married two days before the trial began. She was an unwilling witness for the prosecution, but Hoskyn was none the less convicted. His appeal to the Court of Appeal was dismissed, but his appeal to the House of Lords succeeded. As a result of this decision the question whether a case comes within the common law exception or the broader provisions of the Theft Act 1968 which are about to be discussed is almost devoid of practical importance. The exception would only apply where the Theft Act would not, if the accused's spouse were held to be compellable on a charge of forcible abduction followed by marriage.

(2) *Theft Act* 1968, s. 30(2)

Before the Theft Act 1968 came into force there were ill-defined restrictions on the right of one spouse to bring criminal proceedings against the other; but s. 30(2) provides that:

> "A person shall have the same right to bring proceedings against that person's wife or husband for any offence

[9] *R.* v. *Verolla,* [1963] 1 Q.B. 285; [1961] 2 All E.R. 426.
[10] *R.* v. *Wakefield* (1827), 2 Lew. C.C. 279.
[11] *R.* v. *Serjeant* (1826), Ry. & M. 352.
[12] *R.* v. *Lapworth,* [1931] 1 K.B. 117; [1930] All E.R. 340.
[13] [1978] 2 All E.R. 136.

(whether under this Act or otherwise) as if they were not married, and a person bringing any such proceedings shall be competent to give evidence for the prosecution."

The subsection applies to prosecutions by one spouse against another for any offence committed against him or her. Accordingly the case of *Moss* v. *Moss*[14], in which a husband who charged his wife, from whom he was judicially separated, with repeatedly telephoning him with intent to annoy was held incompetent to testify against her, would now be decided differently.

The subsection also applies to prosecutions brought by one spouse against another for offences committed against third parties. If she were the prosecutrix, a wife would be competent on a murder charge against her husband[15]. It is unlikely that she would be held to be compellable if she had second thoughts about the prosecution in spite of the fact that s. 30(2) unlike s. 30(3) says nothing about compellability. Her competence for the defence would be unaffected by s. 30(2).

(3) *Theft Act* 1968, s. 30(3)

Section 30(3) of the Theft Act 1968 reads:

> "Where a person is charged in proceedings not brought by that person's wife or husband with having committed any offence with reference to that person's wife or husband or to property belonging to the wife or husband, the wife or husband shall be competent to give evidence, . . . whether for the defence or for the prosecution, and whether the accused is charged solely or jointly with any other person."

The words "with reference to", though apt to cover offences committed by one spouse against the other, are of wider application, and the subsection is not confined to charges brought under the Theft Act 1968. A charge against a wife for forging her husband's signature is included[16]. Were the facts of *R.* v. *Algar*[17] to recur, Mrs. Algar would be a competent witness and a wife would now be held a competent witness for the prosecution on a charge against her husband for sending her a letter threatening to murder her contrary to s. 16 of the

---

[14] [1963] 2 Q.B. 799; [1963] 2 All E.R. 829.

[15] *Cf. R.* v. *Deacon,* [1973] 2 All E.R. 1145; [1973] 1 W.L.R. 696; p.66, n. 17, *supra.*

[16] *R.* v. *Noble,* [1974] 2 All E.R. 811.

[17] P. 68, *supra.*

Offences against the Person Act 1861, although such a charge was held not to come within the common law exception to the rule of incompetency[18].

The reference to the "defence" in the subsection makes the accused's spouse competent for him and, without his consent, for a co-accused. It is expressly provided that the accused's spouse shall not be compellable under the subsection unless compellable at common law.

ART. 21.—Oath, affirmation and unsworn evidence

The general rule is that all evidence must be on oath, but any witness may affirm if he so desires and unsworn evidence is received in a few cases.

Explanation:

Oath or affirmation.

Originally all evidence had to be on oath, and that oath had to be on the Gospel, It was decided in *Omychund* v. *Barker*[19] that a witness might give evidence on the oath which bound him according to his religion. Witnesses came to be allowed to affirm by various statutes, and the present position is governed by the Oaths Act 1978.

Section 1 prescribes the form in which an oath shall be administered to Christians and Jews. It also allows for the administration of an oath in other forms to those with other religious beliefs. The fact that a person taking an oath has no religious belief does not prevent it from being binding on him[20]. Under s. 5 anyone objecting to being sworn is permitted to make a solemn affirmation, and such an affirmation may be required of any person in relation to whom it is not reasonably practicable to administer an oath in the manner appropriate to his religious belief. An affirmation has the same force and effect as an oath which means that a false affirmer may be punished as a perjurer.

Unsworn evidence

We have seen that a child of tender years may give his evidence unsworn in criminal proceedings and that the accused

---

[18] *R.* v. *Yeo,* [1951] 1 All E.R. 864n.

[19] (1745), 1 Atk. 21.

[20] S. 4(2).

may make an unsworn statement from the dock. Other witnesses, who need not be sworn, or affirm, include a witness called solely for the purpose of producing a document[1], a judge or barrister testifying from the well of the court concerning a case in which he was involved[2] and the Sovereign.

ART. 22.—Examination-in-chief

1. A witness may generally not be asked leading questions in examination-in chief.

2. A witness may generally not be asked whether he made a statement before the hearing to the same effect as his testimony and such statement may generally not be proved by another witness. Exceptions to this general rule (sometimes called the "rule against self-corroboration" or the "rule against narrative") are discussed in Articles 23 and 24.

3. Provided the requisite conditions are fulfilled, a witness may refresh his memory by referring to a document prepared or checked by him.

Explanation: A witness is liable to have three sets of questions put to him, in examination-in-chief, in cross-examination and in re-examination. The object of the examination-in-chief, which is conducted by or on behalf of the party calling the witness, is to elicit evidence favourable to that party's case. It must be confined to evidence directly relevant to an issue in the case, and questions relating solely to the credit of the witness are not allowed. The object of cross-examination, conducted by or on behalf of the opposite party, is (a) to elicit evidence directly relevant to the issue which is favourable to the cross-examiner's case and (b) to discredit the witness. The object of re-examination is to obviate the effects of the cross-examination, and it must be confined to points arising therefrom[3]. Nothing more need be said about re-examination. The rest of this article and Articles 23 and 24 are primarily concerned with examination-in-chief, and Article 25 is concerned with cross-examination.

---

[1] *Perry* v. *Gibson* (1843), 1 Ad. & El. 48.
[2] *Hickman* v. *Berens,* [1895] 2 Ch. 638.
[3] *Prince* v. *Samo* (1838), 7 Ad. & El. 627.

(1) *Leading questions*

A leading question is not, as is sometimes supposed, necessarily an important one. It is a question which suggests the desired answer. An example would be "did Jones attack you as soon as you met him on the first of January?" The question should be split up and made to take some such form as,"When did you meet Jones?" "What happened when you met him?"

There are several situations in which leading questions are permitted. These include undisputed matters, cases in which it is necessary to bring the witness's mind to the point in issue by jogging his memory, and cases in which the opposite party consents to leading questions. But there is no fixed list of situations in which leading questions may be asked in-chief.

To illustrate the first two situations which have just been mentioned, the following is the beginning of almost any examination-in-chief. "Is your name John Smith?" "Are you a baker?" "Do you live at 1, Any Street, Anywhere?" In a divorce case in which the marriage is not denied by the respondent, the examination might well continue: 'Were you married to the respondent on 1st January 1970, at St. John's Church, Tooting?" "Did you live happily with the respondent until last June?" At a much later stage it may be necessary to bring the witness's mind to the point in issue by means of leading questions. If occurrences in the evening of January 1st are important issues in the case, the petitioner may be led to them by some such question as "Did you have tea with your mother on January 1st?" to be followed, if the petitioner assents to that question by "What happened when you got home?"

Leading questions are allowed in cross-examination.

There is a type of question which is sometimes called "leading", but which may also simply be called "improper", which does not suggest the desired answer but assumes the existence of a disputed fact. An example would be "What did you do after Jones attacked you?", put to a witness who had not previously deposed to an encounter with Jones. Questions assuming the existence of disputed facts are disallowed in-chief. They would also generally be disallowed in cross-examination.

(2) *Prior consistent statements*

The general rule at common law is that a witness may not be

asked whether he has previously said much the same thing as he now says in court, and the fact that he has done so may generally not be proved by another witness. The rule is most important when applied to statements made before the hearing by a party; this is why it is sometimes justified as a prohibition on evidence which could easily be manufactured. It is theoretically distinct from the rule against hearsay, because the purpose for which the statements are tendered is to establish the truth of what the witness has just said in court, not to establish the truth of what he or someone else said out of court. At most the fact that the statement was made does no more than enhance the credibility of the witness, a purpose for which questions are generally inadmissible.

In *R.* v. *Roberts*[4] the accused was charged with murdering a girl by shooting her as she was letting him into her house. The defence, in support of which he gave evidence, was that the gun went off accidentally while he was trying to make up a quarrel with the girl. Two days later he told his father that the defence would be accident. The trial judge would not allow the father to prove this conversation, and the Court of Criminal Appeal held that the judge had been right.

It will be convenient to deal with the exceptions to the rule in separate articles because, although they are still dependent on the common law in criminal cases, the Civil Evidence Act 1968 governs in civil cases.

(3) *Refreshing memory in court*

Provided four conditions are fulfilled, a witness may refer to a document in court in order to refresh his memory before answering particular questions. The four conditions are (a) that the document should have been made substantially at the same time as the occurrence of the events to which the witness is required to depose, (b) that the document should have been made by or under the supervision of the witness, or checked, or simply accepted as true by him, (c) that the document should be produced to the court or the opposite party on demand and (d) that the document should generally be the original.

(a) *Contemporaneity.*—Contemporaneity is a question of fact. Six months would be too long a time lag[5], but, in *Burrough* v. *Martin*[6], a mariner was allowed to refresh his memory by

---

[4] [1942] 1 All E.R. 187.

[5] *Jones* v. *Stroud* (1825), 2 C. & P. 196.

[6] (1809), 2 Camp. 112.

reference to the ship's log-book, compiled soon after the events related therein.

In *R.* v. *Simmonds*[7] notes made by customs officers at the first opportunity on their return to their office after lengthy interviews were held to comply with the requirement of contemporaneity, and it was said to be a course commonly adopted by police officers to read their notes of such interviews when giving their evidence-in-chief.

It has been said that the rule that a witness may only refresh his memory from a contemporaneous document is merely a rule of practice affecting the weight of the evidence[8], but this statement of a Divisional Court is hard to reconcile with some of the authorities[9].

(b) *Authorship of the document.*—*Burrough* v. *Martin* shows that the document need not necessarily have been made by the witness himself. The log-book was only supervised by him. A prosecution witness is regularly allowed to refresh his memory by reference to the statement written out by the police officer to whom he gave it shortly after the events to which it relates[10]. It is sufficient if the document was read by the witness at a time when the facts were fresh in his memory although he had nothing to do with its making provided he accepted it as true[11]. A witness has been allowed to refresh his memory as to a date by referring to an article which appeared in a newspaper contemporaneously with the events to which he was referring[12]. He said that, when he read it, he believed it to be true.

(c) *Production of document and cross-examination.*—The document must be handed to the opposite party to enable him to inspect it and, if he so desires, to cross-examine the witness with regard to its contents. Cross-examining merely on the parts of a document, by which the witness's memory was refreshed, does not make it evidence in the case. When cross-examining on a document used to refresh memory, however, the cross-examiner should be careful about referring to parts of the document which do not directly relate to the subject on

---

[7] [1969] 1 Q.B. 685.

[8] *R.* v. *Governor of Gloucester Prison, ex parte Miller,* [1979] 2 All E.R. 1103.

[9] E.g. *R.* v. *Woodcock,* [1963] Crim. L.R. 263; *R.* v. *Graham,* [1973] Crim. L.R. 628.

[10] *R.* v. *Mullins* (1848), 12 J.P. 776.

[11] *R.*v. *Mills,* [1962] 3 All E.R. 298, at p. 301.

[12] *Dyer* v. *Best* (1866), L. R. 1 Exch. 152.

which the witness was trying to refresh his memory. If he does refer to other parts they become evidence in the case[13]. This may mean that evidence which would be inadmissible in-chief, and favourable to the cross-examiner's opponent, is let in.

If a document used to refresh memory becomes evidence in the case, it is treated as an exhibit and may be taken out by the jury to assist them in their deliberations. In a civil case the court may also treat its contents as evidence of the facts stated under an exception to the rule against hearsay. S. 3(2) of the Civil Evidence Act 1968 contains an express provision to this effect. Criminal cases are still governed by the common law and, when cross-examination on a document used to refresh memory makes it evidence in the case, the document is only admissible to support the witness's creditworthiness by way of exception to the rule prohibiting the reception of the previous statements of witnesses for this purpose[14].

(d) *The need to produce the original.*—It has been held that a witness may refresh his memory by any book or paper (including a copy[15] or a report based on his original notes[16]) if he can afterwards swear to the fact from his own present recollection. But, if he is only prepared to swear to the fact because he finds it mentioned in some book or paper, the original must be produced[17] if it is available. Even when a witness swears to a fact because it is stated in a document, the document does not become evidence in the case. In *Maugham* v. *Hubbard*[18] a witness was called to prove the receipt of money. Being unable to recollect this fact, he was shown an unstamped receipt signed by himself. He then said that he had no doubt that he received the sum specified in it, although he did not recall having done so. It was held that this was sufficient evidence of the payment in spite of the prohibition on the use of unstamped receipts in civil litigation.

> "The paper itself was not used as evidence of the receipt of the money but only to enable the witness to refresh his memory; and when he said that he had no doubt that he had

---

[13] *Gregory* v. *Tavernor* (1833), 6 C. & P. 280; *Senat* v. *Senat*, [1965] P. 172; [1965] 2 All E.R. 505.

[14] *R.* v. *Virgo* (1978), 67 Cr. App. Rep. 323.

[15] *Burton* v. *Plummer* (1834), 2 Ad. & E. 341.

[16] *Horne* v. *McKenzie* (1839), 6 Cl. & Fin. 628.

[17] *Doe d. Church and Phillips* v. *Perkins* (1790), 3 Term Rep. 749.

[18] (1828), 8 B. & C. 14.

received the money, there was sufficient parol evidence to prove the payment."[19]

In such a case the witness is really vouching for the accuracy of a record made by him, but it is his testimony and not the record which is regarded as the evidence. The witness presently swears that what he formerly wrote was true[20].

Police notes.—What has been said in this article has an important bearing on the use that can be made of a police officer's notes.

There is no objection to an officer consulting his notes before he gives evidence in court. The mere fact that the officer took notes immediately after an interview or other occurrence does not make them evidence in the case. Even if the officer states in-chief that he took notes, the notebook itself does not become evidence. This is on account of the rule against self-corroboration. Conversely, if, in answer to questions put to him in cross-examination, the officer says that he made notes, the cross-examiner has no right to call for the notes, although, as a matter of practice, it may be wise to let him see them.

If the cross-examiner suggests that the officer's evidence is a recent fabrication, the officer's notebook may be put in evidence in order to rebut the suggestion.

Everything that has been said so far assumes that the officer does not use his notes to refresh his memory in court. If he does do this, he must allow the defence to see the notes and they may also be inspected by the jury. In appropriate cases, portions of an officer's notebook relating to irrelevant matters may be sealed up.

Where two officers have been conducting an investigation, there is no objection to their collaborating over the preparation of their notes. If there has been collaboration, this fact should be made plain to the court[1].

In *R.* v. *Mills*[2], a police officer was allowed to refresh his memory by referring to his notes taken from a tape-recording made by him of an incriminating conversation between two prisoners in their cells. The officer heard the original conversation, and the case is no authority on the admissibility of tape-

---

[19] Lord TENTERDEN.

[20] *R.* v. *Bryant* (1946), 31 Cr. App. Rep. 146.

[1] *R.* v. *Bass,* [1953] 1 Q.B. 681; [1953] 1 All E.R. 1064.

[2] [1962] 3 All E.R. 298.

recordings, a matter considered in Article 64.

In *R.* v. *Cheng*[3] it was held that a police officer might refresh his memory from a statement prepared by him for use in the committal proceedings from his notebook which was not available at the trial. In *Attorney-General's Reference No. 3 for 1979*[4] it was held that a police officer might refresh his memory from his notebook compiled from jottings made two hours earlier at an interview with the accused. It was also held that the jottings should have been made available to the accused.

Refreshing memory out of court.—Although there is generally no objection to an ordinary witness looking at a written statement of his evidence before he goes into court, it was once said to be bad practice for prosecution witnesses to be given copies of statements made by them to the police[5]; but this practice has since been sanctioned by the Court of Appeal even though the witnesses could not have refreshed their memories from the statements in court because they were not made substantially contemporaneously with the events to which they related[6]. When witnesses' memories have been refreshed out of court in this way, it is desirable, though not essential as a matter of law, that the opposite party should be informed of that fact[7].

ART. 23.—Proof of the previous consistent statements of witnesses in criminal cases

In criminal cases the following previous consistent statements of witnesses may be proved under exceptions to the general rule prohibiting the proof of such statements mentioned in clause 2 of Article 22:—

1. Statements forming part of the *res gestae;*
2. statements made at such a date as to negative a suggestion of recent fabrication by the witness of his evidence;
3. statements constituting complaints by the victim of a sexual offence;
4. statements made by the accused to the police;

---

[3] (1976), 63 Cr. App. Rep. 20.
[4] (1979) Cr. App. Rep. 411.
[5] *R.* v. *Yellow and Thay* (1932), 96 J.P. 826.
[6] *R.* v. *Richardson,* [1971] 2 Q.B. 484; [1971] 2 All E.R. 773.
[7] *R.* v. *Westwell,* [1976] 2 All E.R. 812.

5. statements forming part of the identification of the accused by a witness for the prosecution.

Explanation:

(1) *Res gestae*

If the previous statement was made contemporaneously with the incident to which it relates, it may be received to prove the consistency of the maker when he gives evidence in court, because, as it is sometimes put, the words form part of the *res gestae*. They are part of the story and have especial probative value because the witness has not had time to invent a false story or to forget significant facts. In *R.* v. *Roberts*[8], for example, shortly after the girl was shot, the accused told some friends that the gun went off accidentally; and the friends were allowed to prove what the accused said to them as part of the *res gestae*. *R.* v. *Fowkes*[9] is a classic example of the reception of a previous statement of a witness as part of the *res gestae*. A man commonly known as "the butcher" was charged with murder. The deceased's son gave evidence that he and a police officer were sitting in a room with his father when a face appeared at the window through which the fatal shot was then fired. At the trial he said that he thought the face was that of "the butcher". He was allowed to swear how he had shouted "There's Butcher" when the face appeared, and the police officer, who had not seen the face, was allowed to depose to the shouting. Obviously a jury would attach great significance to the instantaneous and contemporaneous identification as allaying any doubts that might have been occasioned by the witness's hesitancy at the trial. The words indicating identification at the time of the incident may therefore have been received as evidence of the facts stated under an exception to the rule against hearsay.

(2) *Negativing fabrication*

If it is alleged that a witness's testimony is a recent concoction, a previous statement made by him to someone else, or in a note made for his personal use, becomes admissible.

---

[8] P. 75, *ante*.

[9] Stephen's Digest of the Law of Evidence, 12th edition, p. 8.

The witness will usually be asked about his previous consistent statement in re-examination, but the cross-examination of A suggesting that he and B collaborated to fabricate their evidence might justify a question to B in his examination-in-chief about a statement made before the alleged fabrication.

A suggestion put to the accused's wife in cross-examination that she had invented part of her evidence after consultation with her husband allows a statement made by her to a solicitor before she had seen her husband after the events in question to be proved by her in re-examination[10].

An allegation that a police officer is fabricating his testimony allows his notebook to be put in evidence[11], although the book could not have been put in but for the cross-examination. To enable a previous statement to be proved under this head, the cross-examination must be reducible to some such question as the following: "When did you first invent that story?" It is not enough that the cross-examination should suggest that the witness is a liar, or that it should refer to a statement inconsistent with his testimony previously made by him, or that the whole of his testimony is false[12].

(3) *Complaints*

On charges of sexual offences (including those against males)[13] the terms of a complaint made by the victim may be narrated both by the victim and by the person to whom it was made. Two conditions have to be fulfilled to render the complaint admissible: (a) it must have been made at the earliest opportunity that reasonably presented itself, and (b) it must not have been made in response to any inducement or leading question[14]. The terms of the complaint are admissible to prove the consistency of the conduct of the complainant with the story told by him or her in the witness box and as something tending to negative consent when that is in issue. Consent is in issue on a charge of rape, but not on charges of unlawful intercourse with young girls. The terms of the complaint do not corroborate the complainant's testimony, nor are they any

---

[10] *R.* v. *Oyesiku* (1972), 56 Cr. App. Rep. 240.
[11] *R.* v. *Benjamin* (1913), 8 Cr. App. Rep. 146.
[12] *Fox* v. *General Medical Council,* [1960] 3 All E.R. 225.
[13] *R.* v. *Camelleri,* [1922] 2 K.B. 122.
[14] *R.* v. *Lillyman,* [1896] 2 Q.B. 167; *R.* v. *Osborne,* [1905] 1 K.B. 551.

evidence of the facts complained of. Accordingly, when, on a charge of incest with a girl of five, the girl does not give evidence, her grandmother ought not to be called to prove the terms of a complaint made to her by the girl. Consent is not in issue, and there is no testimony the consistency of which can be established by the complaint[15].

(4) *Statements of the accused*

It is the regular practice of the prosecution to give in evidence statements made by the accused to the police at any time[16] even though they are "self-serving", i.e., favourable to him. These self-serving statements do not, unless they are proved as part of a confession, constitute evidence of the facts stated[17]; but, if the accused gives evidence to the same effect, they may be relied on by him as proof of consistency, and, whether he gives evidence or not, they are admissible as evidence of his reaction which is part of the general picture which the jury has to consider[18].

(5) *Identification of the accused*

When a witness is asked about his identification of the accused his answer will often involve the direct or indirect proof of a previous statement of his. Such statements may form part of the *res gestae* as in *R.* v. *Fowkes*[19], but the identification may have taken place far too long after the commission of the crime to which the witness deposes for there to be any question of the statement forming part of the *res gestae*.

ART. 24.—Proof of the previous consistent statements of witnesses in civil cases

1. The previous consistent statement of a witness may be proved in a civil case with the leave of the court under s. 2 or s. 4 of the Civil Evidence Act 1968 and when so proved the statement is evidence of the facts and matters of opinion stated and dealt with therein[20].

---

[15] *R.* v. *Wallwork* (1958), 42 Cr. App. Rep. 153.
[16] *R.* v. *Pearce* (1979), 69 Cr. App. Rep. 365.
[17] *R.* v. *Storey* (1968), 52 Cr. App. Rep. 334.
[18] *R.* v. *Donaldson* (1976), 64 Cr. App. Rep. 59.
[19] *Supra.*
[20] See Civil Evidence Act 1972 extending the 1968 Act to statements of opinion.

2. Statements made at such a date as to negative recent fabrication by the witness of his evidence are admissible without the leave of the court under s. 3(1) of the Civil Evidence Act 1968 as evidence of the facts and matters of opinion stated and dealt with therein.

3. A previous consistent statement of a witness may still be proved in a civil case without the leave of the court as evidence of consistency if the statement forms part of the *res gestae*.

Explanation:

(1) *The Civil Evidence Act s. 2*

Section 2 (1) of the Civil Evidence Act 1968 reads as follows:

> "In any civil proceedings a statement made, whether orally or in a document or otherwise, by any person whether called as a witness in those proceedings or not, shall, subject to this section, and to rules of court, be admissible as evidence of any fact stated therein, of which direct oral evidence by him would be admissible."

The rules of court mentioned in s. 2 (1) are made under powers conferred by s. 8. Rules have been made for the High Court and County Court, apart from bankruptcy, but, as yet, no rules have been made for the Magistrates' Courts. The rules require the party who wishes to tender the statement in evidence to serve notice of his intention to do so on all opposite parties[21]; but, if it considers it just, the court may allow the statement to be proved although no notice was given[1]. Whether or not the notice was served, s. 2 (2) of the Act provides that the statement may not be given in evidence without the leave of the court and generally not before the end of the maker's examination-in-chief. The object of the last mentioned restriction is to prevent a party who finds that his witness is not "coming up to proof", i.e. repeating what he said to the party's solicitor, from eking out the examination-in-chief by reference to the witness's proof of evidence.

If the leave of the court is given, the statement is admissible as evidence of the facts stated; it is an "admissible hearsay statement' as defined on p. 15. As the greater includes the lesser, a witness's previous statement received as evidence of the

---

[21] R.S.C. Ord. 38, rr. 21–2.

[1] Ord. 38, r. 29.

facts stated may also be used to prove his consistency, but the converse is not true. In the ordinary case in which the previous statement is identical with the testimony, the distinction is non-existent, but it becomes important if a witness who has been ill or grown senile since he made the statement gives his evidence haltingly or in a confused manner. This happened for no apparent reason, apart from the fact that the trial took place five years after the accident with which it was concerned, in *Morris* v. *Stratford-on-Avon R.D.C.*[2], and the Court of Appeal held that the trial judge had rightly given leave for a statement given by one of the defendants' witnesses to their solicitor nine months after the accident to be received although no notice of desire to give the statement in evidence had been served. The Court stressed the desirability of giving notice whenever it was thought that leave to give the statement in evidence might be sought, but in the particular case the defendants had no reason to suppose that the witness would give his evidence in a confused and inconsistent manner.

Exceptions.—There are three exceptions to the rule that the previous consistent statement of a witness may not be proved under s. 2 until the conclusion of his examination-in-chief. In the first place, the court may allow the statement to be proved by an earlier witness when it is thought desirable to do this in order to prevent the necessity of recalling that witness after the maker of the statement has given his evidence-in-chief.

Secondly, the court may give leave for the statement to be proved during the witness's examination-in-chief on the ground that to prevent the witness from narrating the statement in the course of his evidence would adversely affect the intelligibility of that evidence[3]. There has in the past been too great a tendency for witnesses to be interrupted by counsel or the court when they make such remarks as "Then I said to ... ."

Finally, if the witness is an expert called to give his opinion in accordance with rules made under the Civil Evidence Act 1972, which applies Part 1 of the 1968 Act to statements of opinion, his report made pursuant to those rules may be proved at the beginning of his examination-in-chief or at any other time which the court orders[4].

---

[2] [1973] 3 All E.R. 263; *cf. Ford* v. *Lewis,* [1971] 2 All E.R. 983.
[3] Section 2 (2).
[4] R.S.C. Ord. 38, r. 43.

Overlap with s. 4.—Section 4 of the Civil Evidence Act 1968 deals with the admissibility of statements contained in documents constituting records. It is discussed in Article 40. All that need be said here is that there is a harmless overlap between s. 2 and s. 4. For example, a witness is called to prove that he delivered ten tons of coal at X on 1st January. He reported this fact to his employer's clerk on 2nd January and the clerk made an entry in a book. The entry could be proved either by the witness or by the clerk under either s. 2 or s. 4. The overlap is harmless because requirements identical with those already discussed concerning notice, the leave of the court and the time at which such leave should be given apply to cases in which the supplier of information contained in a record admissible under s. 4. is called as a witness.

(2) *Negativing fabrication*

In civil, no less than in criminal cases, the previous consistent statements of witnesses may be proved as of right in order to rebut a suggestion of fabrication. The only bearing that the Civil Evidence Act has on the matter is that s. 3 (1) (b) provides that where, in any civil proceedings, a previous statement of a witness is proved for the purpose of rebutting a suggestion that his evidence has been fabricated, that statement shall, by virtue of the subsection, be admissible as evidence of the facts stated therein of which direct oral evidence by the witness would be admissible.

(3) *Res gestae*

Section 1(1) of the Civil Evidence Act 1968 provides that:

> "In any civil proceedings a statement other than one made by a person while giving oral evidence in those proceedings shall be admissible as evidence of any fact stated therein to the extent that it is so admissible by virtue of any provision of this part of this act or by virtue of any other statutory provision or by agreement of the parties, but not otherwise."

This precludes the reception of a witness's previous consistent statement as part of the *res gestae* when tendered as evidence of the facts stated therein; but it is at this point that the fact that the lesser does not include the greater becomes crucial. There is nothing in the Act to preclude the reception of a witness's previous statement for the purpose of proving consistency provided that it can be said to form part of the *res gestae* by virtue of the common law. In *Milne* v. *Leisler*[5], the question was whether the plaintiff contracted to sell goods on the footing that A, to whom the goods were delivered, was the agent of B, or on the basis that A was acting on his own behalf. On the first assumption, the defendant was liable in conversion, but not on the second. After the plaintiff had sworn that A purported to contract as agent for B, he was allowed to put in evidence letters written by him to his firm's representative referring to the sale and asking for inquiries to be made concerning the solvency of B. Normally, letters by a party to his agent are excluded as irrelevant or too remotely relevant, because of the facility with which a man can manufacture evidence for himself. But, in this instance, the letters were received, not as direct proof of the sale to B (evidence of the facts stated), but on account of their strong tendency to confirm the plaintiff's testimony. The crucial facts were that the letters could be regarded as part of the events to which the plaintiff was deposing. If a witness says that, in consequence of the naming of a referee, he made certain inquiries in order to determine whether a particular person should be a party to a contract of sale to which he also deposes, the letters containing those inquiries are better evidence than his testimony. Were the facts of *Milne* v. *Leisler* to recur, it seems that, notwithstanding s. 1 (1) of the Civil Evidence Act 1968, the letters could be received to confirm the plaintiff's testimony.

ART. 25.—**Cross-examination**

1. A witness may be asked in cross-examination whether, before the hearing of the case, he made a statement orally or in writing, which is inconsistent with his testimony relating to the issues in the case. If he does not admit the statement, it may be proved by another witness[6].

2. Subject to important exceptions, a witness's answers in cross-examination to credit are final; but the cross-examiner may call a witness to swear that a previous witness's reputation for veracity is such that he ought not to be believed on oath[7], or

---

[5] (1862), 7 H. & N. 786.

[6] Criminal Procedure Act 1865, s. 4 and s. 5.

[7] *R.* v. *Brown and Hedley* (1867), L.R. 1 C.C.R. 70.

that his physical or mental condition is such as to render his evidence unreliable[8].

3. At a criminal trial, the accused is protected against cross-examination to credit by s. 1 (f) of the Criminal Evidence Act 1898, discussed in Article 80.

Explanation:

Cross-examination generally

All witnesses are liable to be cross-examined except those called for the sole purpose of producing a document and a witness who has not been examined in-chief because he was called by accident[9]. The cross-examination may be by or on behalf of all parties other than the party calling the witness. This means that a defendant or accused may be cross-examined by his co-defendant[10] or co-accused[11] as well as by the plaintiff or prosecution.

There are two main types of cross-examination, cross-examination to the issue and cross-examination to credit.

Cross-examination to the issue is designed to elicit statements concerning the facts in issue, or relevant to the issue, which are favourable to the cross-examiner's case. If it is conducted on behalf of the plaintiff or prosecutor, it is subject to a rule of practice that the evidence on which a party wishes to rely should normally be in before the close of that party's case. Accordingly, it is only in unusual circumstances that the cross-examiner is allowed to put questions about matters concerning which his witnesses have not said anything in-chief[12]. When cross-examination to the issue is conducted on behalf of the defence, the witness under cross-examination must normally have his attention drawn to any point on which he is likely to be contradicted by the defence witnesses, so that he can have an opportunity of commenting on it[13].

The exclusionary rules apply just as much to evidence elicited in cross-examination to the issue as they do to evidence

---

[8] *Toohey* v. *Metropolitan Police Commissioner*, [1965] A.C. 595; [1965] 1 All E.R. 506.

[9] *Wood* v. *Mackinson* (1840), 2 Mood. & R. 273.

[10] *Allen* v. *Allen*, [1894] P. 248, at p. 254; *Dryden* v. *Surrey C.C. and Stewart*, [1936] 2 All E.R. 535.

[11] *R.* v. *Hilton*, [1972] 1 Q.B. 421; [1971] 3 All E.R. 541.

[12] *R.* v. *Rice*, [1963] 1 Q.B. 857; [1963] 1 All E.R. 832.

[13] *Browne* v. *Dunn* (1893), 6 R. 67.

in-chief. If a witness under cross-examination says he was told something by someone, the rule against hearsay applies to the same extent as it does to the evidence in-chief of the party on whose behalf the cross-examination is being conducted. In *R. v. Gillespie and Simpson*[14], a prosecution for larceny and false accounting, documents prepared by sales girls who were not called as witnesses were put to the accused in cross-examination and their truth was not admitted, but the accused were nevertheless called upon to read them out. This procedure was held to have been improper; the sales girls not having been called as witnesses, their statements were inadmissible hearsay. If a document is put to a witness in cross-examination and he accepts it as true it becomes evidence; if the witness does not admit the truth of the statements in the document it is, as the Court of Appeal put it, "non-evidence".

Cross-examination to credit, as its name implies, is designed to suggest that the witness is not the kind of person whose evidence can be regarded as trustworthy.

There is a third kind of cross-examination which may or may not be regarded as separate from the second. It is sometimes called "cross-examination to credibility". The questions do not suggest that the witness is deliberately lying, but merely that, for a variety of reasons, he may be mistaken.

Much greater latitude is allowed to the cross-examiner than is accorded to the person conducting the examination-in-chief. Leading questions may be put in cross-examination to the issue as well as in cross-examination to credit. The cross-examination to credit may include questions suggesting that the witness has made statements inconsistent with his present testimony, that he has a criminal record, is biased or has been guilty of disreputable conduct such as to suggest that he is a liar. But the judge has a discretion to disallow questions in cross-examination, and it is contrary to professional etiquette for counsel or a solicitor to put disparaging questions to a witness unless his instructions give him reasonable grounds for supposing that they are justified. Moreover, an over-rigorous cross-examination may rebound against the cross-examiner. This is partly because it may arouse the antipathy of the tribunal of fact, and partly because it may render evidence admissible in re-examination which would not have been admissible in-chief.

---

[14] (1967), 51 Cr. App. Rep. 172.

For example, suggestions made in the cross-examination of a police officer that he acted as an *agent provocateur* and had no reason to suspect the accused of anything when he visited his house, may lead to revelations, in re-examination, about the accused's known record, which would have been inadmissible in-chief. We have already seen that cross-examination on the contents of a document used to refresh memory must sometimes be conducted with caution on account of the possibility that it may render evidence admissible which could not have been given in-chief. If a document in the possession of a witness (though not being used to refresh his memory) is called for in his cross-examination, and read by the cross-examiner, the party calling the witness may insist that the document be put in evidence[15]. Although the point is not covered by authority, it is difficult to escape the conclusion that, in such circumstances, the contents of the document may be treated as evidence of the facts stated under an exception to the hearsay rule.

Special rules govern cross-examination with regard to previous inconsistent statements, the finality of a witness's answers in cross-examination to credit or credibility, and the protection of the accused against cross-examination to credit.

Previous inconsistent statements

At common law it was permissible to ask in cross-examination about inconsistent statements, but there were certain difficulties in connection with proving them, which were removed by statute in 1854. The governing legislation is now the Criminal Procedure Act 1865, ss. 4 and 5. This applies to civil as well as criminal cases, but with an important difference owing to s. 3 of the Civil Evidence Act 1968.

When the fact that a witness made a statement inconsistent with his testimony is proved or admitted in a criminal case, the effect is simply to weaken or totally destroy the value of that testimony. The contents of the statement do not constitute positive evidence of the facts stated. If a witness tells the police that the accused participated in a crime and later swears in court that this was not so, the judge cannot tell the jury to choose which of these contradictory assertions to believe. He can only advise them to disregard the witness's evidence altogether[16].

---

[15] *Stroud* v. *Stroud,* [1963] 3 All E.R. 539.

[16] *R.* v. *White* (1922), 17 Cr. App. Rep. 60.

Under s. 3 (1) of the Civil Evidence Act 1968 an inconsistent statement received under s. 4 or s. 5 of the Criminal Procedure Act 1865 is admissible as evidence of any fact stated therein of which direct oral evidence of the maker would have been admissible. Accordingly, if the crime in the example given in the last paragraph had been a riot and the proceedings took the form of a civil claim for damage caused by it, the judge could have told the jury that they might choose which of the contradictory statements to believe, and, if there had been no jury, he could have chosen for himself. Of course, on the principle that the greater includes the lesser, inconsistent statements proved as a result of cross-examination in civil cases may simply be treated as sufficient to neutralize the maker's testimony. A statutory provision that a statement is admissible as evidence of the facts stated does not preclude its use for the purpose for which it is admissible at common law, and there would have to be good reason, such as evidence that the witness had been "got at", to justify the reception of the earlier statement as a hearsay statement[17].

Finality of answers in cross-examination to credit

The great difference between cross-examination to the issue and cross-examination to credit is that, whereas the witness's answers to the former may always be contradicted by other evidence adduced in due course by the cross-examiner, answers in cross-examination to credit are usually final. The distinction between the two types of cross-examination is not always easy to draw but it is clear enough in most cases. On a charge of stealing, the question whether a witness for the prosecution has been convicted, or has kept bad company, or been involved in some scandal, plainly goes to credit only, but the facts of the leading case of *Attorney-General* v. *Hitchcock*[18] show that difficult problems can arise. The defendant was charged with using a cistern for making malt without complying with certain statutory requirements. Spooner gave evidence of the use of the cistern and was asked in cross-examination on behalf of the defendant whether he had not told Cook that the excise officers had offered him £20 to say that the cistern had been used. He denied that he had ever made such a statement, and it was held that Cook could not be called on behalf of the defendant to contradict Spooner. The fact that he had been offered a bribe

[17] See p. 15, *ante*, for the latter term.

[18] (1847), 1 Exch. 91.

by the excise officers would not have affected his credit, though his receipt of a bribe would have shown bias; but the offer would have been relevant to the issue as tending to show lack of confidence in their case on the part of the excise officers. It could not, however, have been proved by Cook's hearsay statement.

On charges of rape and indecent assault upon an adult woman with intent to commit rape, the prosecutrix may be asked in cross-examination whether she has had intercourse with the accused on occasions other than that charged and her denial may be contradicted on account of the relevance of the fact to the issue of consent[19]. The prosecutrix's intercourse with other men is also relevant to that issue, though to a considerably less degree, but it has been held to go to credit only, and her denials cannot be contradicted[20]. As a result of s. 2 (1) of the Sexual Offences (Amendment) Act 1976, the prosecutrix cannot be asked in cross-examination about her sexual experience with other men without the leave of the judge which may only be given if he is satisfied that its refusal would be unfair to the defendant. The subsection imposes a similar restriction on the adduction of evidence relating to the prosecutrix's sexual experience with men other than the defendant. Leave might be granted if the prosecutrix denied that she was a prostitute in response to a question allowed by the judge, for the fact that she offered herself to others for gain has been held to be relevant to the issue of consent and not merely to credit[1].

Exceptions

There are three exceptions to the rule that a witness's answers to cross-examination to credit are final.

(1) *Previous inconsistent statements.*—First, if he denies that he has previously made a statement inconsistent with his testimony, the statement may be proved by another witness under s. 4 of the Criminal Procedure Act 1865 which applies to civil and criminal cases.

(2) *Previous convictions.*—Secondly, if the witness denies that he has been previously convicted, the conviction may be

---

[19] *R.* v. *Riley* (1887), 18 Q.B.D. 481.

[20] *R.* v. *Holmes* (1871), L.R. 1 C.C.R. 334.

[1] *R.* v. *Bashir and Mazur*, [1969] 3 All E.R. 692; *R.* v. *Krausz* (1973), 57 Cr. App. Rep. 466.

proved by the production of the appropriate certificates under s. 6 of the Criminal Procedure Act 1865 which also applies to civil and criminal cases. In civil cases a witness may not be asked about convictions which are "spent" within the meaning of the Rehabilitation of Offenders Act 1974 which prohibits reference to convictions which have been followed by specified trouble free periods. Questions about spent convictions are permitted in criminal cases, but a practice direction requires reference to them to be avoided as far as possible. Subject to these restrictions, s. 6 of the 1865 Act allows a witness to be asked whether he has been convicted of any offence. There is no such express restriction to such convictions as those for perjury or those involving dishonesty.

(3) *Bias*.—Finally, a witness who denies that he is biased in favour of one of the parties may be contradicted by other evidence on the point. In *Thomas* v. *David*[2], an action on a bill of exchange, one of the plaintiff's witnesses was asked whether she was his mistress, and it was held that the defendant might call witnesses to prove this fact after she had denied it.

> "If the question had been whether the witness had walked the streets as a common prostitute, I think that that would have been collateral to the issue, and that, had the witness denied such a charge, she could not have been contradicted."[3]

A witness may likewise be contradicted if he denies in cross-examination that he has repeatedly quarrelled with one of the parties[4].

Witness's bad reputation for veracity

After a witness has given evidence, the opponent of the party calling him may call another witness to swear that the reputation of the first witness as a liar is so notorious that he ought not to be believed on oath. This course is seldom adopted. When it is, the witness must confine himself. in-chief to evidence of reputation.

Physical or mental condition of witness

In *Toohey* v. *Metropolitan Police Commissioner*[5], the accused were

---

[2] (1836), 7. C. & P. 350.

[3] COLERIDGE, J.

[4] *Dunn* v. *Aslett* (1838), 2 Mood. & R. 122.

[5] [1965] A.C. 595; [1965] 1 All E.R. 506.

charged with assaulting a boy of sixteen with intent to rob him. The boy's case was that the accused had demanded money and cigarettes, taken him up an alley, and assaulted him in the course of searching him. The accused's defence was that they had found the boy in a state of hysteria exacerbated by drink and were helping him home. The House of Lords held that the accused should have been allowed to call a police surgeon to swear that the boy was in an hysterical condition when brought to the police station, that he smelt of drink and that drink was liable to exacerbate hysteria. The surgeon's evidence was relevant to the issue because it assisted in the resolution of the question whether the alleged assault accounted for the hysteria, or whether the hysteria accounted for the allegation of assault. The primary importance of the decision of the House of Lords is that it sanctions the calling of a witness to impugn the reliability of an opponent's witness on medical grounds. The point was made that, where appropriate, a subsequent witness might be called to swear to the fact that a previous witness had impaired vision or hearing which rendered his evidence about certain matters unreliable.

The accused's shield

We have seen that the Criminal Evidence Act 1898 allows the accused to give evidence on his own behalf in all criminal cases. Section 1 (f) provides him with a shield against cross-examination to credit. This is especially valuable to a prisoner who has previously been convicted or misconducted himself. If he was treated in exactly the same way as any other witness, counsel for the prosecution could always ask him questions about his previous convictions and past offences, and the jury might be too ready to infer that he was guilty of the crime charged because he was the kind of person who would commit such a crime. The general effect of s. 1 (f) is that the accused is only liable to be cross-examined on his record in the exceptional cases in which it can be proved in-chief by the prosecution, or when he throws his shield away. He does this if he gives, or adduces, evidence of good character, casts imputations on a witness for the prosecution, or testifies against a co-accused. The interpretation of s. 1 (f) is considered in Article 80.

ART. 26.—**Unfavourable and hostile witnesses**

A party may not impeach the credit of his own witness; but,

if the witness proves unfavourable, he may contradict him by other evidence relating to the issue and, if given leave by the judge to treat the witness as hostile, he may also ask whether he has made a statement inconsistent with his testimony and contradict him with that statement if it is denied[6].

Explanation: A witness is to some extent regarded as being "on the side of" the party calling him, or a member of that party's team. Accordingly, however uncooperative the witness may be, the party calling him may not cast doubt on his credit by, for example, asking him about previous inconsistent statements, previous convictions or disreputable conduct. A witness who simply fails to prove the fact which he is called to prove is said to be "unfavourable", and an unfavourable witness must be distinguished from a "hostile" or "adverse" witness. A hostile witness is one who shows that he is not desirous of telling the truth at the instance of the party calling him. It is necessary for the party calling a witness to obtain leave from the judge to treat the witness as hostile, if the circumstances warrant the adoption of such a course.

(1) *Unfavourable witnesses*

The rule that a party may not impeach his own witness does not prevent him from calling other witnesses to give evidence contradicting that of his earlier witnesses. For example, if a witness called to prove that A and B were partners fails to do so, another witness may be called by the same party to prove the partnership, although the effect of his testimony would be to contradict the earlier witness. If the law were otherwise the result of a case might depend on the mere chance as to which of several witnesses was first called by the same party[7].

In civil cases, a party may contradict his unfavourable witness by means of the previous statement of that witness if the court gives leave for the statement to be admitted under s. 2 of the Civil Evidence Act 1968.

(2) *Hostile witnesses*

When leave has been given to treat a witness as hostile he may be asked about previous inconsistent statements, and these may be proved if they are denied. The witness may also, like an

---

[6] Criminal Procedure Act 1865, s. 3.

[7] *Ewer* v. *Ambrose* (1825), 3 B. & C. 746.

unfavourable witness, be contradicted by other evidence relevant to the issue. Although even a hostile witness may not be discredited by general evidence of bad character, the examination becomes more like a cross-examination once the leave has been granted. It has been said that, if counsel for the prosecution is aware of a contradictory statement made by a Crown witness, he should always show it to the judge and ask leave to treat the witness as hostile[8]. Leave to treat a witness as hostile is probably given more sparingly in civil than in criminal cases. In criminal cases, it is not unheard of for a Crown witness to contradict his deposition, as well as statements made by him to the police.

If, in a criminal case, the witness is treated as hostile, and the statement or deposition is proved or admitted, it does not become evidence of the facts stated. It merely neutralises the witness's adverse testimony[9] but, in a civil case, statements admissible by virtue of s. 3 of the Criminal Procedure Act 1865 (which applies to civil as well as criminal proceedings) may be proved as evidence of the facts stated under s. 3 (1) of the Civil Evidence Act 1968.

ART. 27.—Recalling a witness, evidence in rebuttal and the calling of witnesses by the judge

The judge has a discretion to allow a party to recall a witness, to allow evidence in rebuttal to be given by a party after his case has been closed, and, in criminal cases, to call a witness himself. In general, the discretion will only be exercised sparingly.

Explanation:

Recalling a witness

It sometimes happens that a party desires to recall a witness either because there is something which he has forgotten to ask him, or else because of some unforeseen contingency. It is necessary to obtain the leave of the judge and, although the judge has a complete discretion in the matter, it does not follow that leave will be given.

---

[8] *R.* v. *Fraser and Warren* (1956), 40 Cr. App. Rep. 160.
[9] *R.* v. *Golder, Jones and Porritt,* [1960] 3 All E.R. 457.

Evidence in rebuttal

The power to allow further evidence to be called by a party after he has closed his case is exercised very sparingly. The principal illustrations of its exercise, and of the refusal to exercise it, are provided by criminal cases in which the prosecutor wishes to call rebutting evidence. When the evidence relates to a material, as opposed to a purely formal, point, the judge will only give leave to call it if it relates to a matter which the prosecutor was unable to foresee. It has even been said that the matter must be one which no human ingenuity could have foreseen[10]. At least the evidence must have been regarded by the Crown as only marginally relevant so far as its case was concerned and rendered substantially relevant by the case for the defence[11].

In *R.* v. *Day*[12], for instance, the trial judge allowed the prosecution in a case of forgery to call a handwriting expert after the case for the prosecution had been closed. The accused was convicted, but his conviction was quashed by the Court of Criminal Appeal because the evidence was of a kind the necessity of which should have been foreseen from the outset.

In *R.* v. *Flynn*[13], on the other hand, the Court of Criminal Appeal held that the trial judge had rightly allowed evidence in rebuttal of a last minute alibi to be given after the closing speeches had been made.

An example of a purely formal omission which the court will usually allow to be remedied, even after the close of the case for the prosecution, would be a case in which the Crown failed to prove that the leave of the Director of Public Prosecutions had been obtained, when such leave is necessary, before the prosecution was begun[14].

Calling of witnesses by judge

In a civil case, the judge has no power to call a witness himself without the consent of the parties[15], but he may do so in a criminal case if the interests of justice so require[16]. The judge must not appear to be supplementing the prosecution's

---

[10] *R.* v. *Frost* (1839), 4 State Tr. N.S. 85, at col. 376.
[11] *R.* v. *Levy* (1966), 50 Cr. App. Rep. 198.
[12] [1940] 1 All E.R. 402.
[13] (1957), 42 Cr. App. Rep. 15.
[14] *Price* v. *Humphries,* [1958] 2 Q. B. 353; [1958] 2 All E.R. 725.
[15] *Re Enoch and Zaretsky, Bock & Co.,* [1910] 1 K.B. 327.
[16] *R.* v. *Harris,* [1972] 2 K. B. 587.

case by calling a witness[17], although a witness called by the judge is not cross-examined in the full sense, the judge will, in addition to putting questions himself, usually allow the parties to ask questions[18].

No witness may ever be called once the judge has summed up to the jury, even if the jury ask for the witness's evidence[19].

ART. 28.—**Privilege generally**

A witness may claim to be privileged from:

1. answering incriminating questions in criminal and civil cases;
2. disclosing communications made to him by his spouse during the marriage but only in criminal cases[20];
3. giving evidence to prove that marital intercourse took place between him and his spouse at any period but only in criminal cases[1];
4. if a lawyer, disclosing communications made to him by his client without the client's consent, and, if a client, from disclosing communications made to him by his lawyer;
5. disclosing communications passing between himself and his patent agent, his patent agent and other persons, and himself and other persons for the purpose of any pending or contemplated proceedings under the Patents Act 1977[2];
6. producing any deed or other document relating to his title to any land in criminal proceedings;
7. in civil proceedings, disclosing a "without prejudice" communication made to him without the consent of the parties to the communication.

Explanation: A privilege may always be waived, and with the exception of "without prejudice" communications, matters

---

[17] *R.* v. *Cleghorn,* [1967] 2 Q.B. 584; [1967] 1 All E.R. 996; *cf. R.* v. *Tregear,* [1967] 2 Q.B. 574; [1967] 1 All E.R. 989.

[18] *Coulson* v. *Disborough,* [1894] 2 Q.B. 316, at p. 318.

[19] *R.* v. *Gearing,* (1966), 50 Cr. App. Rep. 18.

[20] Criminal Evidence Act 1898, s. 1 (d).

[1] Matrimonial Causes Act 1965, s. 43 (1).

[2] Patents Act 1977, s. 104.

covered by privilege may always be proved by the evidence of other witnesses. For instance, there seems to be no reason why a stolen document, the subject of legal professional privilege, should not be given in evidence[3], and a communication between spouses overheard[4] or intercepted[5] may likewise be proved by a third party.

Details concerning the first four privileges mentioned in the article are given in the succeeding articles. The privilege with regard to proceedings under the Patents Act is based on s. 104 of the Patents Act 1977, and is too specialised for further discussion. At common law a witness was privileged from producing his title deeds. This privilege is said to have been based on the complexity of the old land law as the deeds when produced might have disclosed a defect in the witness's title. It was abolished, so far as civil cases are concerned, by s. 16 of the Civil Evidence Act 1968, and it is difficult to see how it could very often apply in practice in a criminal case. Certainly it does not call for any further discussion in this book.

In many cases the privilege is claimed in interlocutory civil proceedings for discovery or leave to administer interrogatories, and the claim may relate to the production of a document or thing as well as to the answer to a question. When a question in respect to which a witness might claim privilege is put in court, the judge or one of the counsel concerned in the case usually informs the witness of the existence of the privilege.

The first six privileges mentioned in the article are coming to be called "private interest" privileges in contrast with the "public interest" privileges, or "immunities", discussed in article 68. These include the protection of state secrets. In some instances public interest privileges cannot be waived and they cannot be circumvented by the use of secondary evidence where that is available. What is called a privilege must then be regarded as an absolute exclusionary rule, hence their treatment in a different part of this book. But the separation of private and public interest privileges is purely a matter of convenience for there is a *continuum* of relevant evidence which may be excluded running from legal professional communi-

---

[3] *Lloyd* v. *Mostyn* (1842), 10 M. & W. 478, at pp. 481–2; *Calcraft* v. *Guest*, [1898] 1 Q.B. 759.

[4] *R.* v. *Simons* (1834), 6 C. & P. 540.

[5] *Rumping* v. *Director of Public Prosecutions*, [1964] A.C. 814; [1962] 3 All E.R. 256, H.L.

cations, through without prejudice statements to state secrets[6]. Without prejudice statements are dealt with in art. 33 because there is no doubt that they can be waived. They could, however, equally well have been treated as a public interest privilege because there is very little doubt that some of these privileges can be waived.

ART. 29.—The privilege against self-incrimination

No one is bound to answer any question or to produce any document or thing if to do so would, in the opinion of the judge, have a tendency to expose the deponent or his spouse to any criminal charge, penalty or (in criminal cases) forfeiture which the judge regards as reasonably likely to be preferred or sued for[7].

Explanation: It is a deeply rooted principle of the common law that no one should be obliged to criminate himself out of his own mouth. Civil actions for penalties or forfeitures are liable to be oppressive, and this accounts for the other limb of the privilege; but s. 16 (1) (a) of the Civil Evidence Act 1968 abolishes the rule whereby a person cannot be compelled to answer any question or to produce any document or thing if to do so would tend to expose him to a forfeiture; the section is confined to civil cases. The privilege against self-incrimination does not extend to questions tending to expose the witness to any other civil liability[8] (including liability to an affiliation order)[9] or to a finding of adultery[10]. The privilege applies to answers to any questions tending to criminate, and not merely to direct questions on the subject, but the mere statement by the witness that the answer would tend to criminate him is not conclusive, for the court must consider whether there is any reasonable probability of this result[11].

---

[6] See *per* Lord SIMON OF GLAISDALE in *D.* v. *N.S.P.C.C.*, [1978] A.C. 171, at p. 233.

[7] *Blunt* v. *Park Lane Hotel*, [1942] 2 K.B. 253, at p. 257; [1942] 2 All E.R. 187, at p. 190.

[8] Witnesses Act 1806.

[9] *S.* v. *E.*, [1967] 1 Q.B. 367; [1967] 1 All E.R. 593.

[10] *Blunt* v. *Park Lane Hotel*, [1942] 2 K.B. 253; [1942] 2 All E.R. 187.

[11] *R.* v. *Boyes* (1861), 1 B. & S. 311.

Section 14 (1) of the Civil Evidence Act 1968 makes it clear that, in civil cases, the privilege is confined to incrimination under the law of any part of the United Kingdom, but extends to the incrimination of the witness's spouse. Both the extension[12] and the restriction[13] probably apply in criminal cases by virtue of the common law.

Statutory exceptions

An accused giving evidence on his own behalf under the Criminal Evidence Act 1898 cannot object to answering a question because of its tendency to criminate him as to the offence charged. There are other statutes under which the privilege cannot be invoked in special proceedings such as examinations in bankruptcy. Under s. 31 (1) of the Theft Act 1968, a witness may not refuse to answer any questions in proceedings for the recovery or administration of property or the execution of a trust on the ground that to do so might incriminate him or his spouse of an offence under the Act; but the witness's answers are not admissible against him in subsequent proceedings for an offence under the Act or, unless they married after the answer was given, his spouse. Several other statutes contain a similar provision.

The right to silence

Though, strictly speaking, confined to answers given by a witness in court, the privilege against self-incrimination lies at the root of what is sometimes spoken of as the "right to silence". Subject to a very few statutory exceptions[14], a person commits no offence by refusing to answer questions put to him by someone who is endeavouring to discover whether and by whom an offence has been committed. In general his failure to reply to such questions cannot be made the subject of adverse comment, and, as such, it certainly does not amount to an admission of the truth of any charge mentioned in the question. If, in spite of having had every opportunity of disclosing it at an earlier date, the accused does not raise a particular defence until the day of his trial, it may be in order for the judge to draw the jury's attention to this fact, but if

---

[12] *R.* v. *All Saints Worcester* (1817), 6 M. & S. 194, at p. 201.

[13] *Re Atherton,* [1912] 2 K.B. 251, at p. 255.

[14] For examples see Official Secrets Act 1920, s. 6 and the Road Traffic Act 1972, s. 162.

more is said, "it, may give rise to the inference that a jury is being invited to disregard the defence put forward because the accused exercised his right of silence."[15]

It generally makes no difference whether the police questions which the accused did not answer were addressed to him with or without the usual caution, for the caution is simply a reminder to the suspect of his common law right not to answer[16]. When the police are not involved and two people may be treated as being on equal terms, the fact that one of them does not deny a charge made by the other may be treated as evidence of a tacit admission of its truth. In *Parkes* v. *R.*[17] the accused had been convicted of the murder of a young woman. Her mother came out of the room where she had found her bleeding from stab wounds and asked him why he had done it. He said nothing, and, when the deceased's mother took hold of him, he threatened her with a knife. The Judicial Committee held that the jury had been properly directed that there was evidence from which they might infer the accused's acceptance of the truth of the mother's charge. The parties may sometimes be treated as being on equal terms when one of them is a police officer, as when the solicitor of the other is present. Subject to the jury's being properly directed, the accused's failure to answer questions might then be treated as an acceptance of adverse suggestions implied in them[18].

The other aspect of the right to silence is the accused's right not to give evidence at his trial mentioned on p. 64.

The privilege against self-incrimination is also the basis, or one of the bases, of the exclusionary rule relating to confessions which are not "voluntary" within the meaning of that term discussed in Article 46, and of the judge's discretion to exclude evidence the reception of which would render the accused's trial unfair[19].

ART. 30.—**Communications between spouses in criminal cases**

In a criminal case "No husband shall be compellable to disclose any communication made to him by his wife during

---

[15] VISCOUNT DILHORNE in *R.* v. *Gilbert* (1977), 66 Cr. App. Rep. 237, at p. 244.

[16] *Hall* v. *R.,* [1971] 1 All E.R. 322.

[17] [1976] 3 All E.R. 380.

[17] *R.* v. *Chandler,* [1976] 1 All E.R. 105.

[19] See the speech of Lord DIPLOCK in *R.* v. *Sang,* [1979] 2 All E.R. 1222.

the marriage, and no wife shall be compellable to disclose any communication made to her by her husband during the marriage."

Explanation: The article quotes s. 1 (d) of the Criminal Evidence Act 1898. The privilege is that of the spouse *to* whom the communication is made. Accordingly, if a wife is giving evidence against her husband in a case in which she is competent to do so, he cannot prevent her from disclosing an admission made by him to her.

The identically worded s. 3 of the Evidence (Amendment) Act 1853 (repealed so far as civil proceedings are concerned by the Civil Evidence Act 1968) was restrictively interpreted by the Court of Appeal in *Shenton* v. *Tyler*[20]. It was held that the privilege only endures so long as the recipient of the communication is the husband or wife of the person making it. The result was that a widow could be obliged to answer interrogatories concerning communications made to her by her late husband with regard to a secret trust. If this construction is applied to s. 1 (d) of the Criminal Evidence Act, it would mean that a divorced wife, giving evidence for her former husband when competent to do so, could be obliged to disclose an admission made by him during the marriage.

Shenton v. *Tyler* decided that the privilege is purely statutory. There is not, as was sometimes supposed, a broader privilege protecting the maker of the communication, and enabling the spouses to prevent disclosure of their intercepted communications by third parties. This latter point was decided by the House of Lords in *Rumping* v. *Director of Public Prosecutions*[21], in which a man charged with murder had written a letter virtually confessing the crime to his wife. The letter was intercepted, and it was held that it might be proved as part of the prosecution's case.

ART. 31.—Questions to spouses concerning intercourse in criminal cases

1. "The evidence of a husband or wife shall be admissible in any proceedings to prove that marital intercourse did or did

[20] [1939] Ch. 620; [1939] 1 All E.R. 827.
[21] [1964] A.C. 814; [1962] 3 All E.R. 256, H.L.

not take place between them during any period.[1]"

2. In a criminal case "A husband or wife shall not be compellable in any proceedings to give evidence of the matters aforesaid."[2]

Explanation: At common law there was a rule, which came to be known as the rule in *Russell* v. *Russell*[3], under which spouses were not permitted to give evidence of non-access during the marriage tending to bastardise a child born in wedlock. The rule applied to criminal cases[4] but it was abolished by the Law Reform (Miscellaneous Provisions) Act 1949 and the governing statute is now the Matrimonial Causes Act 1973, s. 48 (1) of which is quoted in the article.

The Act of 1949 conferred an entirely new privilege on spouses against giving evidence of intercourse, whether or not the legitimacy of a child was affected. This provision was repeated in successive Matrimonial Causes Acts, but it was repealed, so far as civil proceedings are concerned, by s. 16 of the Civil Evidence Act 1968. The Matrimonial Causes Act 1973 preserves that part of s. 43 (1) of the Matrimonial Causes Act 1965 which is set out in clause 2 of the article. There are not likely to be many criminal cases in which the question of the availability of the privilege will arise, and it is arguable that, having regard to its context, s. 43 (1) has no application to criminal proceedings; if this is so, however, there is no reason why the subsection should have been preserved.

ART. 32.—Legal professional privilege

In civil and criminal cases, confidential communications passing between a client and his legal adviser need not be given in evidence by the client and, without the client's consent, may not be given in evidence by the legal adviser if made either

(1) to enable the client to obtain or the adviser to give legitimate legal advice; or

(2) with reference to litigation which is actually taking place or was in the contemplation of the client.

---

[1] Matrimonial Causes Act 1973, s. 48 (1).

[2] Matrimonial Causes Act 1965, s. 43 (1).

[3] [1924] A.C. 687.

[4] *R.* v. *Carmichael* [1940], 1 K.B. 630; [1940] 2 All E.R. 165.

The privilege is overridden by the necessity of disclosing information which may lead to the acquittal of someone accused of crime.

Communications passing between the legal adviser or client and third parties need not be given in evidence by the client and, without the consent of the client, may not be given in evidence by the legal adviser if they come within (2) above.

Explanation: The term "legal adviser" refers to solicitors and barristers, but the privilege protects communications by the client or his agent with the clerk or other subordinate of the adviser and *vice versa*. The term "communications" must be taken to include drafts, notes and other documents incidental to the obtaining and giving of advice or the conduct of litigation. So far as communications between lawyer and client are concerned, nothing turns on the distinction between the matters covered by heads (1) and (2) in the article, but the distinction is crucial when communications passing between the lawyer or client and third parties come to be considered.

1. *Communications between client and legal adviser*

The privilege extends to communications passing between a client and his foreign legal adviser and, if litigation is pending or contemplated, it makes no difference whether the proceedings are English or foreign[5].

Facts excluded.—The privilege does not prevent the disclosure of facts discovered during the relationship of lawyer and client. It has accordingly been held that a barrister can state in court whether a book contained a particular entry when it was produced to him by his client[6].

Legitimate advice.—The privilege is confined to the obtaining of legitimate legal advice. It would not apply where advice is sought concerning the safest way of committing a crime[7]. But it would apply to a letter from a solicitor warning his client that he would be criminally liable if he pursued a particular course of conduct as the communication would not have been in furtherance of crime[8]. It is said that the privilege does not

---

[5] *Re Duncan,* [1968] p. 306; [1968] 2 All E.R. 395.
[6] *Brown* v. *Foster* (1857), 7 H. & N. 736.
[7] *R.* v. *Cox and Railton* (1884), 14 Q.B.D. 153.
[8] *Butler* v. *Board of Trade,* [1971] Ch. 680; [1970] 3 All E.R. 593.

extend to communications made to facilitate the commission of fraud by the client, but, assuming the fraud to be non-criminal, the term is restrictively construed in this context. It does not include an inducement of breach of contract[9].

Limitation and waiver.—The privilege must yield to the principle that, at a criminal trial, no one should be able to refuse to answer questions or produce documents which might lead to the acquittal of the accused[10].

Like other private interest privileges, legal professional privilege may be waived expressly or by implication, but the waiver of privilege affecting a conversation between a party to litigation and his solicitor does not entail a waiver of privilege relating to briefs and other documents brought into existence for the purpose of the litigation[11].

Privileged documents obtained by third parties.—In *Calcraft* v. *Guest*[12] the originals of the proofs of witnesses and notes on the evidence in an action brought by the plaintiff's predecessor in title had come into the possession of the defendant. They belonged to the plaintiff and contained matter relevant to his action. Before returning them the defendant took copies and the Court of Appeal, while affirming that the rule "once privileged always privileged" applied to the documents, allowed the defendant to put the copies in as part of his case. This is an illustration of the doctrine of English law that illegally or improperly obtained evidence is admissible if it is relevant, but this does not affect the rights of the person entitled to a privileged document against the person in possession of it. He may be able to obtain an unrestricted injunction against its use, or the use of a copy, which would protect him in subsequent civil litigation[13], but the court will not grant an injunction that a privileged document, or a copy of such a document, which has accidentally come into the possession of a government department, may not be used by it in a public prosecution against the owner[14].

---

[9] *Crescent Farm (Sidcup) Sports Ltd.* v. *Sterling Offices Ltd.*, [1972] Ch. 553; [1971] 3 All E.R. 1192.

[10] *R.* v. *Barton*, [1972] 2 All E.R. 1192.

[11] *Doland (George) Ltd.* v. *Blackburn, Robinson, Coates and Co.*, [1972] 3 All E.R. 959.

[12] [1898] 1 Q.B. 759.

[13] *Lord Ashburton* v. *Pape*, [1913] 2 Ch. 469.

[14] *Butler* v. *Board of Trade*, [1971] Ch. 680; [1970] 3 All E.R. 593.

2. *Communications between lawyer or client and third parties*

When litigation is not contemplated, communications between the legal adviser and third parties to enable him to obtain information before giving his opinion are not privileged. This was decided in the leading case of *Wheeler* v. *Le Marchant*[15] where the defendant was obliged to produce reports, made to his solicitor by a surveyor, with regard to property that became the subject of litigation which was not contemplated when the reports were made. Counsel's opinion taken by a solicitor is always privileged either because the counsel is the legal adviser for the purposes of the rule or else because he is the *alter ego* of the solicitor[16].

Communications between the client or his agent and third parties are likewise only privileged if made for the purpose of obtaining information to enable the legal adviser to advise concerning pending or contemplated litigation. In *Alfred Crompton Amusement Machines, Ltd.* v. *Customs and Excise Commissioners*[17], the company notified the Commissioners in 1967 that they were dissatisfied with the agreed formula under which it had been paying purchase tax. The prescribed procedure in such a case was that the Commissioners should state an opinion on the basis on which tax ought to be paid and, if this were not accepted, the parties should proceed to arbitration. The Commissioners stated their opinion in 1968, although they had anticipated arbitration since 1967. In the arbitration proceedings they claimed privilege (1) in respect of communications with their salaried legal advisers in order to obtain advice; (2) communications with their legal advisers in order to obtain evidence for use in the anticipated arbitration; (3) internal communications with their officers and agents concerning the assessment of the purchase tax payable by the company; and (4) documents received in confidence from third parties concerning the value of machines sold by the company. The House of Lords held that professional privilege attached to the first[18] and second sets of communication; but by a majority they held that no professional privilege attached to the third and fourth sets because they came into existence solely in order to enable the Commissioners to form an

---

[15] (1881), 17 Ch. D. 675.

[16] *Bristol Corporation* v. *Cox* (1884), 26 Ch.D. 678.

[17] [1974] A.C. 405; [1973] 2 All E.R. 1169.

[18] This point was not argued in the House of Lords.

opinion about the basis of assessment of the tax, and not at all for the purpose of assisting the Commissioners' contentions in the arbitration.

Where the communications have a dual or multiple purpose, as when an inquiry is held by the British Railways Board into the cause of an accident both with a view to preventing its repetition, and laying information before the Board's solicitor in the event of litigation, the question is whether the latter was the dominant purpose[19].

Other confidential or professional communications

Apart from the privilege relating to proceedings under the Patents Act mentioned in Article 28 there is no privilege protecting other confidential communications as a matter of law, although they are frequently protected in practice because a witness is not in fact pressed to disclose them and the judge may have a discretion to disallow questions concerning them[20]. As a matter of law no privilege protects communications between priest and penitent or doctor and patient. Similarly, a journalist is not privileged against disclosing the name of his informant[1], although, in actions of defamation in which fair comment or qualified privilege is pleaded, interrogatories will not be allowed concerning a journalist's source of information[2].

ART. 33.—**Statements made without prejudice**

The contents of a statement made without prejudice cannot be put in evidence in a civil case without the consent of both parties to the litigation.

Explanation: "Without prejudice" means "without prejudice to the legal rights of the maker of the statement." The parties frequently make "without prejudice" statements as part of an endeavour to settle a dispute, and, were it possible to disclose the statement, it might be prejudicial to the rights of the maker, because an offer to settle could be construed as an admission of

---

[19] *Waugh* v. *British Railways Board,* [1979] 2 All. E.R. 1196.

[20] The House of Lords was evenly divided on the position "when it comes to the forensic crunch" in *D.* v. *N.S.P.C.C.,* [1978] A.C. 171.

[1] *A.-G.* v. *Mulholland and Foster,* [1963] 2 Q.B. 477; [1963] 1 All E.R. 767.

[2] R.S.C. Ord. 82, r. 6.

the soundness of the opponent's case. There is no magic in the words used by the parties in order to produce the cloak of the privilege as long as it is clear that the statement in question was intended to be without prejudice. If the first of a series of letters is headed "without prejudice", the privilege may attach to the rest of the correspondence[3].

The privilege applies although the only outstanding issue between the parties is costs. Thus, without the consent of the parties, a judge may not look at "without prejudice" correspondence in order to see whether one party could have saved costs by accepting a favourable offer at an early stage of the litigation[4]. In determining whether one of the parties has been unduly dilatory, however, a judge may take into account the fact that there were "without prejudice" negotiations, although he may not refer to their terms.

The "without prejudice" cloak only covers communications connected with the attempt to compromise litigation, although this may extend to reports obtained by one of the parties from a third party[5]; libel is nonetheless a libel because contained in a letter headed "without prejudice", and such a letter may be relied on as an act of bankruptcy if it contains a statement that the writer is unable to pay his debts as they fall due[6]. A binding agreement as to liability leaving the question of *quantum* open, may be proved by "without prejudice" correspondence[7].

If estranged spouses employ the good offices of a mediator, statements made by either of them to him are privileged, and he may only disclose them in court with the consent of both parties[8]. Such consent is also necessary before evidence can be given of the terms of a "without prejudice" conversation by someone who was present when it took place[9].

ART. 34.—**Opinion**

1. The general rule is that witnesses must speak to the facts which they have observed, not to their opinion, i.e. the inferences which they draw from those facts.

---

[3] *Paddock* v. *Forester* (1842), 3 Man. & G. 903.
[4] *Walker* v. *Wilsher* (1889), 23 Q.B.D. 335.
[5] *Rabin* v. *Mendoza,* [1954] 1 All E.R. 247.
[6] *Re Daintrey, Ex parte Holt,* [1893] 2 Q.B. 116.
[7] *Tomlin* v. *Standard Telephones & Cables Ltd.,* [1969] 3 All E.R. 201.
[8] *Henley* v. *Henley,* [1955] P. 202; [1955] 1 All E.R. 590 n.
[9] *Theodoropoulas* v. *Theodoropoulas,* [1964] P. 311; [1963] 2 All E.R. 772.

2. Expert witnesses may be asked for their opinion on matters calling for special knowledge such as questions of art and science; and any witness may be asked to give his opinion concerning a number of non-technical matters when it would be impracticable for him to give his evidence in any other form.

3. Section 3 of the Civil Evidence Act 1972 provides that, in civil proceedings, an expert may give his opinion on an issue in the proceedings; and declares that any witness may state his opinion on such an issue as a way of conveying relevant facts personally perceived by him.

Explanation:

(1) *The general rule*

The basis of the general rule stated in the article is that it is the function of the jury, or the judge when there is no jury, to draw inferences from facts stated by witnesses. If witnesses were allowed to state their inferences (the same thing as expressing their opinions) without restriction, the jury might act on those inferences instead of coming to their own conclusion. The issues in a case must be determined by the court or jury, not by the opinion of witnesses. Accordingly it has been said that although a bystander may have a complete and full view of a motor accident, he can only inform the court of what he saw and may not express an opinion on the question whether either or both of the parties was negligent[10]. Similarly, a lay witness may not be asked whether he thinks that someone charged with drunken driving had proper control of his car[11]. There are, however, many situations in which it would be difficult, if not impossible, to receive evidence if witnesses were not allowed to state their opinions on certain matters, and this accounts for the two groups of exception to the general rule.

(2) *Exceptions*

(a) *Experts*.—When matters, such as the cause of the silting up of a harbour[12], calling for special knowledge, are in issue, or relevant to the issue, it would be absurd to disallow evidence of opinion if only because the witness is better qualified to

---

[10] *Hollington* v. *Hewthorn & Co. Ltd.*, [1943] K.B. 587, at p. 595; [1943] 2 All E.R. 35, at p. 40.

[11] *R.* v. *Davies*, [1962] 3 All E. R. 97.

[12] *Folkes* v. *Chadd* (1782), 3 Doug. K.B. 157.

draw inferences than the court. It is impossible to draw up a list of matters with regard to which expert evidence is admissible. The words "art and science" used in the article are not exhaustive, for expert evidence may be received on questions of accountancy and foreign law, as well as on more strictly scientific questions such as the cause of death or illness. There are, however, certain questions, such as the ordinary meaning of English words, or the reasonableness of a motorist's conduct, on which expert opinion evidence is inadmissible because the court is as well equipped to draw the necessary inferences as the witness. Special knowledge is not called for on such matters.

Thus, a jury or judge sitting alone is as well qualified as any expert to decide whether an article sent through the post is "indecent or obscene" within the meaning of s. 11 of the Post Office Act 1953, and evidence of witnesses as to the effect that the article had on them is irrelevant[13]. Generally speaking, on a prosecution under the Obscene Publications Act 1959, expert evidence is irrelevant and inadmissible on the question whether an article is "such as to tend to deprave and corrupt"[14], but it may be admissible in the exceptional case in which the tendencies of the article to deprave or corrupt a particular class of the community such as young children is in issue[15]. On similar principles it has been held that, when there is no question of insanity or diminished responsibility, a psychiatrist may not give evidence of his opinion concerning the mental state of the accused at the time of the crime charged because he is no more of an expert on the past intent of an ordinary man than the court or jury[16]. Although a psychiatrist may give expert opinion evidence on behalf of one co-accused as to whether the other was more likely by reason of his disposition to have murdered the deceased when that other alleges that his co-accused was the prime mover[17], he may not give expert opinion evidence that a mentally normal accused is likely to fly into a rage when his girl friend confesses infidelity because this is a tendency well known to all jurors[18].

---

[13] *R.* v. *Stamford,* [1972] 2 Q.B. 391; [1972] 2 All E.R. 427.

[14] *R.* v. *Anderson,* [1972] 1 Q.B. 304; [1971] 3 All E.R. 1152.

[15] *Director of Public Prosecutions* v. *A. and B. C. Chewing Gum, Ltd.,* [1968] 1 Q.B. 159; [1967] 2 All E.R. 504; questioned by VISCOUNT DILHORNE in *Director of Public Prosecutions* v. *Jordan,* [1977] A.C. 699, at p. 722.

[16] *R.* v. *Chard* [1971], 56 Cr. App. Rep. 268.

[17] *Lowery* v. *R.,* [1974] A.C.85; [1973] 3 All E.R. 662.

[18] *R.* v. *Turner,* [1975] 1 All E.R. 70.

It is for the judge to decide whether a witness is sufficiently qualified to testify as an expert. The witness must be skilled in the branch of knowledge under review, though he need not have acquired such knowledge in the course of his professional duties. Thus, a solicitor who has made a special study of handwriting may testify as a handwriting expert[19].

(b) *Non-experts.*—In many cases, although the answer to a question does not call for specialised knowledge, it would be difficult or impossible for a witness to give his evidence without referring to his opinion. Such questions as, "Is the prisoner the man you saw on the first of January?" "Is that your wife's signature?" and "How fast was the car travelling?" call for an answer in terms of an opinion, but the replies are nonetheless regularly received in evidence. Any witness may be asked whether he thinks that the accused had been drinking[20], because that is a compendious mode of ascertaining whether the accused displayed those symptoms, lurching gait, slurred voice, etc., from which people normally infer that other people have been drinking. In these situations the facts upon which the witness's opinion was based will emerge in the course of further questioning. It is impossible to draw up a closed list of cases falling within the second exception to the general rule. Items frequently included in it are speed, the identity of persons, things, and handwriting, age and the state of the weather.

(3) *Ultimate issues*

The fact that, in all cases, the decision whether to accept evidence must be taken by the judge or jury accounts for what was once thought to be a rigid common law rule that no witness must be asked the very question in issue between the parties. It has been said that someone engaged in a particular trade must not be asked whether he considers a covenant in restraint of trade to be reasonable, although he may inform the court of the dangers against which the covenantee requires protection[1]. It is, however, easy to think of cases in which the answer to such a question might be of assistance to the tribunal of fact, for example an issue might be whether a person purporting to have particular skills actually possessed them. So far as criminal cases are concerned, there is no doubt that the

---

[19] R. v. *Silverlock,* [1894] 2 Q.B. 766.

[20] *R.* v. *Davies,* [1962] 3 All E.R. 97.

[1] *Hayes* v. *Doman,* [1899] 2 Ch. 13.

rule, if it exists at all, has many exceptions. When insanity is pleaded, a doctor may be asked whether he considers that the accused was capable of distinguishing right from wrong at the material time although this is one of the matters to be decided by the jury under the Mcnaghten rules[2]. Cases of this nature led Lord PARKER, C.J., to suggest that, with the advances of science, more and more inroads have been made into the old common law principles[3].

Section 3 (1) of the Civil Evidence Act 1972 provides that, in any civil proceedings, a witness's opinion may be given on any relevant matter (including an issue in the proceedings) on which he is qualified as an expert. Having regard to the views of Lord PARKER which have just been mentioned, it is open to question whether this means that there is a vast difference between the civil and criminal law on this question; but the latter continues to be governed by the common law.

Section 3 (2) of the Civil Evidence Act 1972 provides that, in any civil proceedings, the opinion of a non-expert, if given as a way of conveying relevant facts personally perceived by him, is admissible on any relevant matter (including an issue in the proceedings). The statutory provision is declaratory of the common law, for a non-expert's testimony on such questions as identity, age and handwriting is unquestionably admissible in civil and criminal proceedings alike although the latter are unaffected by any statute.

---

[2] *R.* v. *Holmes*, [1953] 2 All E.R. 324.

[3] *Director of Public Prosecutions* v. *A. and B. C. Chewing Gum, Ltd.*, [1968] 1 Q.B. 159; [1967] 2 All E.R. 504.

CHAPTER 5

Corroboration

ART. 35.—**When corroboration is required**

1. The general rule, in civil and criminal cases alike, is that the court may act on the testimony of one witness.

2. Corroboration is required as a matter of law:

(a) in criminal cases, before there can be a conviction for perjury[1], for various sexual offences[2] or on the unsworn evidence of a child[3];

(b) in civil cases, before there can be a finding in favour of the complainant in affiliation proceedings in which the mother gives evidence[4].

3. There can be no conviction for exceeding the speed limit solely on the evidence of one witness to the effect that, in his opinion, the accused was driving at a speed exceeding the limit[5].

4. In criminal cases a warning of the danger of convicting on uncorroborated evidence must be given when the evidence is

---

[1] Perjury Act 1911, s. 13.

[2] Sexual Offences Act 1956, ss. 2–4, 22–3.

[3] Children and Young Persons Act 1933, s. 38.

[4] Affiliation Proceedings Act 1957, s. 4 (1) as substituted by Affiliation Proceedings (Amendment) Act 1972.

[5] Road Traffic Regulation Act 1967, s. 78A inserted by Road Traffic Act 1972, s. 203.

that of an accomplice, or the sworn evidence of a child, and on trials for sexual offences, other than those in relation to which corroboration is necessary as a matter of law.

5. Rules of practice concerning corroboration apply in matrimonial causes.

Explanation:

(1) *The general rule and its exceptions*

One of the distinguishing features of English legal procedure is the fact that, as a matter of law, the uncorroborated evidence of one witness will normally suffice. In practice the jury and justices may well hesitate to convict on the word of one witness when there are no confirmatory circumstances, but legal rules prohibiting them from doing so are exceptional.

There are four groups of exception to the general rule. First, there are a very few criminal cases in which the evidence of two witnesses is essential to a conviction. An example is provided by the personation of voters at elections[6]. They are of no importance from the point of view of the general law and nothing more need be said about them. Secondly, there are cases in which corroboration is necessary as a matter of law. In these cases, the jury must be directed not to convict in the absence of corroboration, and a conviction or finding of paternity in its absence will be set aside on appeal. Thirdly, there are criminal cases in which the jury must be warned of the danger of convicting on uncorroborated evidence. Provided the warning is given, a conviction in the absence of corroboration is perfectly proper but, if there is no warning, the conviction will be set aside by the Court of Appeal, even if there is corroboration (unless the Court is prepared to apply the proviso to s.2(1) of the Criminal Appeal Act 1968 and dismiss the appeal on the ground that no miscarriage of justice has occurred). Fourthly, corroboration is required as a matter of practice in certain situations in matrimonial causes.

(2) *When corroboration is required as a matter of law*

In the case of perjury, what has to be corroborated is the falsity of the oath or statement in respect of which the accused is charged. The requirement of corroboration extends to the various offences akin to perjury, mentioned in the Perjury Act 1911.

[6] Representation of the People Act 1949, s. 146 (5).

The sexual offences in respect of which corroboration is required as a matter of law are the procuration of women for the purpose of prostitution, and the use of various unlawful means in order to have sexual intercourse. There cannot be a conviction on the evidence of one witness only unless his evidence is corroborated " in some material particular by evidence implicating the accused". Corroboration is not required as a matter of law in the cases of rape and indecent assault.

As we saw on p. 62, *ante,* children are allowed to give unsworn evidence in criminal cases. When they do so, as witnesses for the prosecution, the accused cannot be convicted "unless their evidence is corroborated by some other material evidence in support thereof implicating him".

In affiliation cases in which evidence is given by the mother the court may not adjudge the defendant to be the father "unless her evidence is corroborated in some material particular by other evidence to the court's satisfaction".

(3) *Speeding*

Strictly speaking, there is no requirement of corroboration before there can be a conviction for exceeding the speed limit. What is prohibited is a conviction on one witness's opinion of the speed at which the accused was driving; but this has the effect of imposing a requirement of corroboration. A witness's view, based solely on his personal observation, concerning the speed at which a vehicle was travelling is nothing more than his opinion. We saw in Article 34 that evidence of opinion is generally inadmissible, but the question of a motorist's speed is among the matters on which even the evidence of non-expert opinion has to be received by way of exception to the general rule.

The effect of the relevant statutory provision, now s. 78A of the Road Traffic Regulation Act 1967, is that there must usually be two witnesses deposing to their opinion that the accused exceeded the speed limit. But a police witness's statement that he drove behind the accused between two points, together with his statement of the reading on the speedometer of the police car over the relevant period, constitutes *prima facie* evidence against the accused. It will therefore be sufficient to support a conviction if the accuracy of the speedometer is not successfully challenged[7].

---

[7] *Nicholas* v. *Penny,* [1950] 2 K.B. 466; [1950] 2 All E.R. 89.

(4) *Criminal cases in which a warning is necessary*

The law requiring a warning of the danger of convicting on uncorroborated evidence has been built up by the practice of the judges in criminal cases over the last hundred years. Most of the case-law is concerned with accomplices, but there is now no doubt that a warning must be given in the other two cases mentioned in the article, sexual offences other than those in relation to which corroboration is required as a matter of law, and cases in which children give sworn evidence.

The primary meaning of "accomplice" is any party to the crime charged, whether he is a principal, or someone who merely aids and abets its commission. Before the distinction between felonies and misdemeanours was abolished, it was held that an accessory after the fact must be treated as an accomplice; presumably there will be a similar holding in the case of someone who impedes the apprehension or trial of a person guilty of an arrestable offence[8]. An *agent provocateur* is not an accomplice for the purpose of the law governing corroboration, even when he is a party to the crime[9]. It is for the judge to decide whether there is any evidence that the witness is an accomplice and for the jury to determine whether he is in fact an accomplice.

So far as the requirement of the warning is concerned there are two extended meanings of the expression "accomplice". First, a receiver is the accomplice of the thief who steals the goods he receives[10]. Secondly, a party to other crimes committed by the accused is an accomplice although he was not a party to the crime charged[11], provided that the commission of such other crimes by the accused is admissible evidence against him at his trial for the crime charged.

These points were made in the judgment of the House of Lords in *Davies* v. *Director of Public Prosecutions*[12]. This was a murder trial in which it was held that a witness for the prosecution was not an accomplice although he was a member of the same gang of youths as the accused, and had joined with him in the assault on the deceased before the accused had stabbed the deceased with a knife. The witness did not know of the existence of the knife. All the observations in the judgment

---

[8] Criminal Law Act 1967, s. 4.

[9] *Sneddon* v. *Stevenson*, [1967] 2 All E.R. 1277.

[10] *R.* v. *Jennings* (1912), 7 Cr. App. Rep. 242

[11] *R.* v. *Mohamed Farid* (1945), 173 L.T. 68.

[12] [1954] A.C. 378; [1954] 1 All E.R. 507.

were confined to cases in which the accomplice is called as a witness for the prosecution.

Two or more people may be jointly tried for the same offence and one may incriminate the other by his evidence. In the case of an accomplice giving evidence for the defence, everything said above ought to be applicable. Before *R.* v. *Prater*[13], the authorities were not in complete agreement, but the position is clarified by this case. Prater, Welham and others were charged with conspiracy to defraud. Welham gave evidence on his own behalf and implicated Prater. No warning was given and Prater was convicted. The Court of Criminal Appeal said that the warning in such a case was "desirable"; but it is not essential as a matter of law, as it is when the accomplice is called by the prosecution[14].

Even when a child is allowed to give evidence on oath, it has long been customary for the judge at a criminal trial to warn against the danger of convicting on such testimony in the absence of corroboration.

The warning is also necessary in sexual cases. Although, once it has been given, there may be a conviction if the jury is satisfied of the truth of the witness's testimony, convictions have often been quashed for want of such a warning even when there has been ample corroborative evidence[15].

(5) *Matrimonial causes*

In *Alli* v. *Alli* [16], Sir JOCELYN SIMON, P., said that it was necessary to distinguish between two situations in which questions concerning corroboration can arise in a matrimonial cause. The first situation comprises cases in which a sexual crime, such as rape or buggery, is alleged against the husband, and cases in which a willing participant in adultery has given evidence against the other alleged adulterer. In this situation, by parity of reasoning with the requirements of the criminal law concerning the corroboration warning, an appellate court will interfere in a matrimonial cause if it does not expressly appear that the court below has warned itself about the dangers of acting on uncorroborated evidence. In all other cases, the court will look for corroboration on account of the gravity of

---

[13] [1960] 2 Q.B. 464; [1960] 1 All E.R. 298.
[14] *R.* v. *Stannard*, [1965] 2 Q.B. 1; [1964] 1 All E.R. 34.
[15] *R.* v. *Trigg*, [1963] 1 All E.R. 490.
[16] [1965] 3 All E.R. 480.

the issues involved, but it may act without it and, even if it does so without any reference to the point, the decision will not necessarily be set aside on appeal.

Other possible cases

It is sometimes said that corroboration is required as a matter of practice in other cases, but there are no fixed rules.

Owing to the absence of the principal witness, it is natural to look for corroboration when a claim is made against the estate of a deceased person but, if a single uncorroborated witness carries conviction, the court may act on his evidence[17].

The correctness of a single witness's identification of the accused is often the crucial issue in a criminal case, but there is no fixed rule requiring a warning of the danger of convicting when such a witness's evidence is uncorroborated whether he was[18], or was not[19], acquainted with the accused before the commission of the crime. There are, however, special rules with regard to identification evidence which are mentioned on p. 312.

ART. 36—Witnesses who cannot corroborate

The unsworn evidence of a child cannot corroborate the unsworn evidence of another child; and the evidence of an accomplice who was a party to the crime charged cannot corroborate the evidence of another party.

Explanation: It was once thought that a witness whose evidence required corroboration or a warning of the dangers of acting on it without corroboration could not corroborate the evidence of another witness whose evidence was itself subject to these infirmities, but two decisions of the House of Lords have shown that this is not so.

In *Director of Public Prosecutions* v. *Hester*[20], it was held that the unsworn evidence of a child could be corroborated by the sworn evidence of another child and vice versa although,

---

[17] *Re Hodgson, Beckett* v. *Ramsdale* (1885), 31 Ch.D. 177, at p. 183.
[18] *Arthurs* v. *A.-G. for Northern Ireland* (1970), 55 Cr. App. Rep. 161.
[19] *R.* v. *Long* (1973), 57 Cr. App. Rep. 871.
[20] [1973] A.C. 296; [1972] 3 All E.R. 1056.

before there can be a conviction on the former, it must be corroborated as a matter of law, and a warning is necessary before there can be a conviction on the latter when uncorroborated. The House of Lords recognised, however, that the unsworn evidence of one child cannot be corroborated by the unsworn evidence of another child. This is because the statutory provision that, where the unsworn evidence is admitted by virtue of s. 38 of the Children and Young Persons Act 1933 the accused shall not be liable to be convicted unless it is "corroborated by some other material evidence", refers to evidence admitted otherwise than by virtue of s. 38.

In *Director of Public Prosecutions* v. *Kilbourne*[1], the accused was convicted of buggery and gross indecency with two groups of youths in respect of acts committed with one group in 1970 and with the other group in 1971. The evidence of members of each group was admissible on charges concerning the other on account of the similarity of the conduct alleged against the accused in every instance, but the Court of Appeal quashed the convictions because the boys concerned in the 1971 offences were parties to other crimes committed by the accused when the 1970 charges were under consideration and vice versa; they therefore came within the extended definition of an accomplice mentioned on p. 116, *ante*. The House of Lords restored the convictions because there is no absolute rule that an accomplice cannot corroborate another accomplice, although the speeches seem to have approved of a rule laid down in earlier cases that the evidence of one party to a crime could not be corroborated by that of another party to the same crime.

The two decisions which have just been mentioned may therefore be treated as authority for the proposition stated in the article.

The evidence of the wife of one accomplice can corroborate the evidence of another whether or not he is called and whether or not he is a co-accused[2].

---

[1] [1973] A.C. 729; [1973] 1 All E.R. 440.

[2] *R.* v. *Willis*, [1916] 1 K.B. 933; *R.* v. *Evans*, [1965] 2 Q.B. 295; [1964] 3 All E.R. 401.

ART. 37.—The nature of corroboration and the functions of judge and jury

1. Corroboration is confirmatory evidence implicating the person against whom it is required in a material particular; it may consist of the express or implied admission or other relevant conduct of such person; but not of the previous statement of the witness whose evidence requires corroboration.

2. When directing the jury about corroboration the judge must usually identify the items of evidence which are and are not capable of amounting to corroboration.

Explanation: The statutory provisions set out on p. 115, *ante*, justify the proposition that corroboration must implicate the person against whom it is required in a material particular, and it was held in *R.* v. *Baskerville*[3] that this requirement applies when the evidence is that of an accomplice. It may safely be assumed that this is so in all cases in which a warning must be given. This means that it is not enough that a piece of evidence should tend to confirm the truth of any part of the testimony to be corroborated. It must confirm that part of the testimony which suggests that the crime was committed by the accused. If a witness says "The accused and I stole the sheep and I put the skins in a certain place", the discovery of the skins in that place does not corroborate the witness's evidence as against the accused. But if the skins were found in the accused's house, this would corroborate because it tends to confirm the statement that the accused had some hand in the theft[4].

Express and implied admissions

In affiliation proceedings the respondent's admission of intercourse, or of other acts of intimacy, is capable of constituting corroboration. If the admission is contained in a letter produced and identified by the mother there is corroboration of her evidence, because, once the handwriting has been proved by her, the contents of the letter constitute a separate item of evidence—an admission received under an exception to the rule against hearsay[5].

---

[3] [1916] 2 K.B. 658.

[4] *R.* v. *Birkett* (1839), 8 C. & P. 732.

[5] *Jeffrey* v. *Johnson,* [1952] 2 Q.B. 8; [1952] 1 All E.R. 450.

Silence may amount to an implied admission if it is natural to expect a reply. If the accused was silent when charged by a police officer, that cannot constitute corroboration on account of the right to silence mentioned on p. 100; but if the accused and his accuser stand on an equal footing, the accused's silence may be treated as an admission. In *R.* v. *Cramp*[6] a girl's father met the accused in the street and said, "I have here those things which you gave my daughter to produce abortion". The accused did not reply and this was held to tend to corroborate the daughter's evidence.

Lies out of court may or may not amount to an implied admission. If the accused tells the police that he broke into a house in order to "have a bit of kip" there, the fact that the jury believe an accomplice's statement that he and the accused jointly broke into the house in order to steal does not entitle them to treat the accused's lie to the police as corroboration of the accomplice's evidence; but an out-of-court denial of an opportunity, if proved false, may suggest that advantage was taken of the opportunity. Thus, in *Credland* v. *Knowler*[7], a young girl swore that the accused committed an offence against her in his house. The fact that the accused ultimately admitted that he had falsely stated that he was not at home at the material time was treated as corroboration of the evidence against him.

An admission of a type sufficient to constitute corroboration may be provided by the testimony of the person against whom it is required. In *R.* v. *Dossi*[8], a man was charged with an indecent assault on a little girl, and in his evidence admitted to having fondled her "platonically". This was held to be some corroboration of the girl's evidence.

Failure to give evidence cannot amount to corroboration because to hold otherwise would militate against the rule that the accused is not obliged to give evidence[9].

It has been said that lies in court can never amount to corroboration[10] but there is authority to the contrary, and the generality of the statement has been questioned[11]. In *Corfield* v. *Hodgson*[12], for instance, the mother alleged in affiliation

---

[6] (1880), 14 Cox C.C. 390.
[7] (1951), 35 Cr. App. Rep. 48.
[8] (1918), 13 Cr. App. Rep. 158.
[9] *R.* v. *Jackson*, [1953] 1 All E.R. 872.
[10] *R.* v. *Chapman and Baldwin*, [1973] Q.B. 774; [1973] 2 All E.R. 624.
[11] *R.* v. *Boardman*, [1974] 2 All E.R. 958, at p. 963.
[12] [1966] 2 All E.R. 205.

proceedings that intercourse with the respondent took place on the way home from a dance. The respondent denied in-chief that he had taken the girl home, but admitted this in cross-examination, and it was held that his lie in-chief corroborated the mother's testimony.

Other relevant conduct

Any other conduct of the person against whom corroboration is required may corroborate if it is a relevant fact on the issue of his liability on the occasion into which the court is inquiring. Obvious examples are previous or subsequent acts of intercourse or familiarity in sexual cases, and rehearsals of an alleged robbery. We have already seen that, in *Director of Public Prosecutions* v. *Kilbourne*[13], similar conduct by the accused in 1971 corroborated evidence given against him in respect of charges of offences in 1970 and vice versa.

Previous statement and distressed condition

A witness cannot corroborate himself; hence his previous statements, whether proved by him or by another witness do not constitute corroboration. We have seen that complaints in sexual cases are admissible to prove consistency, but they do not corroborate the complainant's evidence.

"The girl cannot corroborate herself, otherwise it is only necessary for her to repeat her story twenty-five times in order to get twenty-five corroborations of it."[14] In many cases, the prosecutrix's distressed condition will do no more than her complaint, but if a witness testified to having seen her go on to a moor with the accused and come away shortly afterwards in a distressed condition, that latter fact will corroborate her testimony[15].

Functions of judge and jury

In a case in which there is no corroboration the judge should direct an acquittal when corroboration is required as a matter of law. If there is no corroboration in a case in which the judge must warn the jury of the dangers of acting on uncorroborated evidence, it is especially important that he should inform them

---

[13] P. 119, *ante*.

[14] *R.* v. *Whitehead,* [1929] 1 K.B. 99, at p. 102, *per* Lord HEWART, C.J.; see *R.* v. *Christie,* [1914] A.C. 545.

[15] *R.* v. *Redpath* (1962), 46 Cr. App. Rep. 319; cf. *R.* v. *Knight,* [1966] 1 All E.R. 647.

of this fact when there is an item of evidence, such as a complaint of a sexual assault, which they might believe to be corroborative. When directing them about corroboration, the judge must tell the jury what it is–independent evidence of some material fact which implicates the accused person and tends to confirm that he is guilty of the offence[16]. The most recent authorities go further and insist that, at any rate in cases of any complexity, he should indicate what evidence in the case is and is not capable of being corroboration[17].

---

[16] *R.* v. *Clynes* (1960), 44 Cr. App. Rep. 158.

[17] *R.* v. *Reeves* (1978), 68 Cr. App. Rep. 33; *R.* v. *Charles and Others* (1976), 68 Cr. App. Rep. 334n.

CHAPTER 6

Hearsay

ART. 38.—The rule against hearsay

A statement other than one made by a person while giving oral evidence in the proceedings is inadmissible as evidence of any fact or opinion stated.

Explanation: The rule against hearsay applies to oral and written statements. It has never been authoritatively formulated, but the formulation adopted in the article does not differ substantially from that of a number of other text-writers, and it is based on s. 1 of the Civil Evidence Act 1968. This formulation means that there are two entirely different situations in which the rule operates, that in which the maker of the statement is called as a witness, and that in which he is not called.

Maker called

It is unnecessary to say much more about the first of these situations. The common law ban on the proof of a witness's previous statements was mentioned in Article 22. It prohibits the reception of the statement as evidence of consistency as well as evidence of the facts stated; and, subject to the possible exception of statements received as part of the *res gestae*[1], even when a statement is admitted under an exception to the ban mentioned in Article 22, it is not admitted as evidence of the facts stated. The reason why the previous statements of witnesses may not be proved in-chief for this purpose is that, in the ordinary case where the statement and the testimony are identical, the latter can at most only bolster up the witness's credibility; while, if the witness is prevaricating or hesitant, it is wrong to allow him to eke out his testimony with a statement which he did not make on oath or when subject to cross-examination. The framers of the Civil Evidence Act 1968 took the view that, subject to the control of the court, these statements should be admissible as evidence of the facts stated and ss. 2 and 4 of the Act, discussed in Article 24, are primarily designed to cater for the case in which there is a good reason for supposing that the earlier statement is more reliable than the testimony.

At common law, a previous inconsistent statement admitted by, or proved against, a witness under cross-examination

[1] P. 80, *ante*.

merely neutralises his testimony; it is inadmissible as evidence of the facts stated. Such a statement may be treated as evidence of these facts under s. 3 of the Civil Evidence Act 1968. The common law continues to apply to criminal cases both as regards statements proved in-chief, and as regards statements proved in cross-examination. In civil and criminal cases alike the informal admission of a party, whether elicited in the cross-examination of the maker, or proved by another witness, is admissible as evidence of the facts stated, and informal admissions are discussed in Article 42. The cross-examination of a witness on a previous statement with which he has refreshed his memory may render parts of the statement admissible evidence of the facts stated in a civil case[2].

Maker not called

When the maker of the statement is not called as a witness, the reasons for the rule against hearsay may seem to be more convincing than they are in the cases in which he is called. The essence of the matter is that B's statement may not be narrated by A as evidence of its truth, because B cannot be cross-examined and the court has no opportunity of considering his demeanour; furthermore B will usually not have been on oath. In many instances there will be no chance of checking the accuracy with which A has repeated B's words. These are excellent reasons for requiring the maker of the statement to be called whenever that is reasonably possible, but they are poor reasons for rejecting the statement when it is impossible, impracticable or even highly inconvenient. This is why the rule against hearsay has been relaxed in civil cases and why many people think that it should also be relaxed in criminal cases.

Illustrations

A few illustrations of the application of the rule to criminal cases in which the maker of the statement was not called may be helpful. When examining them, or when considering the possible application of the rule against hearsay to any case, the student should always ask himself for what purpose is the statement put in evidence? What fact is the statement tendered to prove? If it is a fact expressly or impliedly asserted by the statement, the hearsay rule applies and the statement will be inadmissible, unless the case can be brought within an exception to the rule.

---

[2] P. 77, *ante*.

In *Sparks* v. *R.*[3], an appeal from Bermuda, the accused, a white man, was charged with an indecent assault on a girl between three and four years old. About an hour and a half after the event the child told her mother that a coloured boy did it. The child did not give evidence and the Judicial Committee held that the trial judge had rightly rejected the evidence of what she said to her mother, although the accused's appeal against conviction was allowed on other grounds.

In *Nicholas* v. *Penny*[4], the court stated that the fact that the speedometer on a police car was in working order could not be proved by the driver's statement of what he had been told about the results of tests carried out on the previous day, since this would be to receive inadmissible hearsay evidence.

In *R.* v. *Saunders*[5], it was necessary for the prosecution to prove that the accused were carrying on business at the material time. It was held that a police officer ought not to have been asked whether, as a result of inquiries, he concluded that any business had been carried on. This case should serve as an object lesson to those who believe that the rule against hearsay only applies to evidence given in the form of a direct narration of someone else's statement: "A told me that", etc. The rule is equally applicable when the witness says "I learned that" or "From information supplied I gathered that" provided, in each instance, that the fact learnt or gathered is the fact which the party calling the witness is seeking to prove.

In *Jones* v. *Metcalfe*[6], a witness swore that he saw a lorry driver cause an accident and reported the matter to a police officer to whom he repeated the number of the lorry, but he did not give any further evidence identifying the accused as the lorry driver. Another police officer swore that he interviewed the accused who admitted driving a lorry of the number mentioned by the witness, but denied having caused an accident. It was held by the Divisional Court that there was no case to answer on a charge of careless driving because the accused had not been identified by admissible evidence as the driver who caused the accident to which the witness deposed. The police officer's note and repetition of the number was hearsay. Had the police officer to whom the number was dictated been the one who

---

[3] [1964] A.C. 964; [1964] 1 All E.R. 727.
[4] [1950] 2 K.B. 466; [1950] 2 All E.R. 89.
[5] [1899] 1 Q.B. 490.
[6] [1967] 3 All E.R. 205.

gave evidence, the decision would have been the same[7], because the object of the evidence as to the number dictated to him by the lay witness would still have been to prove that that was the number perceived by the witness. Had the witness of the accident kept a note of the lorry number, or sworn that he saw the police officer write the number down from his dictation, he could have used either note to refresh his memory, but then the evidence of identity would have been the witness's testimony and not the note.

Opinion

The hearsay rule applies as much to evidence of opinion as to evidence of fact. In a criminal case, a letter written by a doctor, since deceased, stating that he carried out a *post mortem* examination on 2nd January which led him to infer that A died of a certain illness before midnight on 1st January is inadmissible as evidence of the cause and time of A's death, although the doctor's direct testimony to the same effect as his letter would have been admissible evidence of expert opinion.

Interpreters

No hearsay problem arises if evidence is given through an interpreter at the trial. He simply informs the court of the meaning of the words spoken by the witness. But, when a suspect is questioned by a police officer with the aid of an interpreter, the rule against hearsay is infringed if the interpreter is not called to give evidence as well as the officer. All the officer can do is to tell the court what the interpreter told him the suspect had said. He is thus narrating to the court what the interpreter told him as evidence of the facts stated by the interpreter (the words of the suspect)[8]. The interpreter should be called to inform the court of the words used by the suspect and their meaning. The administrative directions attached to the Judges' Rules of 1964 provide for the signature by the suspect of his statement in his own language and the preparation of an official translation which the interpreter can produce to the court as an exhibit.

Assertive conduct

Although there is no authority on the point, signs and gestures, meant to be assertive, are presumably governed by

---

[7] *R.* v. *Maclean* (1968), 52 Cr. App. Rep. 80.
[8] *R.* v. *Attard* (1958), 43 Cr. App. Rep. 90.

the rule against hearsay to the same extent as words. If a witness says, "X signalled to me that Y was inside the house", the evidence would be just as inadmissible to prove the fact that Y was inside the house as would the witness's statement that X told him that Y was in the house.

Implied assertions

The rule extends to exclamatory statements, not intended by their maker to be assertive, if the court is asked to treat them as equivalent to the assertion of some fact. Thus, in *Teper* v. *R.*[9], it was held that a police officer's evidence that he heard a woman exclaim to the driver of a passing car "Your place burning and you going away!" was inadmissible evidence of the accused's presence at a fire which he was alleged to have started some twenty-five minutes earlier. The driver of the car bore some resemblance to the accused, and the officer narrated the woman's statement as equivalent to an assertion, made by her to the officer, that the driver was in fact the accused.

It has even been suggested that the rule against hearsay applies to conduct which was not intended to be assertive if reliance is placed on the conduct as an implied assertion of someone other than the witness who is testifying. For example, it has been said that the plaintiff in an action on a marine insurance policy, in which the seaworthiness of a ship was in issue, would not be allowed to prove seaworthiness by calling a witness to say that a sea captain, since deceased, examined the ship and thereafter embarked on it with his family[10]. If the captain had told the witness that the ship was seaworthy, the witness would not have been allowed to narrate that statement as evidence of seaworthiness; but it may be said that deeds speak louder than words, and there is no modern authority obliging an English Court to apply the rule against hearsay in such a case.

If the rule were to be held to extend to assertions implied from conduct not intended to be assertive, as distinct from verbal utterances not intended to be assertive, its scope would be unduly wide. Not only would it cover implied assertions of opinion (as in the hypothetical case of the sea captain); but it would also cover assertions of love or hate to be implied from affectionate or vindictive action, and a vast number of exceptions to the rule would have to be recognised. Such

---

[9] [1952] A.C. 480; [1952] 2 All E.R. 447.

[10] *Wright* v. *Doe d. Tatham* (1837), 7 Ad. & El. 313, at p. 387.

developments could theoretically take place at common law, but it is to be hoped that this will not happen, because the intention of the latest major statute on the subject, the Civil Evidence Act 1968, is, in effect, to abolish the rule against hearsay so far as first hand hearsay is concerned.

First and second hand hearsay

By "first hand" hearsay is meant a statement made by A and proved either by the production of the document in which A made the statement, or by the oral evidence of a witness who heard or otherwise perceived the making of the statement by A. If a witness swears that A told him that B had said something, or if a document asserts that the author was told something by another person or that the author is repeating what he read in another document, the hearsay is "second hand". The distinction is important because repetitions of statements are frequently inaccurate. If a witness swears that A told him that B had said that C told him that he had seen D assault E, it would not be safe for the court to place any reliance on the witness's testimony as hearsay evidence of the assault. Hearsay upon hearsay is suspect; we shall see that there are cases in which it must be received as evidence of the truth of the original assertion, but usually only where there is some special feature enhancing the probability of the accuracy of the repetition.

Exceptions to the rule against hearsay

(1) *Civil cases*

The effect of the Civil Evidence Act 1968 is that, provided certain conditions are fulfilled, the court must admit all first hand hearsay and it has a discretion to do so when those conditions are not fulfilled. Provided certain conditions are fulfilled, the court must admit documentary records containing first or second hand hearsay, it has a discretion to admit such records even though the conditions have not been fulfilled. The result of the act is that, in civil cases, all exceptions to the rule against hearsay are statutory. Apart from those under which hearsay statements[11] are admissible under various sections of the Civil Evidence Act 1968, it is unnecessary to mention many of them in this book; but there is a complication due to the fact that the 1968 Act has not yet been extended to Magistrates' Courts where, so far as the general law of hearsay is concerned,

[11] P. 15, *ante*.

the common law, modified by the Evidence Act 1938, still prevails in civil proceedings just as it prevails in criminal proceedings without such modification.

(2) *Criminal cases*

In criminal cases, whether in the Crown Court or in Magistrates' Courts, the common law still governs the exceptions to the hearsay rule as well as its definition and scope. There are many statutory exceptions, although only those of some general interest are mentioned in this book.

Arrangement of this chapter

Articles 39–41 deal with the admissibility of hearsay statements in civil proceedings other than those before Magistrates; Articles 42–45 deal with the admissibility of hearsay statements in civil and criminal proceedings; Articles 46–54 deal with the admissibility of hearsay statements in criminal proceedings; while a brief resumé of the position in Magistrates' Courts is attempted in Article 55.

ART. 39.—Statements of persons not called as witnesses admissible under s. 2 of the Civil Evidence Act 1968

1. In civil cases a statement made by someone who is not called as a witness is admissible as evidence of any fact or matter[12] stated by agreement of the parties and, with or without such agreement, provided the following conditions are fulfilled:—

(a) The statement was either made in a document or proved by the direct oral evidence of any person who either heard or otherwise perceived it being made; and

(b) the maker of the statement is dead, or beyond the seas, or unfit by reason of his bodily or mental condition to attend as a witness, or cannot with reasonable diligence be identified or found, or cannot reasonably be expected to have any recollection of matters relevant to the accuracy of the statement having regard to the time which has elapsed since it was made; and

(c) the party desiring to give the statement in evidence has served the notice required by rules of court on all other parties to the proceedings[13].

---

[12] Civil Evidence Act 1972, s. 1.

[13] Civil Evidence Act 1968, ss. 1–2.

2. The court has a discretion to admit a statement coming within clause 1 above notwithstanding that the conditions specified in clauses 1 (b) and 1(c) have not been fulfilled.

Explanation:

Section 1 (1) of the Civil Evidence Act 1968 provides that

> "In any civil proceedings a statement other than one made by a person while giving oral evidence in those proceedings shall be admissible as evidence of any fact stated therein to the extent that it is so admissible by virtue of any provision of this part of this Act or by virtue of any other statutory provision or by agreement of the parties, but not otherwise."

This has the effect of abolishing all common law exceptions to the rule against hearsay (other than the exception relating to the admissibility of hearsay evidence by agreement of the parties).

Section 2 (1) provides that

> "In any civil proceedings a statement made, whether orally or in a document or otherwise, by any person, whether called as a witness in those proceedings or not, shall, subject to this section and to rules of court, be admissible as evidence of any fact stated therein of which direct oral evidence by him would be admissible."

This has the effect of admitting all hearsay evidence subject to the provisions of the rest of the section and to the rules of court authorised by s. 8. The admissibility of such evidence when the maker of the statement is called as a witness was discussed in Article 24, and no further details are required.

Agreement

One of the differences between the rules of evidence in criminal and civil cases is that they may be waived by the parties to the latter. The reception of hearsay evidence by agreement in civil proceedings is thus but an instance of a broad permission for the reception of otherwise inadmissible evidence; but the rules of court made under the Civil Evidence Act provide a ready means of evidencing the agreement when the maker of the statement is available. A party desiring to give in evidence a statement admissible under s. 2 must serve notice of his intention on all other parties to the proceedings. The notice must give particulars of the statement and it must be served whether or not the maker is available to give evidence, and whether or not the party desiring to give the statement in evidence proposes to call the maker. If the maker is available, the party upon whom the notice is served can, by counter-notice, require him to be called. If the party upon whom the notice is served does not serve a counternotice, and if the maker of the statement is not called, hearsay evidence is received by virtue of the Act and by what amounts to the agreement of the parties. This is the effect of Ord 38, rr. 21, 22 and 26 of the Rules of the Supreme Court, and there are corresponding provisions in the County Court Rules and the Matrimonial Causes Rules. Order 38, r. 32 provides a disincentive to the service of a counternotice by empowering the court to make the party serving it bear the costs if it is considered unreasonable to have required the maker of the statement to be called.

Conditions of admissibility under s. 2 when maker unavailable

The first condition on which hearsay evidence is admissible under s. 2 is the outcome of s. 2 (3) which provides that

> "Where in any civil proceedings a statement which was made otherwise than in a document is admissible by virtue of this section, no evidence other than direct oral evidence by the person who made the statement or any person who heard or otherwise perceived it being made shall be admissible for the purpose of proving it."

The provision for proof by the direct oral evidence of the person who made the statement applies to cases, with which we are not concerned at this stage, in which the maker of the statement is called as a witness.

The subsection has the effect of restricting hearsay evidence admissible under s. 2 to first hand hearsay. "Document" is broadly defined so as to include, in addition to a document in writing, maps, plans, photographs, tape recordings and films[14]; but, in order that it should be admissible under s. 2, the statement must, if not proved by someone who heard it, have been "made in a document" by the person for whose oral evidence it is a substitute. If A writes out on a piece of paper "The number of the car I saw was ——", the piece of paper would clearly be admissible as a document containing A's

[14] Section 10.

statement; this would presumably also be the case if A dictated the statement to someone else; but if A were to dictate to someone else "Y told me that the car he saw bore the number ——", the statement in the document would be that of A, and Y's statement would be inadmissible under s. 2 because it was neither made in a document nor proved by the direct oral evidence of someone who heard it.

The second condition on which hearsay evidence is admissible under s. 2 when the maker of the statement is not called as a witness is that one of the five reasons specified in clause 1 (b) of the article for not calling him should be present. The framers of the Act took the view that, subject to the contrary agreement of the parties, the evidence in civil proceedings should generally continue to take the form of direct testimony but that, when such testimony was not available, first hand hearsay should be admissible. The first four reasons for not calling the maker of the statement mentioned in the article do not call for comment. The fifth covers the case where, though it would be perfectly possible to call him, it would be pointless to do so because he cannot reasonably be expected to recollect the matters about which he would be required to testify. Suppose that the sole matter on which A could give relevant evidence is whether B's call upon him took place on the first or second of January, and suppose that A wrote a letter to C dated the second of January stating that B called yesterday then, if A were called as a witness two years later, it would, generally speaking, be unreasonable to expect him to remember the date of B's call. The best he could do would be to refresh his memory by reference to the letter and depose to the first of January as the date of the interview because of his confidence in the accuracy of his former account of then recent events. The letter would be held admissible under s. 2 even if A were not called.

The rules of court require the party serving notice of his desire to give in evidence a statement admissible by virtue of s. 2 to specify which, if any, of the five reasons for not calling the maker of the statement exists; his opponent may then only serve a counternotice requiring the maker to be called if he contends that the reason does not exist, and this issue may be determined at or before the trial. The specified reasons are disjunctive. If it can be shown that the maker of the statement is beyond the seas, it is not also necessary for the party tendering it to prove any attempt on his part to call him[15].

[15] *Piermay Shipping Co. S.A.* v. *Chester,* [1978] 1 All E.R. 1233.

The third condition of admissibility under s. 2 is the service of the notice of the desire to give the statement in evidence required by rules of court, and it does not call for further comment.

Evidence as to credibility of maker

Evidence is admissible for the purpose of destroying or supporting the credibility of the maker of a statement admitted under s. 2 if it would have been admissible had the maker been called as a witness and denied the allegations made against him in cross-examination. This means that evidence may be given with regard to the maker's bias, previous convictions, unreliability on oath and inconsistent statements[16].

Statements in former proceedings

Section 2 (3) of the Civil Evidence Act 1968 contains a proviso under which a statement made while giving oral evidence in some other legal proceedings (civil or criminal) may be proved in any manner authorised by the court. Testimony in former proceedings between the same parties was admissible at common law, but, under s. 2 of the Civil Evidence Act, such testimony is admissible even if the parties were different. For example, the statements made by a witness in the course of his evidence at a criminal trial for robbery may be proved at the hearing of a claim against an insurance company in respect of that robbery. The party desiring to give a statement made in former proceedings in evidence under s. 2 of the Civil Evidence Act must serve notice to that effect on all other parties; any party may apply for directions as to how the statement is to be proved. It is necessary to apply to the court for such directions because it may be desirable that other evidence in the former proceedings affecting that mentioned in the notice should be proved with it.

Implied assertions

For the purposes of the Civil Evidence Act "statement" includes any representation of fact, whether made in words or otherwise. Does this include exclamatory statements not intended by their maker to be assertive[17]? If it is desired to prove that A was in a particular place at a particular time, can a witness prove, as a statement to be admitted under s. 2, that he

---

[16] Section 7.

[17] See p. 129, *ante*.

heard someone say "Hello A" at that place and time? If it is desired to prove that a workman was not wearing protective spats, can a witness prove that he heard the workman's mate (since deceased) exclaim "What! No spats?" It is submitted that statements of this sort do imply representations of fact, the presence of A, and the absence of spats, but the application of the Act to statements not intended to be assertive is perhaps not as clear as it might have been. The Act certainly does not extend to non-verbal conduct which was not intended to be assertive such as that of the deceased sea captain mentioned on p. 129, *ante*.

Probate actions

It sometimes happens that a party to a probate action wishes to prove statements made by the deceased as evidence of the facts stated. Indeed he may wish to prove the deceased's account of the contents of his lost will. In such a case, there would be no point in serving the opposite party with notice of intention to prove the statements of the deceased because the opposite party will not be able to contest the death of the deceased; accordingly, the rules of court provide that no notice need be served in such a case[18]. Section 2 (1) of the Civil Evidence Act 1968 provides that a statement rendered admissible by its provisions shall be evidence of any fact of which direct oral evidence by the maker would be admissible. This is not an easy concept to apply to a statement made by the deceased in a probate action relating to his will, but it is to be hoped that the courts will not be deterred from receiving such a statement in evidence.

Undefended divorces

The object of the notice is to enable the opposite party to consider whether he wishes the maker of the statement to be called as a witness if he is available, to consider the validity of any reasons given for not calling the witness and generally to make inquiries concerning the circumstances of the statement. There is therefore no point in serving such a notice in undefended proceedings and the Matrimonial Causes Rules accordingly provide that the notice need not be served in undefended divorce cases.

---

[18] R.S.C. Ord. 38, r. 21 (3).

Extension to opinion

Section 1 of the Civil Evidence Act 1972 provides that, with the exception of s. 5 which is concerned with computerised records and is discussed in the next article, the hearsay provisions of the 1968 Act shall apply in relation to statements of opinion as they apply in relation to statements of fact subject to the necessary modifications. References to a fact stated in a statement are to be construed as references to a matter of opinion stated therein. If a doctor, since deceased, had told A that he believed, in consequence of a post mortem examination, that B had died of lung cancer, A could prove the statement under s. 2 (3) of the 1968 Act as evidence of the cause of A's death. The matter stated is one of which direct oral evidence by the doctor would have been admissible, and A is someone who heard the statement being made. A similar statement by a deceased non-expert could not be proved as evidence of the cause of death because it is not a matter on which "direct oral opinion evidence by him would be admissible".

Discretion

Under R.S.C. Ord. 38, r. 29 the court has a discretion to allow a statement admissible under s. 2 to be proved although no notice of desire to give it in evidence has been served, or even if the requirement of a counternotice that the maker of the statement should be called as a witness has not been met. In theory this is a wide inclusionary discretion. It would enable a court to permit a solicitor to give evidence of what a proposed witness said to him as evidence of the facts stated, although the witness was in court; in practice any court would of course be most unlikely to act in this way. The court may refuse to give directions concerning the proof of statements made in former proceedings admissible under s. 2, but, with this one exception, there is no exclusionary discretion with regard to statements admissible under s. 2. Once it is proved that the conditions mentioned in clause 1 of the article are satisfied, the statement must be admitted. An example of the exercise of the inclusionary discretion where the maker of the hearsay statement gives evidence is provided by *Morris* v. *Stratford-on-Avon R.D.C.*[19].

---

[19] P. 84, *ante*.

ART. 40.—Records admissible under s. 4 and s. 5 of the Civil Evidence Act 1968

1. In civil cases a statement contained in a document is admissible as evidence of any fact stated therein of which direct oral evidence would be admissible if the document is, or forms part of, a record compiled by a person acting under a duty from information which was supplied by a person (whether acting under a duty or not) who had, or may reasonably be supposed to have had, personal knowledge of the matters dealt with in that information and which, if not supplied by that person to the compiler of the record directly, was supplied by him to the compiler of the record indirectly through one or more intermediaries each acting under a duty[20].

2. In civil cases a statement contained in a document produced by a computer is admissible as evidence of any fact stated therein of which direct oral evidence would be admissible, provided the conditions specified in s. 5 (2) of the Civil Evidence Act 1968 are satisfied[1].

Explanation: There is no definition of a "record" in the Civil Evidence Act; all that is required is that there should be a document containing information supplied to its maker directly or indirectly by one or more persons. A police officer takes a statement from a bystander who witnessed an accident; the officer's notebook would presumably be held to constitute a record. The foreman of a factory collects information from a number of workmen concerning work done by them. In due course the information is passed on to the officer in charge of records; the resultant compilation is a record although it is not a full reproduction of anyone's oral or written statement.

(1) *Records admissible under s. 4*

The example of the police officer's notebook shows that there is an overlap between s. 4 of the Civil Evidence Act 1968, part of which is abstracted in clause 1 of the article, and s. 2, upon which Article 39 is based. The oral statement of the bystander could be proved by the police officer as a statement under s. 2, or the notebook could be treated as a record containing the statement admissible under s. 4. The overlap is

---

[20] Civil Evidence Act 1968, s. 4 (1).

[1] Section 5 (1).

of no practical significance because (agreement apart) the person who originally supplied the information from which a record admissible under s. 4 is compiled must either be called as a witness, or be unavailable because he is dead, beyond the seas, unfit, untraceable, or else must be shown to be someone who cannot reasonably be expected to have any recollection of the matter dealt with in the information. There are rules of court concerning the notice which must be served on opposite parties by someone who desires to give in evidence a record admissible by virtue of s. 4 and the counternotice which may be served. These rules correspond to those mentioned in Article 39, and everything said there with regard to the admissibility of first hand hearsay (as a statement) applies to the admissibility of such hearsay (as a record). The supplier of the information is to all intents and purposes in the same position as the maker of a statement admissible under s. 2.

The importance of s. 4 lies in the fact that it permits the reception of hearsay which is not first hand or even second hand. A lorry driver informs a fellow servant that he delivered a load at X; the fellow servant makes a note of this fact and passes the note on to another servant who destroys it after entering the delivery in a book. This process can be continued for any length without affecting the admissibility of the ultimate record, provided the compiler and all the intermediaries were acting under a duty.

The duty

The existence of the duty to pass the information on and to compile the record reduces the chances of erroneous repetition which is the great weakness of hearsay upon hearsay. Section 4 (3) reads

> "Any reference in this section to a person acting under a duty includes a reference to a person acting in the course of any trade, business, profession or other occupation in which he is engaged or employed or for the purpose of any paid or unpaid office held by him."

It is not clear how far this provision is from being exhaustive. If, after an accident, A, a police officer acting under a duty, records a statement by B, who did not see the accident, that C told him that one of the drivers was driving without lights, and it proves to be impossible to trace C, is the record admissible? The answer turns upon the question whether B could be said to have been acting under a duty to pass the information on to A. Is a mere social duty, or the moral duty of citizens to help the police, sufficient?

Further points

Everything said in Article 39 with regard to evidence of the credibility of the maker of the statement applies to the original supplier of the information from which a record admissible under s. 4 is compiled. Everything said in Article 39 about the discretion of the court also applies to records. It has been said that a transcript of a witness's evidence in former proceedings is admissible both as a statement under s. 2 and as a record under s. 4[2]; it has even been suggested that a transcript of the judge's summing-up in a criminal case is admissible in subsequent civil proceedings as a record under s. 4[3] although it is perhaps open to question whether the judge "supplies" information to the shorthand writer, even if (contrary to the view taken with regard to the Evidence Act 1938) the witness "supplies" information to the shorthand writer[4].

A statement of opinion is admissible under s. 4 if it would have been admissible had it been made in the course of giving oral evidence by the person who originally supplied the information from which the record was compiled; but if the statement of opinion concerned a matter on which the supplier of the information would have been qualified to give oral expert evidence, personal knowledge on his part is not required[5]. People who give opinions about the causes of disasters cannot be said to have personal knowledge of such matters, but an expert's opinion on the cause of an accident may nonetheless be admissible under s. 4 if the other conditions of admissibility mentioned in the section are satisfied.

(2) *Records admissible under s. 5—computerised records*

Computerised records may be based on information of which no one had personal knowledge, as when a record is made of the movements of a machine when no one is anywhere near it, and they may also be based on remote hearsay. The conditions of admissibility mentioned in s. 5 (2) of the Act are

---

[2] *Taylor* v. *Taylor,* [1970] 2 All E.R. 609.
[3] *Ibid.*
[4] See *Barkway* v. *South Wales Transport Co., Ltd.,* [1949] 1 K.B. 54.
[5] Civil Evidence Act 1972, s. 1 (2).

that the document should have been produced during a period when the computer was being used for certain activities, that the computer was regularly supplied with information relating to those activities, that the computer was in working order, and that the information contained in the document reproduces or is derived from information supplied to the computer in the course of the activities for which it is used. Section 5 contains a number of elaborate provisions and R.S.C. Ord. 38, r. 24 gives details of the contents of the notice which must be served by someone who wishes to give the computerised record in evidence. The notice must give the names of the persons responsible for the arrangement of and supply of information to the computer. Computerised records of opinion are inadmissible under s. 5.

ART. 41.—Statements and records admissible under s. 9 of the Civil Evidence Act 1968

1. The following hearsay statements formerly admissible at common law are now admissible in civil proceedings by virtue of s. 9 of the Civil Evidence Act 1968:

(a) informal admissions made by a party to the proceedings or those in privity with him;
(b) statements in public documents.

2. A statement tending to establish reputation or family tradition formerly admissible under common law rules concerning character, pedigree, proof of marriage, proof of public or general rights and the identity of any person or thing is admissible by virtue of s. 9 of the Civil Evidence Act 1968, in any civil proceedings, in so far as it is not capable of being rendered admissible under s. 2 or s. 4.

Explanation

(1) *Informal admissions and public documents*

The effect of s. 1 (1) of the Civil Evidence Act 1968, set out on p. 132, *ante,* is to abolish all common law exceptions to the hearsay rule so far as civil proceedings are concerned. One very important common law exception is that relating to the informal admissions of a party. Soon after a motor accident the driver of one of the cars involved says to the other "I am afraid the brakes of my car have been in need of attention for a long time". If, at the subsequent trial of an action for damages for negligence, he either admits that he made the statement and seeks to explain it away, or else denies it with the result that a witness on the opposite side is called to prove it, the statement is admissible as a hearsay statement (evidence of the poor condition of the brakes and the driver's knowledge of that fact). The statement could be rendered admissible under s. 2 of the Act, but there is no point in serving a party with notice of his opponent's desire to rely on an informal admission of his. This is the main reason why s. 9 expressly preserves the common law with regard to informal admissions. A further reason for the adoption of that course is that statements of belief in the truth of what someone else said may, in some exceptional circumstances, be held to amount to admissions. The reception of such statements amounts to the reception of second hand hearsay, something which is not possible under s. 2 of the Act and, having regard to the duty requirement, most unlikely to be permissible under s. 4. If A swears that B admitted to him that C was his daughter although her mother was married to another man at the time of her birth, second hand hearsay is being received although inadmissible under s. 2 or s. 4. Hence the need to preserve the common law by s. 9.

Various public documents and records are admissible at common law. They frequently contain second hand or more remote hearsay, as when a report states that the official making it conducted an inquiry into the rights of common enjoyed by the inhabitants of a particular locality and came to certain conclusions enumerated in the report on the basis of what the inhabitants said their ancestors had told them. Section 9 preserves this common law exception to the hearsay rule which would otherwise have been abolished by s. 1 without any replacement in the other sections of the Act.

The above two exceptions to the hearsay rule apply to civil and criminal cases alike and they are discussed in Articles 42 and 43.

(2) *Reputation*

Evidence of reputation may or may not entail the reception of second hand hearsay. If A swears that B told him that, according to the tradition and repute prevailing in her family, C's mother was illegitimate, the proof of that statement is first hand hearsay if reputation is a matter of fact; and it is expressly declared to be such a matter by s. 9 (3) of the Act. In such a case the party desiring to prove the statement concerning the reputation must serve notice on opposite parties. But, if A swears that his mother told him that her mother told her that the tradition and repute prevailing in the family was that C's grandmother was illegitimate, second hand hearsay would be received.

At common law reputation is only admissible evidence in a limited number of cases. These are mentioned in the article, and the effect of s. 9 is that, when the hearsay by which it is to be proved is first hand, s. 2 or s. 4 applies, but the common law is preserved in cases in which reputation is to be proved by second hand hearsay.

Evidence of character is a rarity in a civil case but, in a libel action, the character of the plaintiff is in issue on the question of damages. It may only be proved by evidence of reputation. If A were prepared to swear that B had told him that the plaintiff had a bad reputation, s. 2 would be applicable, but it is much more likely to be the case that B told A that, from what various people had told him, he gathered that the plaintiff had a bad reputation; in that event the defendant could rely on s. 9.

An example of evidence of reputation in matters of pedigree was given above in the illustration of the statements concerning the legitimacy of C's mother and grandmother.It does not call for much imagination to ring the changes so as to produce an illustration of the proof of the existence of a marriage by repute with the aid of first hand and second hand hearsay.

Public or general rights may be proved by first or second hand hearsay evidence of reputation. An example of the first type of evidence would be that of a local inhabitant prepared to swear that his father had simply told him that the reputation prevailing in the locality was that certain classes of inhabitants did or did not enjoy rights of common over a particular piece of land. In such a case, s. 2 of the Act would be applicable, but it would not apply to a case in which the local inhabitant could only swear that his father had told him that he had been told by his father that according to the tradition which had always prevailed in the locality, certain classes of inhabitants had certain common rights; reliance would then have to be placed on s. 9.

In inheritance cases, the question whether a particular ancestor was or was not the ancestor through whom a claim could be traced may turn on his reputation for having committed some notorious act such as a murder.

ART. 42.—Informal admissions

1. The informal admission of a party, or those in privity with him, is admissible evidence against him of the truth of its contents at common law in a criminal case and by virtue of s. 9 of the Civil Evidence Act 1968, which preserves the relevant common law rules, in a civil case.

2. In civil cases, statements which are inadmissible at common law as admissions made by a person in privity with a party may be rendered admissible under s. 2 or s. 4 of the Civil Evidence Act 1968.

Explanation:

(1) *Admissions*

We are here concerned with informal admissions. They must be distinguished from the formal admissions discussed in Article 16. Informal admissions are not made expressly for the purposes of a particular case, and the person making them may endeavour to explain them away at the trial. Informal admissions, like all exceptions to the hearsay rule which are not expressly confined to statements in documents, may be oral or written. Formal admissions, on the other hand, are made for the purpose of the litigation between the parties, they are in writing and they have nothing to do with the rule against hearsay.

Admissions and confessions

Reliance may be placed on an informal admission in a criminal as well as a civil case. In *R.* v. *Simons*[6], for example, a witness was allowed to prove an inculpatory remark which he heard the accused make to his wife on leaving the police court where the committal proceedings had taken place. When the accused is alleged to have made an inculpatory statement to a person having authority over the prosecution, he is said to have made a "confession", and confessions are only admissible if

---

[6] (1834), 6 C. & P. 540.

especially stringent conditions are satisfied. They are discussed in Article 46. The conditions concern threats and inducements. In a civil case the fact that an informal admission was made in consequence of a threat or inducement affects its weight. It does not prevent the informal admission from being proved[7].

Whole statement

It sometimes happens that a statement containing an admission is not entirely unfavourable to the party making it. In such a case, the party relying on the parts of the statement constituting an admission must put the whole statement in evidence.

> "Now, what a prisoner says is not evidence, unless the prosecutor chooses to make it so, by using it as part of his case against the prisoner; however, if the prosecutor makes the prisoner's declaration evidence, it then becomes evidence for the prisoner, as well as against him; but still, like all evidence given in any case, it is for you to say whether you really believe it."[8]

This means that more weight may be attached to the parts of the statement containing the admissions than to the exculpatory parts[9]. If the accused does not give evidence those parts will not have been subject to cross-examination but they may nevertheless be some evidence of the facts stated unlike a bare self-serving statement of the accused unconnected with anything in the nature of an admission[10].

Admissions without personal knowledge

Admissions have been received although the party making them cannot be said to have full personal knowledge of the fact admitted, as when a man charged with incest admits that the girl in question is his daughter, though born to his wife five years before their marriage[11]. But, generally speaking, "if a man admits something of which he knows nothing it is of no real evidential value"[12]. This remark was made in a case in

---

[7] *Ibrahim* v. *R.*, [1914] A.C. 599, at p. 610 *per* Lord SUMNER.

[8] *R.* v. *Higgins* (1829), 3 C. & P. 603.

[9] *R.* v. *McGregor*, [1968] 1 Q.B. 371; [1967] 2 All E.R. 267.

[10] *R.* v. *Donaldson* (1976), 64 Cr. App. Rep. 59 at p. 64.

[11] *R.* v. *Jones* (1933), 24 Cr. App. Rep. 55.

[12] *Comptroller of Customs* v. *Western Lectric Co., Ltd.*, [1966] A.C. 367; [1965] 3 All E.R. 599.

which the issue concerned the falsity of entries recording the place of origin of goods. They bore markings indicating that their place of origin was Denmark or the United States, but the markings were held not to be evidence of the place of origin because of the rule against hearsay. It was also held that the respondent's director's statement that he had no knowledge of the place of origin apart from what was stated on the invoice which referred to the markings did not constitute an admission because it had no more evidential value than the markings themselves.

The two decisions which have just been mentioned, the one of the Court of Criminal Appeal, the other of the Judicial Committee of the Privy Council, may well be irreconcilable, but there was a far higher degree of personal knowledge on the part of the accused in the incest case than on that of the director in the other case. The decisions on handling stolen goods are more consistent with that of the Privy Council. It has been held that the accused's admitted belief, based in part on statements to that effect made to her, that articles of clothing sold to her in public houses at very low prices were stolen, is inadmissible evidence against her of the latter fact, although her admissions of the circumstances of the purchases are admissible evidence against her warranting an inference by the jury that the goods were stolen[13].

Admissions by conduct

Admissions may be implied from a party's conduct. The subornation of witnesses may be construed as an admission of the weakness of the case of the party responsible for the subornation[14], and silence in the face of an informal charge of crime when a reply might have been expected from an innocent man may be treated as some evidence of an admission of guilt[15]. Though failure to answer a letter can seldom be fairly construed as an admission of the truth of its contents[16], it might have this effect in some cases. The problems raised by these cases depend on ordinary principles of relevancy; they concern circumstantial evidence and have little to do with the rule against hearsay.

---

[13] *R.* v. *Hulbert* (1979), 69 Cr. App. Rep. 243.
[14] *Moriarty* v. *London, Chatham and Dover Rail. Co.* (1870), L.R. 5 Q.B. 314.
[15] *R.* v. *Cramp* (1880), 14 Cox C.C. 390.
[16] *Wiedemann* v. *Walpole,* [1891] 2 Q.B. 534.

Statement in the presence of a party

The possibility of inferring an admission from silence or an insufficiently strenuous denial lies at the root of the law governing the admissibility of statements made in the presence of the parties in general, and in the presence of the accused in particular. *R.* v. *Christie*[17] is the leading case. A little boy charged Christie with having indecently assaulted him, and it was held that, although Christie denied the charge, the boy's accusation, made in the presence of his mother and a police officer, might be proved by them. It was for the jury to decide whether the denials were sufficiently strenuous. The mere statement in the presence of a party is never, of itself, evidence of the facts stated; everything depends on the party's reaction to it. But *Christie's* case is usually said to have decided that statements made in the presence of a party are always admissible in evidence. It may sometimes be necessary for the judge to tell the jury to disregard the statement because, after all the evidence has been called, there is nothing suggestive of a possible acceptance of its truth. *R.* v. *Christie* also recognised that, in a criminal case, the judge has a discretion to exclude evidence of a statement made in the presence of the accused, even though it is legally admissible. Examples of the application of the principle underlying *Christie's* case have been given on p. 101.

Privity

The phrase "in privity" used in the article includes predecessors in title, agents and referees, but not co-defendants. (Admissions by privies are sometimes spoken of as "vicarious admissions.")

(a) *Predecessors in title.*—The reception of admissions by predecessors in title is primarily of importance in the land law. The rule is that an admission affecting an interest in land of a party to the litigation, made by his predecessor in title, binds him, provided the predecessor made the admission while he had the interest affected by his statement[18].

(b) *Agents.*—An agent's admission is evidence against his principal or employer provided it was made in the course of an authorised conversation. In *Kirkstall Brewery Co.* v. *Furness*

---

[17] [1914] A.C. 545.
[18] *Woolway* v. *Rowe* (1834), 1 Ad. & El. 114.

Railway Co.[19], the plaintiff claimed damages for loss of a parcel, and it was held that a remark made by the defendant's stationmaster to a police officer, suggesting that the goods had been stolen by a servant of the defendants, could be proved against them. In *Great Western Rail. Co.* v. *Willis*[20], on the other hand, the plaintiff claimed damages for the defendant's failure to deliver cattle promptly, and it was held that a statement by a night inspector to the plaintiff, suggesting that the beasts had been forgotten, was inadmissible as evidence against the defendants. The distinction between the two cases lies in the fact that the stationmaster was authorised to put the police inquiries in motion, and this necessarily included authority to draw attention to suspects, whoever they might be, but the night inspector had no authority to answer inquiries of the kind the plaintiff was making. At common law the admission of negligence by a servant is not evidence against the master merely because the master would be vicariously liable in tort for such negligence if proved[21]. The servant has no authority to carry on negotiations or answer inquiries concerning his master's vicarious liability.

It has been held that if an inspector of weights and measures calls at a company's premises, asks for someone in authority, and is interviewed by a person describing himself as the depot manager, there is *prima facia* evidence that such person is the depot manager with authority to make statements binding the company[1].

The admission of one co-conspirator is evidence against the other if it relates to an act done in furtherance of the conspiracy, but not otherwise. The judge must first find that there is *prima facie* evidence that the parties are acting in furtherance of a common purpose and, once he is satisfied on that point, the admission of one party relating to the conspiracy affects the other, because they are treated as agents for each other[2].

(c) *Referees.*—Statements made by someone to whom a party has referred others for information may be proved against him as admissions concerning the subject-matter of the reference.

---

[19] (1874), L.R. 9 Q.B. 468.
[20] (1865), 18 C.B.N.S. 748.
[21] *Burr* v. *Ware R.D.C.*, [1939] 2 All E.R. 688.
[1] *Edwards* v. *Brookes (Milk) Ltd.*, [1963] 3 All E.R. 62.
[2] *R.* v. *Blake and Tye* (1844), 6 Q.B. 126.

In *Williams* v. *Innes*[3] the defendants were executors of a deceased's estate. They referred the plaintiff to one Ross for information concerning the assets, and it was held that what Ross said could be proved against the defendants for

> "If a man refers another upon any particular business to a third person, he is bound by what this third person says or does concerning it, as much as if that had been said or done by him."

(d) *Co-defendants.*—Except in the case of conspiracy, the extra judicial admission of one co-defendant is no evidence against the other at common law, however much it may implicate him. The implicating statement is, as against that other, inadmissible hearsay. The exception relating to admissions only applies against the person making the admission or those in privity with him. We shall see that the odd consequences of this rule can now be avoided in civil cases but it is still very important in criminal cases. It frequently happens that A, one of two accused, makes a confession implicating B, his co-accused, when B is not present. At the trial, the confession may be used as evidence against A, provided the conditions mentioned in Article 46 were observed. The references to B will not necessarily be excluded[4], but it will be made plain to the jury that nothing said in the confession is evidence against B, and, in some cases, the fact that the confession was going to be used against A would be a ground on which the judge might exercise his discretion to order separate trials. If there is not sufficient evidence against B apart from the references to him in A's confession, there will be no case for him to answer. A cannot be called as a witness for the prosecution as long as he is being tried together with B[5]. If there is a case for B to answer, and A gives evidence on his own behalf in the course of which B is implicated, A's testimony becomes evidence against B although, as we saw in Article 35, it may be desirable to warn the jury with regard to the danger of acting on the evidence of an accomplice given on his own behalf unless it is corroborated. A's testimony is nonetheless evidence against B because the statements incriminating B were made by A when under cross-examination by the prosecution[6]. This is so, even

---

[3] (1804), 1 Camp. 364.

[4] *R.* v. *Walkely and Clifford* (1833), 6 C. & P. 175.

[5] See Article 18.

[6] *R.* v. *Paul*, [1920] 2 K.B. 183.

though the cross-examination was based on statements made in A's confession which, though voluntary and admissible, were not put in evidence by the prosecution because it would have been unfair to B to have proved the confession in-chief[7].

(2) *Civil Evidence Act 1968, s. 2 or s. 4*

Statements which are inadmissible as vicarious admissions by virtue of s. 9 of the Civil Evidence Act 1968, which, as we have seen, simply preserves the common law, may nonetheless be rendered admissible under s. 2 or s. 4 of the Act. Thus, on facts such as those of *Great Western Rail. Co.* v. *Willis*[8], the night inspector's statement could be made admissible under s. 2 if the plaintiff served the defendant with a notice of his desire to give the statement in evidence and no counter-notice was served. If a counter-notice were served, the statement could be proved with the leave of the court if the plaintiff called the inspector, but the court would also have a discretion to allow the statement to be proved without the inspector's being called by the plaintiff[9].

A similar procedure could be adopted in a case in which one of two co-defendants had made a statement implicating the other, and the court would have a similar discretion to dispense the plaintiff from the necessity of calling the maker of the statement. One of the odd results of the common law's exclusion of the extra-judicial admission of one party as evidence against the other, however much it might implicate him, was that, in a divorce case, there might be a finding that A had committed adultery with B on account of A's out-of-court admission, coupled with a finding that B's adultery with A had not been proved because the admission was not evidence against B[10]. Though still a theoretical possibility, such a result is rendered unlikely by the Civil Evidence Act 1968.

ART. 43.—**Statements in public documents**

Statements in a public document, made by an officer acting in pursuance of a public duty, are admissible as evidence of the truth of their contents, in criminal cases by virtue of the

---

7 *R.* v. *Rice*, [1963] 1 Q.B. 857; [1963] 1 All E.R. 832.

8 P. 148, *ante*.

9 R.S.C. Ord. 38, r. 29 (2).

10 *Rutherford* v. *Richardson*, [1923] A.C. 1.

common law[11], and in civil cases by virtue of s. 9 of the Civil Evidence Act 1968, which preserves the relevant common law rules; but the admissibility of statements in public documents is governed by a great variety of special statutes.

Explanation: The expression "statements in public documents" is a convenient description of a heterogeneous mass of exceptions to the hearsay rule consisting of an amalgam of statutory provisions and the common law. The registration of births, deaths and marriages in the United Kingdom is now governed by statute, but, subject to the fulfilment of the conditions mentioned in the article, foreign registers are admissible as evidence of these matters at common law. Old English parochial registers are admissible at common law as evidence of marriages, baptisms and burials. The production of the relevant certificate or book must be supplemented by evidence of identity which may take the form of the bare assertion of a witness that the person named is the person whose birth, death or marriage has to be proved.

The exception covers entries in all manner of public registers, surveys and assessments. At common law, recitals in statutes are evidence of the facts stated in them, as are the contents of parliamentary journals and government gazettes relating to acts of state. The London Gazette is made evidence of a variety of matters by statute.

The principle underlying the exception is that the public nature of the document renders it unlikely that there should be undetected mistakes in it, and, in many cases, the officer compiling it is under a public duty to satisfy himself of the truth of its contents.

Public document

The requirement that the document should be a public one means that it must have been made so as to be retained in order that the public may refer to it. Records compiled by the post office, showing the times at which telegrams are received, are inadmissible under this exception to the hearsay rule because there is no intention that they should be retained for public inspection[12]. A soldier's regimental records are likewise

[11] *Sturla* v. *Freccia* (1880), 5 App. Cas. 623.
[12] *Heyne* v. *Fischel & Co.* (1913), 30 T.L.R. 190.

inadmissible under the exception as evidence of service abroad because they are not intended to be used by the public[13].

Public duty

The relevant officer must be under a duty to record particular facts and satisfy himself of their existence. A certificate has been held to be evidence of the date, as well as the fact, of the birth, death or marriage recorded because this is a matter of which the registrar must be satisfied, and it has also been held that a birth certificate may be evidence of the marriage of the parents of the child mentioned therein[14]; but a death certificate is not admissible evidence of the cause of death mentioned therein under this exception to the hearsay rule[15].

In *R.* v. *Halpin*[16] it was held that allowance must be made for the greater division of labour in modern times with the result that the duty to record may lie on one person and the duty to be satisfied of the existence of the fact recorded on another. Accordingly the fact that the accused was a director of a particular company was held to have been properly proved by the production of the file of statutory returns from the Companies' Registry. An official of the Registry was under a duty to record and preserve the returns for public inspection, and an official of the company was under a duty to be satisfied of the truth of facts stated in its return.

Civil Evidence Act 1968

In so far as the exception is based on other statutory provisions dealing with particular types of document, the Civil Evidence Act 1968 has no bearing on it; s. 9 preserves the following common law rules:

the rule "whereby in any civil proceedings published works dealing with matters of a public nature (for example histories, scientific works, dictionaries and maps) are admissible as evidence of facts of a public nature stated therein";

the rule "whereby in any civil proceedings public documents (for example, public registers, and returns made under public authority with respect to matters of public interest) are admissible as evidence of facts stated therein";

---

[13] *Lilley* v. *Pettit*, [1946] K.B. 401.
[14] *Re Stollery, Weir* v. *Treasury Solicitor*, [1926] Ch. 284.
[15] *Bird* v. *Keep*, [1918] 2 K.B. 692.
[16] [1975] Q.B. 907; [1975] 2 All E.R. 1124.

the rule "whereby in any civil proceedings records (for example the records of certain courts and treaties, Crown grants, pardons and commissions) are admissible as evidence of facts stated therein".

No notice is required to render a document admissible under s. 9, but it must be borne in mind that statements in documents which do not qualify as public documents may often be rendered admissible under s. 2 or s. 4 of the 1968 Act. The post office and regimental records mentioned above would be admissible under s. 4 and, if based on information supplied directly to the compiler of the record by someone with personal knowledge, under s. 2 as well. Now that hearsay statements of opinion are admissible under the Civil Evidence Act 1968, as extended by the Civil Evidence Act 1972, a death certificate may be received as evidence of the cause of death under s. 4.

ART. 44.—**Affidavits and depositions**

In several different situations in civil cases, affidavits may be received as evidence of the facts stated in them and, in several different situations in criminal cases, depositions may be received as evidence of the facts stated in them.

Explanation: The transcript of the evidence given in different proceedings between the same parties is admissible under an exception to the hearsay rule in civil cases by virtue of s. 2 of the Civil Evidence Act 1968[17], and, in criminal cases, at common law provided the subject matter is substantially the same and the witness is unable to attend the second trial through death or illness[18]. We are now concerned with the reading at a particular trial of evidence taken beforehand for the express purpose of being used in that trial when necessary. These exceptions to the hearsay rule are statutory and the Civil Evidence Act is inapplicable.

---

[17] P. 135, *ante*.

[18] *R.* v. *Scaife* (1851), 17 Q.B. 238; *R.* v. *Hall*, [1973] Q.B. 496; [1973] 1 All E.R. 1.

(1) *Affidavits*

An affidavit is a written statement made on oath before a commissioner of oaths or other person authorised to administer oaths. Affidavits are used for a variety of purposes other than the recording of the evidence which may subsequently be read at a civil trial. There are, however, many situations in which affidavit evidence may be used in civil cases. An order may be made at any stage of the proceedings that the whole or part of the evidence be taken by affidavit[19]. The order may make provision for the attendance of the deponent for cross-examination, and, if he does attend the trial, the affidavit becomes incorporated in his testimony. When the deponent does not attend the trial, the affidavit is received as evidence of the facts stated under an exception to the rule against hearsay.

When there is no special order for evidence to be taken on affidavit, the principal occasions on which affidavit evidence is used occur in the Chancery Division where proceedings are often begun by originating summons, and in interlocutory proceedings.

(2) *Depositions*

A deposition is a written record of evidence, given before a magistrate or other official of the court. Depositions are used in a variety of different situations in civil and criminal cases alike, but mainly in criminal cases.

An example of the use of a deposition in a civil action is provided by a case in which an order is made for the taking of the evidence of a particular witness by an examiner before trial. Such an order may be necessary because the witness will, for good reason, be unavailable at the trial[20]. Provision is made for the attendance of all parties and their representatives at the examination, and the witness may be cross-examined. Assuming he does not attend the trial, the witness's deposition may be read. It is received as evidence of the facts stated and therefore, under an exception to the rule against hearsay, but the exception is not a very serious one as the evidence recorded in the deposition will have been given on oath and subject to cross-examination.

Neither is the exception a serious one when depositions are received as evidence of the facts stated in them in a criminal

[19] R.S.C. Ord. 41.

[20] *Ibid.*

case. There are five principal situations in which this may occur.

Two instances are provided by depositions taken at committal proceedings before examining justices. In the ordinary case, the depositions are not used as evidence of the facts stated in them because the deponents appear as witnesses at the trial. It will be recollected that, if a witness contradicts his deposition, it can only be used to cast doubt upon his testimony at the trial[1]. Depositions may be used as affirmative evidence, in the absence of the deponent, when witnesses are ordered to attend the trial conditionally on their receiving notice requiring them to do so, and they have not been notified that their attendance is required.

Depositions taken at the committal proceedings may also be used at the trial if, although the deponent was unconditionally ordered to attend, he is dead, insane, so ill as to be unable to travel, or kept out of the way by means of the procurement of the accused[2]. The existence of one of these conditions of admissibility must be proved by a credible witness. It is not enough merely to show that the deponent is abroad[3].

In each of the above instances, the deposition must be signed by the justice taking it, and it must be proved, either by a certificate signed by that justice, or by the clerk to the examining justices, or else by the oath of a credible witness, that the deposition was taken in the presence of the accused and that he, his counsel or solicitor, had full opportunity of cross-examining the deponent.

Statements admissible under s. 2 of the Criminal Justice Act 1967 may take the place of depositions in the two situations which have so far been mentioned. The conditions of admissibility are (a) that the maker should have signed the statement, (b) that the statement should contain a declaration that the maker believed it to be true and knew that, if it were used in evidence, he was liable to prosecution if this were not the case, (c) that a copy of the statement should have been served on all other parties, and (d) that no other party should have objected to its use.

The third situation in which a deposition may be read at a criminal trial is when someone who might have been willing to give material information relating to an indictable offence is

---

[1] P. 89, *ante*.

[2] Criminal Justice Act 1925, s. 13 (3).

[3] *R.* v. *Austin* (1856), 20 J.P. 54.

dangerously ill. If a Justice of the Peace is satisfied (i) by the representation of a doctor that the person in question is dangerously ill and unlikely to recover and (ii) that it is not reasonably practicable to take the sick person's evidence in the ordinary way before examining justices, the written deposition of the sick person may be taken on oath anywhere. The deposition may be read before examining justices or at the trial provided (a) the deponent is dead, or there is no reasonable probability that he will ever be able to travel or give evidence, (b) the deposition is signed by the justice who took it, and (c) the person (whether prosecutor or accused) against whom the evidence is to be read had reasonable notice of the intention to take the deposition and full opportunity of cross-examining the deponent[4]. The notice to the accused is essential. A deposition cannot be read even if it be proved that the accused's fault accounts for his not having been given notice[5].

The fourth situation in which the deposition of an absent deponent may be read at a criminal trial is when the deposition is that of a child or young person in respect of whom an offence mentioned in the Schedule to the Children and Young Persons Act 1933 is alleged to have been committed. The offences include cruelty to children and various sexual offences now defined by the Sexual Offences Act 1956, and the Indecency with Children Act 1960. Under s. 42 of the Act, the deposition may be taken anywhere instead of before examining justices, provided a Justice of the Peace is satisfied by the evidence of a duly qualified medical practitioner that the attendance in court of the child or young person would involve serious danger to his life or health. The justice must sign the deposition and add a statement of his reasons for taking it together with the names of those present when it was taken.

Under s. 43 of the Act of 1933, the trial court may admit in evidence the deposition of a child or young person taken either in the ordinary way before examining justices or else under s. 42. The court must be satisfied on the evidence of a duly qualified medical practitioner that the deponent's attendance would involve serious danger to his life or health.

A deposition cannot be received under s. 42 or s. 43 of the Act of 1933 as evidence against the accused unless he was given reasonable notice that it would be taken. He, his counsel or

---

[4] Magistrates' Courts Act 1952, s. 41; Criminal Law Amendment Act 1867, s. 6.

[5] *R.* v. *Quigley* (1868), 18 L.T. 211.

solicitor, must have had an opportunity of cross-examining the deponent.

Under s. 27 of the Children and Young Persons Act 1963 a statement made by, or taken from, a child witness in writing shall be admissible in evidence, on prosecutions for sexual offences, of any matter as to which his oral testimony would be admissible. But the section does not apply where, *inter alia*, the defence objects, or the prosecution requires the statement for the purpose of identifying any person. The section is therefore broader than s. 42 and s. 43 of the Act of 1933 in that it applies to any child witness, and not merely to a child in respect of whom the offence has been committed, and it provides for the reception of statements in writing as opposed to depositions. But the section is narrower than the earlier enactments because it is confined to sexual offences and does not apply where the defence objects to its application.

Finally it has been held that the trial court may read a deposition taken at a coroner's inquisition when the deponent committed suicide after the inquest[6]. The deponent had been cross-examined, and parts of the deposition were excluded.

ART. 45—Evidence by certificate, statutory declaration and agreed statement

1. By virtue of various statutory provisions, certain facts may be proved by the production of a certificate or statutory declaration.

2. Under s. 9 of the Criminal Justice Act 1967 the parties to criminal proceedings may agree to the receipt in evidence of written statements.

Explanation:

1. *Certificates*

Greater use is made of evidence by certificate in criminal than in civil cases, although in any civil proceedings, the court could order proof of a particular fact by certificate[7]. Under s. 8 (5) of the Civil Evidence Act 1968 the court may act on the

---

[6] *R.* v. *Cowle* (1907), 71 J.P. 152.

[7] R.S.C. Ord. 38, r. 3.

evidence of a medical certificate in deciding whether a witness is able to attend court.

An example of the use of certificate evidence in a criminal case is provided by s. 41 (1) of the Criminal Justice Act 1948:

> "In any criminal proceedings, a certificate purporting to be signed by a constable, or by a person having the prescribed qualifications, and certifying that a plan or drawing exhibited thereto is a plan or drawing made by him of the place or object specified in the certificate, and that the plan or drawing is correctly drawn to a scale so specified, shall be evidence of the relative position of the things shown on the plan or drawing."

Under s. 41 (5), the defendant may require the attendance at the trial of the person who signed the certificate.

Subject to the prescribed conditions, analysts' certificates are admissible evidence of the quantity of alcohol in the accused's blood in road traffic cases.

A "statutory declaration" is a declaration complying with the conditions of the Statutory Declarations Act 1835. It is made before a commissioner for oaths, and the maker may be prosecuted under the Perjury Act 1911, if he wilfully makes false statements in the declaration. Section 27 (4) of the Theft Act 1968, provides for the use of statutory declarations on charges of theft of goods in the course of transmission (whether by post or otherwise) and of handling goods stolen by such a theft. A statutory declaration made by any person that he dispatched or received or failed to receive any goods or postal packet or that any goods or postal packet when despatched or received by him were in a particular state or condition, is admissible as evidence of the facts stated in the declaration. A copy must be served on the opposite party within seven days of the hearing and, within three days of the hearing, he may give notice requiring the maker to be called.

2. *Agreed statements*

Provided the conditions specified in s. 9 of the Criminal Justice Act 1967 are fulfilled, agreed statements of facts may be admitted in evidence at any criminal trial to the same extent and with the same effect as oral evidence. The principal conditions are that the statement should be signed and contain a declaration of the maker's knowledge that it was made subject to penalties in the event of its being used in evidence if the maker knew it to be false or did not care whether it was true, that a copy should have been served on the opposite party, and that no notice of objection should have been received from the party within seven days. It is also possible for parties to agree to the reception of such a statement at or before the trial, although the provisions with regard to service of a copy of the statement and non-receipt within seven days of notice of objection have not been complied with.

ART. 46.—Confessions in criminal cases, subsequently discovered facts and the Judges' Rules

1. A partial or total confession of guilt in a criminal case is only admissible as evidence for the prosecution against the party who made it if it was voluntary in the sense that it was not obtained from him by fear of prejudice or hope of advantage excited or held out by a person in authority, or by oppression.

2. There is no rule of law that facts discovered in consequence of an inadmissible confession may not be proved by the prosecution.

3. Confessions obtained in contravention of the Judges' Rules or by means of unfair questions may be excluded by the judge in the exercise of his discretion although the conditions mentioned in clause 1 of this article were satisfied.

Explanation: For the purpose of the ensuing discussion a confession includes any incriminating statement even though it does not amount to a full confession of guilt. It is a species of admission, but the subject has to be treated separately on account of the exclusionary rule set out in clause 1 of the article governing admissions made to persons in authority. The rule only applies to statements which the prosecution seek to put in evidence against the party who made them. If one of two accused makes a confession incriminating his co-accused as well as himself, the prosecution cannot rely on it as evidence of its truth against the co-accused on account of the rule against hearsay. This is so even if the confession was voluntary. The hearsay rule also prevents an accused person from relying on the confession of another as evidence of its truth unless that other is his co-accused in which case it will, as between the two accused, be treated as an ordinary admission although the method by which it was obtained may greatly affect its weight.

The reason most commonly given for the law's rigorous insistence on proof of voluntariness when a confession is tendered in evidence by the prosecution is that a confession which was not voluntary within clause 1 of the article might be unreliable; but allowance must be made for the "disciplinary" principle in addition to the "reliability" principle. The reception of confessions induced by even the mildest of police improprieties might encourage undesirable police methods. There is moreover a deep rooted objection, to which reference has already been made[8], to a person's being put under any form of pressure to incriminate himself.

The requirement of voluntariness refers to pressures brought to bear on the accused in order to obtain the confession. The fact that someone makes a confession while in a disturbed mental state does not entitle him to have it excluded as a matter of law, although the confession might be excluded by the judge in the exercise of his discretion if the disturbance was sufficiently great[9].

(1) *The admissibility of confessions*

The requirement of voluntariness in the somewhat special sense mentioned in clause 1 of the article goes back to the eighteenth century, but the formulation of the rule stems from a statement of Lord SUMNER's in the Privy Council in *Ibrahim* v. *R.*[10]. The words "or oppression" were added by Lord PARKER, C.J., in *Callis* v. *Gunn*[11], and they were repeated in the formulation of the exclusionary principle in the introduction to the Judges' Rules of 1964. This formulation has since been approved by the House of Lords on two occasions[12]. As reported, Lord SUMNER spoke of the necessity of proving that the confession was not obtained by fear of prejudice or hope of advantage "exercised" or held out by a person in authority, and the word "exercised" was repeated in the introduction to the Judges' Rules. As Lord HAILSHAM pointed out in *Director of*

---

[8] P. 99, *supra*.

[9] *R.* v. *Isequilla*, [1975] 1 All E.R. 77.

[10] [1914] A.C. 599, at p. 609.

[11] [1964] 1 Q.B. 495, at p. 501.

[12] *Customs and Excise Commissioners* v. *Harz and Power*, [1967] 1 A.C. 760; [1967] 1 All E.R. 177; *Director of Public Prosecutions* v. *Ping Lin*, [1976] A.C. 574; [1975] 3 All E.R. 175.

Public Prosecutions v. *Ping Lin*[13], it does not make sense and his suggestion that Lord SUMNER probably used the word "excited" has been adopted.

Ping Lin's case is of great importance because of the insistence by the House of Lords on a rigorous application of Lord SUMNER's words. The accused was convicted of a conspiracy to contravene the Misuse of Drugs Act 1971 and his conviction was affirmed by the Court of Appeal and House of Lords. He had been taken into custody on being found by police smoking Chinese heroin with friends in his flat in which further significant quantities of the drug were discovered. When interviewed under caution by two police officers he endeavoured to make a bargain under which he would disclose the name of this supplier if released, but he was told that this was not possible. He then admitted that he was a dealer, though only in a small way. He persisted in his endeavour to buy immunity or lenience and the superintendent who was conducting the interview used the following words after reiterating his inability to do a deal: "If you show the judge that you have helped police to trace bigger drug people, I am sure he will bear it in mind when sentencing you." Ping Lin then suggested a means of entrapping his supplier and made further incriminating remarks about his own activities which, however, amounted to little more than an amplification of what had already been said. The House of Lords held that the judge was entitled to find that the accused's self-incrimination was not caused by the superintendent's remark, although that may have contributed to the betrayal of the supplier. While emphasising the factual nature of the inquiry, the House was also of opinion that the case would have been very different if the superintendent's remark had preceded Ping Lin's admission that he was a dealer. It would then have been difficult if not impossible for the judge properly to hold that the confession had not been obtained by the hope held out of a lighter sentence.

The House also stressed the points that the fact that the words alleged to excite a fear or raise a hope were not uttered with the intention of inducing a confession was immaterial, and that nothing in the nature of improper conduct by the person in authority has to be shown in order that the confession should be inadmissible. The judge should ask

---

[13] [1976] A.C. at p. 597.

himself one question and one only: "Have the prosecution proved that the contested statement was voluntary in the sense that it was not obtained by fear of prejudice or hope of advantage excited or held out by a person in authority or . . . by oppression"[14]

Fear of prejudice.—The factual nature of this question militates against the utility of the numerous reported decisions concerning the fear of prejudice or hope of advantage or, as it is frequently put, the "threat or inducement" which will have the effect of rendering a confession inadmissible. What will suffice in the case of a timorous or ignorant suspect may be wholly insufficient in the case of a more robust character. The use or threat of violence by a person in authority would almost certainly render the ensuing confession inadmissible on account of the difficulty of proving that it was not caused by fear of prejudice but confessions have been excluded when the menace was of a less brutal nature. In *R.* v. *Smith*[15] a soldier had been stabbed in a fight and immediately after the episode a regimental sergeant-major put his men on parade saying that he would keep them there until he learnt who had been involved in the fighting. A confession made shortly afterwards by the accused was held to be inadmissible although it was recognised that what the regimental sergeant-major did was a useful course of action to enable further inquiries to be made.

The threat need not relate to the accused or his family. A confession made by someone told by a police officer that, unless he made a statement it would be necessary to detain the woman in whose house he had sought to store stolen goods has been held inadmissible and there seems to be no reason why a threat to maltreat a total stranger should not render a confession made in consequence of it inadmissible[16].

In *Customs and Excise Commissioners* v. *Harz and Power*[17] it was held that statements made to officers of customs and excise should have been excluded as having been made under threat of prosecution for failure to answer questions at an interrogation which the officers were not authorised to conduct. The House of Lords pointed out that if the interrogation had been conducted in a manner authorised by the relevant statute

[14] *Per* Lord HAILSHAM, [1976] A.C. at p. 600.
[15] [1959] 2 Q.B. 35; [1959] 2 All E.R. 193.
[16] *R.* v. *Middleton,* [1974] Q.B. 191; [1974] 2 All E.R. 1190.
[17] [1967] 1 A.C. 760; [1967] 1 All E.R. 177.

the ensuing statement would probably have been admissible because failure to answer would have been an offence and the officers' statement to that effect would have been authorised by statute. The main importance of the decision lies in its rejection of a supposed rule supported by a tenuous line of authority that the threat or inducement must relate to the prosecution of the offence charged.

Hope of advantage.—Typical inducements which have been held to render confessions inadmissible are suggestions that a suspect might have bail or be allowed to leave the police station if he made a statement[18]. Although more depends on the circumstances than the actual words used[19] observations by police officers such as "Speak the truth. It will be better for you", or "The time has come when you had better make a statement"[20], are liable to render a confession inadmissible on account of the implication that if the truth is that the suspect is guilty he may be treated more leniently if he makes a confession[1].

Several decisions can be urged in support of the view that in order to render a confession inadmissible the inducement must be of a temporal nature[2] but it is possible to think of spiritual inducements which would be more influential with some people than temporal ones and, in view of the purely subjective approach required by the House of Lords in *Director of Public Prosecutions* v. *Ping Lin,* it is perhaps doubtful whether the decisions are still good law.

Duration.—A threat or inducement may become ineffective through lapse of time or some other intervening cause. In that event a confession or further confession will be admissible. In *R.* v. *Smith*[3], a further confession made to an investigating officer the day after the one made to the regimental sergeant-major was held to be admissible. In such a case the second confession is admissible although the accused has not been expressly told that the first was inadmissible[4].

---

[18] *R.* v. *Zaveckas,* [1970] 1 All E.R. 413.

[19] *R.* v. *Priestley* (1966), 50 Cr. App. Rep. 183.

[20] *R.* v. *Richards,* [1967] 1 All E.R. 829.

[1] See the judgment of KELLY, C.B., in *R.* v. *Jarvis* (1867), L.R. 1 C.C.R. 96.

[2] E.g. *R.* v. *Wild* (1835), 1 Mood. C.C. 432; *R.* v. *Reeve and Hancock* (1872), L.R. 1 C.C.R. 362.

[3] [1959] 2 Q.B. 35; [1959] 2 All E.R. 193.

[4] *R.* v. *Howes* (1834), 6 C. & P. 404.

Person in authority.—A person in authority is anyone whom the accused might reasonably have considered to have been capable of influencing the outcome of the prosecution. A police officer, magistrate or prosecutor is clearly included. The nature of the charge determines whether an employer is someone in authority. He would be if the charge were one of theft from him by one of his servants but not on a charge brought against a maidservant for murdering her own child[5]. The owner of a house whose goods were stolen from it has been held to be in authority[6].

A confession made to a person in authority is admissible, though made in consequence of a threat or inducement from someone not in authority, if the person in authority was aware of the threat or inducement and did nothing to disassociate himself from it[7].

Although it is now settled that the threat or inducement need not relate to the prosecution[8], it is still the law that the exclusionary rule concerning voluntariness only applies to confessions made to persons in authority, not, for instance, to those made to a fellow prisoner[9].

Oppression.—The following appears to be the only judicial elucidation of the meaning of the word "oppression" in this context[10].

> "[T]his word, in the context of the principles under consideration, imports something which tends to sap, and has sapped that free will which must exist before a confession is voluntary . . . Whether there is oppression in an individual case depends upon many elements . . . They include such things as length of time intervening between periods of questioning, whether the accused person had been given proper refreshment or not, and the characteristics of the person who makes the statement. What may be oppressive as regards a child, an invalid or an old man or somebody inexperienced in the ways of this world may turn out not to

---

[5] *R.* v. *Moore* (1852), 2 Den, 522.

[6] *R.* v. *Wilson and Marshall-Graham,* [1967] 2 Q.B. 406; [1967] 1 All E.R. 797.

[7] *R.* v. *Cleary* (1963), 48 Cr. App. Rep. 116.

[8] *Customs and Excise Commissioners* v. *Harz and Power,* [1967] 1 A.C. 760; [1967] 1 All E.R. 177.

[9] *Deokinanan* v. *R.*, [1969] 1 A.C. 20; [1968] 2 All E.R. 346.

[10] SACHS, L.J., in *R.* v. *Priestley* (1966), 51 Cr. App. Rep. 1(n).

be oppressive when one finds that the accused person is of a tough character and an experienced man of the world".

Functions of judge and jury.—The question whether a confession was in fact made, must, if it is in issue, be determined by the jury[11]. The question whether a confession was voluntary must be determined by the judge at a trial within the trial which will usually be conducted in the absence of the jury. If he concludes that the confession is admissible, he must allow the Crown witnesses to be cross-examined on the method by which it was obtained in the presence of the jury at the trial proper, and the jury must then decide what weight should be attached to the confession[12]. It is only necessary for the judge to draw attention in his summing up to the possible effect of alleged threats or inducements or oppressive questioning on the truth of the confession. He must not tell the jury to disregard it altogether if they have a reasonable doubt concerning its voluntariness[13].

In *R.* v. *Hammond*[14] the Court of Criminal Appeal held that it was proper for counsel for the prosecution to ask the accused in cross-examination at a trial within a trial whether a confession, the voluntariness of which is contested, was true, because that is a fact which could affect the credibility of the accused's evidence concerning the obtaining of the confession, and its truth might be relevant to its voluntariness . This case was not followed by the Privy Council on an appeal from Hong Kong in *Wong Kam-Ming* v. *R.*[15]. The accused had replied to questions put to him in cross-examination on the *voir dire* in terms suggesting that his confession was true. The judge held the confession to be inadmissible but allowed the prosecution to call witnesses at the trial proper to prove the accused's admissions on the *voir dire*. The Judicial Committee held that the accused should not have been asked in cross-examination on the *voir dire* whether the confession was true, and that witnesses should not have been allowed to testify at the trial proper concerning his answers. The conviction was accordingly quashed. The reaction of the English courts to these conflicting decisions remains to be seen.

---

[11] *R.* v. *Roberts,* [1954] 2 Q.B. 329; [1953] 2 All E.R. 340.

[12] *R.* v. *Murray,* [1951] 1 K.B. 391; [1950] 2 All E.R. 925.

[13] *Chen Kwei Keung* v. *R.,* [1967] 2 A.C. 150; [1967] 1 All E.R. 945; *R.* v. *Ovenall,* [1969] 1 Q.B. 17; [1968] 1 All E.R. 933.

[14] [1941] 3 All E.R. 318.

[15] [1979] 1 All E.R. 939.

Onus of proof and corroboration.—The onus of satisfying the judge beyond reasonable doubt that a confession was voluntary is borne by the prosecution[16]. There is no rule of law, or even of practice, that a confession must be corroborated[17].

(2) *Subsequently discovered facts*

In *R.* v. *Warickshall*[18], a woman charged as accessory after the fact to theft made an inadmissible confession in the course of which she said that the property in question was in her lodgings. The property was found there and it was held that this fact might be proved. The court said that the principle respecting confessions:

> "has no application whatsoever as to the admission or rejection of facts, whether the knowledge of them be obtained in consequence of an extorted confession or whether it arises from any other source; for a fact, if it exist at all, must exist invariably in the same manner, whether the confession from which it derives be in other respects true or false."

The court also stated that the facts must be proved without any reference to the inadmissible confession. In many cases, however, the mere proof of the facts, without any reference even to the part of the confession mentioning them, would be useless. In *R.* v. *Gould*[19], someone who was charged with burglary made a statement to a police officer in circumstances which induced the prosecution not to offer it in evidence; but the statement contained an allusion to a lantern which was afterwards found in a particular place, and the officer was asked whether, in consequence of something said by the prisoner, he searched for it. The court required the words used by the prisoner to be proved, and the officer stated that the prisoner had said that he threw the lantern into the pond in which it was found. It seems fairly clear that the finding of the lantern would have had no probative value unless coupled with evidence of the accused's knowledge of its whereabouts. There are, however, subsequent decisions which favour the view taken

---

16 *R.* v. *Thompson,* [1893] 2 Q.B. 12.

17 *R.* v. *Sykes* (1913), 8 Cr. App. Rep. 233.

18 (1783), 1 Leach 263.

19 (1840); 9 C. & P. 364.

in *R.* v. *Warickshall* that no part of the inadmissible confession may be proved in evidence[20].

It is quite clear that there is no absolute rule of law excluding proof of facts discovered in consequence of inadmissible confessions. In this instance, as in that of illegally or improperly obtained evidence generally, English law, unlike that of the United States, has no ban on the "fruits of the poisoned tree"; but the judge has a discretion to exclude them if he thinks it is necessary to do so to secure a fair trial for the accused.[1] All that can be said with certainty of the law is that the cases conflict on the extent to which the discovery of facts in consequence of a confession renders the whole or part of it admissible.

(3) *The Judges' Rules and the discretion to exclude legally admissible confessions*

In 1912 the judges formulated guides to be followed by the police when questioning suspects, and they came to be known as the "Judges' Rules". A new set was published in 1964. Provided it was voluntary within the meaning of clause 1 of this article, a confession obtained in contravention of the Judges' Rules is not inadmissible as a matter of law, but the judge has a discretion to exclude it. In addition to being subject to the principle of voluntariness which has already been stated[2] the rules are expressed to be subject to the following principles: that citizens have a duty (though in most circumstances only a social or moral one) to help a police officer to discover and apprehend offenders; that police officers, otherwise than by arrest, cannot compel any person against his will to come to or remain in any police station; that every person at any stage of an investigation should be able to communicate and to consult privately with a solicitor, even if he is in custody, provided that in such a case no unreasonable delay or hindrance is caused to the processes of investigation or the administration of justice by his doing so[3]; and if a police officer making enquiries of

---

[20] *R.* v. *Berriman* (1854), 6 Cox C.C. 388; *R.* v. *Barker,* [1941] 2 K.B. 381; [1941] 3 All E.R. 33.

[1] *R.* v. *Sang,* [1979] 2 All E.R. 1222, p. 305, *infra.*

[2] P. 159, *ante.*

[3] See *R.* v. *Lemsatef,* [1977] 2 All E.R. 835 (the fear that the subject might make contact with others through his solicitor is not an adequate reason for denying him his right). See also Criminal Law Act 1977, s. 62 (right of arrested person to have information given to someone reasonably named by him).

any person about an offence has enough evidence to prefer a charge against him, he should without delay cause that person to be charged or informed that he may be prosecuted. The rules apply to interrogations concerning "offences", a term which is not defined and on which there is no relevant case-law.

Rule I provides that, when a police officer is trying to discover whether, or by whom an offence has been committed, he is entitled to question any person, whether suspected or not, from whom he thinks that useful information may be obtained. This is so whether or not the person in question has been taken into custody so long as he has not been charged with the offence or informed that he may be prosecuted for it. The person interrogated may be in custody for a different offence than that about which he is being questioned[4].

Rule II provides that as soon as a police officer has evidence (i.e. information which could be put before a court)[5] which would afford reasonable grounds for suspecting that a person has committed an offence, he shall caution that person, or cause him to be cautioned, before putting to him any questions relating to that offence. The caution should be in the following terms: "You are not obliged to say anything unless you wish to do so but what you say may be put into writing and given in evidence." The suggestion that the statement will necessarily be given in evidence against the person interrogated must be avoided, otherwise innocent people might be discouraged from making exculpatory statements.

Rule III provides (a) that where a person is charged with or informed that he may be prosecuted for an offence he shall be cautioned in the following terms: "Do you wish to say anything? You are not obliged to say anything unless you wish to do so but whatever you say may be taken down in writing and given in evidence"; (b) that it is only in exceptional cases that questions relating to the offence should be put to the accused person after he has been charged or informed that he may be prosecuted. Such questions may be put where necessary for the purpose of preventing or minimising harm or loss to some other person or to the public or for clearing up an ambiguity in a previous answer or statement. Before any such questions are put the accused should be cautioned in the following terms: "I wish to put some questions to you about

---

[4] *R.* v. *Buchan,* [1964] 1 All E.R. 502.

[5] *R.* v. *Osbourne and Virtue,* [1973] Q.B. 678; [1973] 1 All E.R. 649.

the offence with which you have been charged [or about the offence for which you may be prosecuted]. You are not obliged to answer any of these questions, but if you do the questions and answers will be taken down in writing and may be given in evidence." "Charged" in this rule means formally charged, not merely "informed of the cause of an arrest on suspicion"[6], and a person who has been told that he will be charged is "charged" within the meaning of this rule[7]. "Informed that he may be prosecuted" is a phrase appropriate to someone who is not under arrest with regard to whom the interrogating officer has decided that a summons may be issued[8].

Rule IV contains important directions about the form in which statements should be taken.

Rule V is aimed at an improper practice said to have been common in some police forces at one time. A written statement would be taken from one of two co-accused, or fellow suspects. If it implicated the other, the statement would be read to that other and, whatever his reply might be, the reading of the statement would be proved at the trial as a statement made in the presence of a party on principles discussed on p. 147, *ante*. The jury would thus be made aware of the fact that the first accused had incriminated the second even if the first did not give evidence.

The rule provides that, if at any time after a person has been charged with, or has been informed that he may be prosecuted for, an offence, a police officer wishes to bring to the notice of that person any written statement made by another person who in respect of the same offence has been charged or informed that he may be prosecuted, he shall hand to that person a true copy of such written statement, but nothing shall be said or done to invite any reply or comment. If that person says that he would like to make a statement in reply, or starts to say something, he shall at once be cautioned or further cautioned as provided by r. III (a).

Rule VI provides that persons other than police officers charged with the duty of investigating offences or charging offenders shall, so far as may be practicable, comply with the

---

[6] *R.* v. *Brackenbury,* [1965] 1 All E.R. 960; *R.* v. *Collier and Stenning,* [1965] 3 All E.R. 136.

[7] *Conway* v. *Hotten,* [1976] 2 All E.R. 213.

[8] *R.* v. *Collier and Stenning, supra.*

Rules. It has been held that they do not apply to a store manager[9].

The Judges' Rules are to some extent a reinforcement of the right to silence which has been previously mentioned[10]. But, long before they were heard of, the courts had exercised a discretion to exclude confessions which, though voluntary within clause 1 of this article, were thought to have been obtained improperly. Anything in the nature of a "cross-examination" of an accused person was greatly deplored. In *R.* v. *Winkel*[11] it was even said that the following utterance constituted a subtle form of cross-examination: "You have been brought here and will be charged with procuring abortion on Beatrice Gregg. She alleges you are responsible for her condition, and you gave her five pounds to get the operation done." While there is no doubt that the Judges' Rules have done nothing to fetter the trial judge's discretion to exclude confessions which he considers to have been improperly obtained, and confer a discretion to exclude confessions obtained in breach of them[12], more recent cases have shown less tenderness towards the accused with regard to what constitutes unfair questioning.

In *R.* v. *Voisin*[13], the accused had been detained for questioning concerning the murder of a woman. The police had not decided to charge him with the murder when, without a caution, they asked him to write "bloody Belgian". He did so and signed his death warrant by writing "bladie Belgiam", words written on a piece of paper found near the deceased's body. The Court of Criminal Appeal held that the evidence had been properly admitted because the writing had been done voluntarily. There was no suggestion of a trap or manufacture of evidence nor was there an "unguarded answer made in circumstances that rendered it unreliable, or unfair, for some reason, to be allowed in evidence against the prisoner". Although reference was made to the Judges' Rules, it is clear that the court was thinking in terms of a more general discretion to exclude improperly obtained confessions. It is, however, also open to question whether the case has much to do with the law concerning the admissibility of confessions.

---

[9] *R.* v. *Nichols* (1967), 51 Cr. App. Rep. 233.
[10] P. 100, *ante*.
[11] (1911), 76 J.P. 191.
[12] *Conway* v. *Hotten, supra,* at pp. 216–7.
[13] [1918] 1 K.B. 531.

The problems it raises have more to do with the admissibility of facts, evidence of which might have been obtained by improper means, and, on this, there is no rigid exclusionary rule in English law. If the officer had said "write bloody Belgian and I will see that you get bail", it seems that the ensuing inscription "bladie Belgiam" would have been admissible as a matter of law, whatever the position with regard to judicial discretion might have been.

In *R.* v. *May*[14], an alleged piece of cross-examination was dealt with purely in terms of voluntariness. May and others had been convicted of shopbreaking. While following the prisoners a police officer saw one of them drop something which turned out to be a jemmy wrapped in newspaper. When taken into custody May was searched, and, in his pocket, there was a small corner piece of the newspaper in which the jemmy had been wrapped. After cautioning May the officer said: "I saw you throw this jemmy away, it was wrapped in this newspaper, and you have now seen that the piece of paper from your pocket fits it exactly." May answered "nicked for a bit of paper, you have done me right now. I'd have got away with it but for that." On appeal it was contended that there had been cross-examination of a prisoner in custody. The appeal was dismissed on the ground that the statement was a voluntary one and admissible. This case was obviously concerned with the proof of a confession as opposed to the proof of a fact and May's utterance would have been inadmissible as a matter of law if the officer had opened with some such remark as "I will shoot you unless you tell me what your reactions are to my discovery".

ART. 47.—Dying declarations of the deceased on charges of homicide

The oral or written declaration of the deceased is admissible evidence of the cause of his death at a trial for his murder or manslaughter, provided he was under a settled hopeless expectation of death when the statement was made, and provided he would have been a competent witness if called to give evidence at that time.

[14] (1952), 36 Cr. App. Rep. 91.

Explanation: The principle underlying this exception to the hearsay rule is that a person would be unlikely to choose to die with a lie on his lips. It came to be settled, that these declarations are only admissible at trials for the murder or manslaughter of the person making them; there is no authority on their admissibility at trials for causing death by dangerous driving, an offence created as recently as 1956.

The requirement that the deceased must have been under a settled hopeless expectation of death does not mean that he must have expected to die immediately, but, if he says that "at present" he has no hope of survival, a belief in the possibility that he will recover is implied, and the statement will be inadmissible[15].

The requirement that the deceased must be someone who would have been a competent witness if he had survived means that the declaration of a dying child of four must be excluded[16].

If the conditions of admissibility mentioned in the article are satisfied, the declaration may sometimes be used in the accused's favour. The deceased's confession of suicide, or his recognition that he was guilty of gross provocation leading to the fatal attack may be utilised by the accused, just as a statement suggesting that the accused's unprovoked attack accounted for the declarant's condition may be used by the prosecution.

ART. 48.—Declarations by deceased persons against pecuniary or proprietary interest in criminal cases

In criminal cases, the oral or written declaration by a deceased person of a fact, which he knew to be against his pecuniary or proprietary interest when the declaration was made, is admissible as evidence of that fact, and of all collateral matters mentioned in the declaration, provided the declarant had personal knowledge of such facts and matters.

Explanation: When Part I of the Civil Evidence Act 1968 is extended to civil proceedings in Magistrates' Courts this

---

[15] *R.* v. *Jenkins* (1869), L.R. 1 C.C.R. 187.
[16] *R.* v. *Pike* (1829), 3 C. & P. 598.

exception to the hearsay rule will be confined to criminal cases although the authorities on which it is based are mainly decisions in civil cases. The four conditions required to bring it into play are: that the declarant should be dead, that the declaration should have been against the declarant's pecuniary or proprietary interest when made, that he should have known that it was against his interest at that time, and that he should have had personal knowledge of the fact which it is sought to prove by the declaration. Nothing need be said about the first condition.

Statements against pecuniary or proprietary interest when made

The simplest example of a declaration against pecuniary interest would be an acknowledgement of indebtedness, but it has been held that a receipt for fees due will suffice because it constitutes a release of a debt and is therefore against the interest of the person giving it. In the old leading case of *Higham* v. *Ridgway*[17], an entry, made by a deceased male midwife, stating that he had delivered a woman of a child on a certain day and referring to the payment of his charges, was received as evidence of the date of the child's birth.

> "If this entry had been produced when the party was making a claim for his attendance, it would have been evidence against him that his claim was satisfied."[18]

A statement which might have involved the declarant in criminal liability is not, for that reason, a statement against pecuniary or proprietary interest[19].

The declaration must have been against pecuniary or proprietary interest when made. Accordingly a reference to an executory bilateral contract is inadmissible under this exception to the rule against hearsay, for the court will not assume that the contract is against the interest of the maker of the statement[20].

It is immaterial that the statement may ultimately prove to be beneficial to the maker. Thus, in *Re Adams, Benton* v. *Powell*[1], the question was whether a woman's will was in existence at the time of her death. A statement by her husband (since deceased), that he had destroyed the original after his wife's death, was

[17] (1808), 10 East 108.
[18] Lord ELLENBOROUGH, C.J.
[19] *Sussex Peerage Case* (1844), 11 Cl. & Fin. 85.
[20] *R.* v. *Inhabitants of Worth* (1843), 4 Q.B. 132.
[1] [1922] P. 240.

received in evidence. He was in possession of his wife's land, and was therefore *prima facie* its owner. The statement referred to the terms of the will and said that it gave him a life interest in the land. This was something less than ownership of the land and therefore the statement was *prima facie* against the husband's interest when made, although it later turned out to be favourable to him as it could be relied on as evidence of the terms of the will.

Declarant's knowledge that statement was against interest

In *Tucker* v. *Oldbury Urban Council*[2], a claim for workmen's compensation was made on behalf of the dependants of a deceased workman. The Court of Appeal held that statements made by him to the effect that the injury to his thumb which caused his death was due, not to his work, but to a whitlow, were inadmissible as evidence of that fact. They were against interest in the sense that they would, if true, disentitle him to workmen's compensation, but he did not know this.

> "Such declarations are admitted on the ground that declarations made by persons against their own interest are extremely unlikely to be false. It follows therefore that to support the admissibility it must be shown that the statement was to to the knowledge of the deceased contrary to his interest."[3]

Deceased's personal knowledge of facts stated

In *Ward* v. *H. S. Pitt & Co.*[4], it was held that a deceased workman's implied assertions that he was the father of the claimant's illegitimate child and that he intended to marry the claimant were inadmissible as evidence of these facts on a claim for dependency for a child under the Workmen's Compensation Acts. The basis of the decision, so far as the statement of paternity was concerned, was that the deceased had no personal knowledge of the fact stated, as the mother might have had intercourse with others. The statement with regard to the intention to marry was inadmissible as a declaration against interest, because it referred to an executory contract.

---

[2] [1912] 2 K.B. 317.
[3] FLETCHER-MOULTON, L.J.
[4] [1913] 2 K.B. 130.

Contrast with admissions

The conditions governing the reception of declarations against interest differ from those governing the reception of admissions in three respects. The maker of a declaration against interest must be dead whereas the maker of an admission must be a party or his privy; an admission need only be adverse to a party's case, it does not have to be against pecuniary or proprietary interest; the maker's personal knowledge of the facts stated is essential to the admissibility of a declaration against interest, whereas a statement of belief will sometimes suffice in the case of an admission.

Collateral matters

Provided the declarant had personal knowledge of collateral facts mentioned in the statement, the statement is admissible evidence of those facts in addition to being evidence of the fact which it was against the declarant's interest to state. In *Higham* v. *Ridgeway*[5], for example, the entry was received, not as evidence of the payment of money to the midwife, but as evidence of the birth of the child.

> "It is idle to say that the word 'paid' only shall be admissible in evidence, without the context which explains to what it refers."[6]

Although the principle on which collateral facts may be proved by declarations against interest may be sound enough, it can produce odd results. Thus in *Taylor* v. *Witham*[7], a receipt, for payment of twenty pounds as interest on a debt for two thousand pounds, enabled the entry to be received as evidence of the amount of the debt due to the declarant, although a deceased person's statement that someone owed him money is normally inadmissible as evidence of that fact at common law.

ART. 49.—**Declarations by deceased persons in the course of duty in criminal cases**

In criminal cases, the oral or written statement of a deceased person made in pursuance of a duty to do an act and record it,

[5] *Supra.*
[6] Lord ELLENBOROUGH, C.J.
[7] (1876), 3 Ch.D. 605.

is admissible evidence of the truth of such parts of the statement as relate to that which it was his duty to record. This applies only if the record was made roughly contemporaneously with the doing of the act, and provided the declarant had no motive to misrepresent the facts.

Explanation: When Part I of the Civil Evidence Act 1968 is extended to civil proceedings in Magistrates' Courts this exception to the hearsay rule will only be relevant to criminal cases although most of the authorities upon which it is based are decisions in civil cases. The principle underlying the exception to the hearsay rule is that the likelihood that the duty would have been properly performed affords some guarantee of the trustworthiness of the statement. The conditions of admissibility are more stringent than those governing the exception mentioned in the previous article. There are five of them. The declarant must be dead; he must have owed a duty both to do an act and record it; the act must have been performed; the statement must have been made roughly contemporaneously with it, and the declarant must have had no motive to misrepresent the facts.

Duty to act and record

In *Price* v. *Torrington*[8], the defendant was sued for the price of beer sold and delivered. Entries which a deceased drayman, who had been employed by the plaintiff, made in the plaintiff's books, were received as evidence of the delivery of the beer. It was his duty to deliver and record the amount delivered. The act must have been recorded in pursuance of a duty; the mere taking of notes, however useful and common it may be, will not of itself suffice to render the notes admissible as evidence of anything written down in them[9].

The act must have been performed

In *Rowlands* v. *De Vecchi*[10] an office book containing a record of letters to be posted kept by a clerk who had since died, was rejected as evidence that a particular letter copied in the book had been posted. The principle that the exception only applies to acts done by the deceased and not to acts to be done by him

---

[8] (1703), 1 Salk. 285.

[9] *Mills* v. *Mills* (1920), 36 T.L.R. 772.

[10] (1882), 1 Cab. & El. 10.

may have been ignored in *R.* v. *Buckley*[11], in which a deceased constable's statement that he intended to go in search of the accused, who was charged with his murder, was received as evidence that the constable had acted as he said he would; the case is, however, of questionable authority and may have been decided on another principle discussed on p. 182.

Contemporaneity

It is impossible to lay down a precise rule with regard to the degree of contemporaneity between the doing of the act and the making of the record. In *Price* v. *Torrington*[12], the entry, made in the evening, related to acts performed in the daytime, and it was received; but, in *The Henry Coxon*[13], entries concerning a collision at sea, made in a ship's log-book two days after the event, were rejected. The cases suggest that the standard of contemporaneity is a strict one[14].

Absence of motive to misrepresent

A further ground for the rejection of the entries in *The Henry Coxon* was that the mate who made them had every reason to misrepresent the facts. The absence of a motive to misrepresent the facts stated is not a condition of admissibility in the case, either of declarations against interest, or of dying declarations, or of statements in public documents[15], although the proved presence of such a motive might well affect the weight to be attached to the statement.

Collateral facts

By way of contrast with declarations against interest, declarations in the course of duty can never be received as evidence of collateral facts. Thus, in *Chambers* v. *Bernasconi*[16], the certificate of an officer, whose duty it was to record the day and hour of an arrest, was rejected as evidence of the place at which the arrest occurred, although this was stated in the certificate, and the officer was dead at the date of the trial.

---

[11] (1873), 13 Cox C.C. 293.
[12] *Supra.*
[13] (1878), 3 P.D. 156.
[14] *Re Djambi (Sumatra) Rubber Estates, Ltd.* (1912), 107 L.T. 631.
[15] *Irish Society* v. *Bishop of Derry* (1846), 12 Cl. & Fin. 641.
[16] (1834), 1 Cr. M & R. 347.

ART. 50.—Declarations by deceased persons concerning pedigree in criminal cases

In criminal cases the oral or written declaration of a deceased person, or declarations to be implied from family conduct, are admissible as evidence of pedigree provided the declarant was a blood relation, or the spouse of a blood relation, of the person whose pedigree is in issue, and provided the declaration was made before the dispute arose.

Explanation: When Part I of the Civil Evidence Act 1968 is extended to Magistrates' Courts, this exception to the hearsay rule will be confined to criminal cases. It is unlikely that resort will frequently be had to it in these cases, and the briefest account of the law, based exclusively on civil decisions, will suffice.

In *Goodright d. Stevens* v. *Moss*[17] the question was whether a child was the legitimate offspring of its parents (then deceased), and Lord MANSFIELD admitted their declarations proved by the person to whom they were made, to the effect that the child was born before their marriage. He said:

> "Tradition is sufficient in point of pedigree; circumstances may be proved. For instance from the hour of one child's birth to the death of its parent, it had always been treated as illegitimate, and another introduced and considered as the heir of the family; that would be good evidence. An entry in a father's family Bible, an inscription on a tombstone, a pedigree hung up in the family mansion, are all good evidence. So are the declarations of parents in their life time."

The requirement that a question of pedigree must be in issue may be illustrated by *Haines* v. *Guthrie*[18]. Infancy was pleaded as a defence to an action on a contract, and an affidavit concerning the date of birth of the defendant, sworn by his deceased father, was held to be inadmissible. "No question of family was raised."

The requirement that the declarant should have been a blood relation, or a spouse of a blood relation, of the person whose pedigree is under investigation means that statements by deceased relations *de iure,* and servants, however intimately

---

[17] (1766), 2 Cowp. 591.
[18] (1884), 13 Q.B.D. 818.

acquainted they were with the family, are excluded. In *Johnson* v. *Lawson*[19], the question was who was the heir at law of one H. L., and declarations by a deceased woman who had been his housekeeper for 24 years were excluded.

In order that it should be inadmissible on the ground that it was made after a pedigree dispute had arisen, it is not essential that the maker of a pedigree declaration should have been aware of the existence of the dispute[20].

ART. 51.—Declarations concerning public or general rights in criminal cases

In criminal cases an oral or written declaration by a deceased person concerning the reputed existence of a public or general right is admissible as evidence of such right provided the declaration was made before a dispute had arisen.

Explanation: When Part I of the Civil Evidence Act 1968 is applied to Magistrates' Courts, this exception to the hearsay rule will be confined to criminal cases. Though resort is more likely to be had to it than to pedigree declarations in these cases, a very brief account of the law will suffice.

A public right is one affecting the entire population, such as a claim to tolls on a public highway or a claim to treat part of a river bank as a public landing-place. A general right is one that affects a class of persons such as the inhabitants of a particular district, or the owners of certain plots of land. The distinction between the two is, in this context, only of importance on a small point to be mentioned shortly.

Not only must the declaration of the deceased have concerned a public or general right; it must also have spoken of the reputed existence of such a right. In *R.* v. *Berger*[1], the question was whether a strip of land formed part of the highway, and an old map was tendered in evidence. It showed the land unfenced and bounded on one side by the road, and on the other by a row of buildings, but it was excluded because it was equivalent to statements of particular facts. This doctrine

---

19 (1824), 2 Bing. 86.

20 *Shedden* v. *A.-G.* (1860), 30 L.J.P.M. & A. 217.

1 [1894] 1 Q.B. 823.

was forced to what has been described as its "logical and ludicrous conclusion" in *Mercer* v. *Denne*[2] where the issue was whether the fishermen of Walmer had a customary right of immemorial antiquity to dry their nets on part of the foreshore. In support of the contention that the custom would not have existed throughout the relevant period, a survey, depositions and old maps were produced. They showed that the sea had run over the portion of foreshore in respect of which the customary right was claimed, but they were rejected as they amounted to statements of particular facts and had nothing to do with the reputed existence of the custom.

Although it may be more difficult to justify in the case of declarations concerning the reputed existence of public or general rights than in the case of pedigree declarations, the requirement that the declaration must have been made before the dispute arose is well established.

Crease v. *Barrett*[3] is about the only authority warranting a distinction between the two classes of right so far as the admissibility of hearsay evidence is concerned. The declarations of deceased landowners who did not enjoy the mining rights under their land were held admissible on an issue concerning the local customary mining rights, but the judgment of PARKE, B., suggests that, whereas in the case of a public right, the declaration of someone wholly unconnected with the locality would be admissible (though very likely valueless), in the case of general rights, some degree of personal knowledge of the matters in issue was essential before statements concerning the reputed existence of such rights could be received.

ART. 52.—**Declarations of contemporaneous bodily or mental states admissible in criminal cases**

In criminal cases a person's declarations about his contemporaneous bodily or mental state are admissible evidence of the existence of those states.

Explanation: When Part I of the Civil Evidence Act 1968 is extended to Magistrates' Courts this exception to the hearsay

---

[2] [1905] 2 Ch. 538.
[3] (1835), 1 Cr. M. & R. 919.

rule will be confined to criminal cases. There does not appear to be any authority on its applicability to cases in which the maker of the statement is called as a witness.

(1) *Bodily states*

When witnesses are allowed to depose to other people's statements concerning their contemporaneous bodily condition as evidence of the existence of that condition, the evidence is received under an exception to the hearsay rule. There is very little authority, and discussion of such authority as there is is confused by references to the *res gestae* doctrine and even by denials that the evidence is received under an exception to the hearsay rule; but there is little doubt about the existence of the exception at common law.

The common law requires the strictest contemporaneity and nothing in the nature of a repetition of the patient's narrative of his or her past symptoms is permitted; still less may the patient's statement be proved as evidence of the cause of the suffering of which complaint is made.

"If a man says to his surgeon: 'I have a pain in the head,' or 'in such a part of my body,' that is evidence, but if he says to the surgeon, 'I have a wound,' and was to add 'I met John Thomas who had a sword and ran me through the body with it,' that would be no evidence against John Thomas."[4].

(2) *State of mind*

Declarations of someone other than the witness who was testifying have been allowed to show his belief that defamatory statements referred to the plaintiff[5], his political opinions[6], his dislike of his child[7], and his fear of some burglars which prevented him from reporting their conduct to the police[8].

Declarations of intention to prove an act.—Intention is a state of mind, but the decisions on the reception of contemporaneous declarations of intention, other than those accompanying a relevant act[9], present a certain amount of difficulty. The upshot is that, although such declarations may be received as evidence of the declarant's intention at the time, and to raise a

---

[4] *R.* v. *Nicholas* (1846), 2 Car. & Kir. 246, at p. 248.
[5] *Du Bost* v. *Beresford* (1810), 2 Camp. 511.
[6] *R.* v. *Tooke* (1794), 25 State Tr. 344, at p. 390.
[7] *R.* v. *Hagan* (1873), 12 Cox C.C. 357.
[8] *R.* v. *Gandfield* (1846), 2 Cox C.C. 43.
[9] See Article 57.

presumption of fact that the intention continued for some little time afterwards, declarations of intention to do an act are inadmissible as evidence that the act was in fact performed, unless they can be brought under the wholly distinct exception to the hearsay rule relating to the admissions of a party.

In *R.* v. *Thomson*[10], the accused was charged with having performed an abortion on a woman who had since died. The Court of Criminal Appeal held that the trial judge had rightly refused to allow him to ask a prosecution witness in cross-examination whether the deceased had told her, first, that she intended to operate on herself, and secondly, that she had in fact done so. The court did not distinguish between the two statements. Proof of the statement that she had already operated on herself as evidence of the fact would clearly have infringed the rule against hearsay. It was therefore perhaps inevitable that the court should hold that a statement of intention to perform an act was inadmissible as evidence that the act was in fact performed, when a statement that the act had already been performed would be inadmissible as evidence of performance. In *R.* v. *Buckley*[11], a statement by a deceased police officer that he intended to go in search of the accused at dusk was received, apparently as evidence that the officer in fact went in search of the accused, but no reasons were given for the decision and it is doubtful whether it can be supported on any ground. If the deceased's statement is regarded as having been made in the course of duty, the case is in conflict with *Rowlands* v. *De Vecchi*[12]. If it is regarded as a statement of intention tendered to prove the performance of the act intended, the case is inconsistent with *R.* v. *Wainwright*[13] in which similar evidence was excluded, and appears to have been overruled by *R.* v. *Thomson*.

R. v. *Thomson* was not cited in *R.* v. *Moghal*[14], a decision of the Court of Appeal in which A had been convicted of murder by aiding and abetting B who had been tried separately and acquitted. The prosecution conceded that B was the actual killer, and the Court, while affirming the conviction, held that B's tape-recorded declaration of intention to kill the deceased would have been admissible, had the judge been asked to rule

---

[10] [1912] 3 K.B. 19.
[11] (1873), 13 Cox C.C. 293.
[12] (1882), Cab & El. 10, p. 177 *supra*.
[13] (1875), 13 Cox C.C. 171.
[14] (1977), 65 Cr. App. Rep. 56.

on the point, in support of A's contention that he was an unwilling frightened spectator of the murder. The relevance of the declaration of intention would presumably have been to show that B's state of mind with regard to the deceased was such that she might well have "Gone it alone." The case does not conflict with *R.* v. *Thomson* because the declaration would not have been admitted to prove the killing.

If, in *R.* v. *Thomson,* the accused had told a witness that he had operated on the deceased, his statement could of course have been proved against him as an admission. Had he told a witness that he intended to operate on the deceased, his statement could have been proved on similar principles as a remark damning to his case. But admissions can only be made by parties, and the deceased was not a party to the proceedings in *R.* v. *Thomson.*

ART. 53.—Statements received as part of the res gestae in criminal cases

An oral statement made by a person involved in an exciting event in issue and approximately contemporaneous with it is admissible in criminal cases as evidence of the facts stated, provided it was made in such conditions of involvement or pressure as to exclude the possibility of concoction or distortion to the advantage of the maker or the disadvantage of the accused[15].

Explanation: When Part I of the Civil Evidence Act 1968 is made applicable to Magistrates' Courts this exception to the hearsay rule will be confined to criminal cases. We will see in Article 57 that "*res gestae*" is a blanket phrase covering the admissibility at common law of evidence by way of exception to a number of exclusionary rules. The proposition in the article simply covers one aspect of the doctrine under which statements which would normally be excluded as hearsay if tendered as evidence of the facts stated may be received. There is relatively little English authority and that which there is is in need of review in the light of the latest pronouncements of the Privy Council; this accounts for the rather vague formulation of principle in the article which is directly derived from those pronouncements.

---

[15] *Ratten* v. *R.,* [1972] A.C. 378, at p. 391, per Lord WILBERFORCE.

We have already seen an example of the reception, as part of the *res gestae,* of a statement relating to a contemporaneous event when discussing *R.* v. *Fowkes* on p. 80. It will be recollected that a police officer was allowed to state what a previous witness had said when a face, identified as that of the accused, appeared at the window. In that case it made no difference whether the statement was received as original evidence (something which proved the consistency of a witness) or as hearsay (evidence of the facts stated); but there are other cases, in which the maker of the statement was not called as a witness, in which there is no doubt that the statement was admitted under a special exception to the rule against hearsay.

In *R.* v. *Foster*[16], for instance, the accused was charged with manslaughter by the dangerous driving of a carriage. A witness was allowed to narrate what the deceased said immediately after he had been run down, and the report makes it plain that the statement was received as evidence of the cause of the deceased's injuries. It was not received as a dying declaration on the principles discussed in article 47 because there was no evidence that the deceased was aware of the fact that he was in a dying condition; nor was there any question of the statement having been made in the presence of the accused, in which case it might have been received on the principles discussed on p. 147.

The principle underlying this exception to the hearsay rule was as succinctly stated as it is ever likely to be in the old case of *Thompson* v. *Trevanion*[17], a civil action for an assault on the plaintiff's wife. She was then an incompetent witness, but HOLT, C.J., held that "what the wife said immediate upon the hurt received and before she had time to devise or contrive anything for her own advantage might be given in evidence".

In *Ratten* v. *R.*[18], the decision of the Judicial Committee of the Privy Council on which the article is based, the accused had been charged and convicted of murdering his wife by shooting her. His defence was that the gun had gone off accidentally while he was cleaning it. The accused and the deceased were the only adults in the house at the time, and there was evidence that the deceased was alive and apparently normal at 1.12 p.m. The accused said that, after he had phoned for an ambulance, the police phoned him at about 1.20 p.m. The prosecution

[16] (1834), 6 C. & P. 325.
[17] (1693), Skin. 402.
[18] [1972] A.C. 378; [1971] 3 All E.R. 801.

called a telephone girl who swore that, at about 1.15 p.m., a woman with a frightened hysterical voice had phoned from the accused's house asking for the police. The woman having rung off, the girl spoke to the police who, in their turn, had phoned the accused. The Judicial Committee held that the girl's evidence had been rightly received and therefore affirmed the conviction. On one view the disputed evidence was not a hearsay statement for it was relevant, both as contradicting the accused's evidence that his call for the ambulance was the only one going out of the house between 1.12 and 1.20, by which time Mrs. Ratten was indubitably dead, and as showing that the only adult woman in the house was in an hysterical state, but the Judicial Committee also held that the girl's evidence was admissible as proof of an implied assertion by the deceased that someone was attacking her. Lord WILBERFORCE formulated the principle of admissibility on the lines stated in the article.

The test of contemporaneity coupled with the absence of any opportunity of concoction probably rules out written statements[19], but it also casts doubt on two earlier English decisions which seem to have required that the statement should have formed "part of the event in issue", whatever that may mean. In *R.* v. *Bedingfield*[20], a man was charged with the murder of the woman with whom he had been living. His defence was that she had cut her throat. It was held that a witness who saw the deceased come out of a house clutching her throat could not be allowed to swear that she heard the deceased say something like: "See what Bedingfield has done to me", because this was something stated by the deceased "after it was all over, whatever it was". In *R.* v. *Gibson*[1], a man was charged with unlawful wounding. It was held that a witness ought not to have been allowed to swear that he heard a woman say: "The man who threw the stone went in there", pointing to the premises on which the accused was found. The statement was made immediately after a stone had been thrown, but according to *Teper* v. *R.*[2], the explanation of the decision was that the words were not directly connected with the assault as they were prompted by the sight of a man quitting the scene of the crime and by a desire to bring him to

---

[19] *Tustin* v. *Arnold & Sons* (1915), 84 L.J.K.B. 2214.
[20] (1879), 14 Cox C.C. 341.
[1] (1887), 18 Q.B.D. 537.
[2] [1952] A.C. 480; [1952] 2 All E.R. 447.

justice. Both these cases may well be held to have been wrongly decided.

In *R.* v. *Nye and Loan*[3] Nye was charged with driving with an excess of alcohol in his blood and Loan was charged with assaulting Lucas. The prosecution's case was that Loan was a passenger in a car driven by Nye which ran into the back of Lucas's car. Lucas got out of his car and was immediately assaulted. He spent the short interval, before the arrival of the police, in his car recovering from the shock. He then identified Loan and not Nye as his assailant, pointing to him and saying to a police officer "That man assaulted me." The officer proved the identification and the Court of Appeal held that it was sufficiently contemporaneous with the assault as well as being spontaneous. Lucas was in no condition to concoct a story and it was unlikely that he would have mistaken his assailant. The Court eschewed such questions as "was the identification part of the event or transaction in issue."

ART. 54.—Records admissible in criminal cases under the Criminal Evidence Act 1965

In any criminal proceedings, where direct oral evidence of a fact would be admissible, any statement made by a person in a document which is, or forms part of, a record is admissible as evidence of that fact provided the following conditions are satisfied:

1. the record relates to any trade or business and was compiled in the course of that trade or business;

2. the record was compiled from information directly or indirectly supplied by persons who have, or may reasonably be supposed to have, personal knowledge of the matters dealt with;

3. the person who supplied the information is either (a) dead, or (b) beyond the seas, or (c) unfit by reason of his bodily or mental condition to attend as a witness, or (d) cannot with reasonable diligence be identified or found, or (e) cannot reasonably be expected (having regard to the time which has elapsed since he supplied the information and to all the circumstances) to have any recollection of the matters dealt with in the information.

---

[3] (1977), 66 Cr. App. Rep. 252.

Explanation: The Criminal Evidence Act 1965, was passed in order to obviate the principle effects of the decision of the House of Lords in *Myers* v. *Director of Public Prosecutions*[4] according to which motor manufacturers' records were inadmissible at common law as evidence of the numbers on cylinder blocks placed in engines by workmen who had long since ceased to be identifiable or to have any recollection of the matter. If the workmen had been identified and proved to have been dead, the records would have been admissible as statements made by deceased persons in the course of duty[5].

Although its wording is, to a large extent similar to that of s. 4 of the Civil Evidence Act 1968, mentioned on p. 138, the scope of the Act of 1965 is much narrower because it is confined to records kept for trade or business purposes. Thus, in *R.* v. *Gwilliam*[6], it was held that, even if a consignment note relating to goods supplied by the Home Office Supply and Transport Store to the police were a record, the body in question was not carrying on a trade or business. In *R.* v. *Crayden*[7] it was held that the medical records of a National Health Service hospital are not records of a trade or business within the meaning of the 1965 Act. The position with regard to the records of a hospital outside the Health Service was left open.

A mere file of correspondence is not a record[8]. In *R.* v. *Jones and Sullivan*[9] it was said that the term referred to a document containing a history of events in time which were not evanescent. Accordingly a bill of lading issued in Hong Kong and the cargo manifest were held to be records within the meaning of the Act. They showed what goods were shipped, where they came from and on what ship they were carried. The fact that the records were produced out of the jurisdiction was held to be immaterial for the Act deals with procedure and not the substantive law. The Court did not agree that a consignment note could never be a record.

The 1965 Act is more permissive than s. 4 of the 1968 Act in that it does not require proof of any duty on the part of the compiler of the record, or of intermediate suppliers of the

---

[4] [1965] A.C. 1001; [1964] 2 All E.R. 881.
[5] Article 49.
[6] [1968] 3 All E.R. 821.
[7] [1978] 2 All E.R. 700.
[8] *R.* v. *Tirado* (1975), 59 Cr. App. Rep. 80.
[9] [1978] 2 All E.R. 718.

information to him. Certain computerised records may come within the 1965 Act, but others may be excluded by the requirement of personal knowledge on the part of those supplying the information from which the record was compiled[10].

ART. 55.—Hearsay in Magistrates' Courts

1. The rules governing the admissibility of hearsay statements in criminal cases generally apply to proceedings in Magistrates' Courts as well as to proceedings in the Crown Court.

2. In civil proceedings in Magistrates' Courts hearsay statements are admissible under the exceptions to the hearsay rule mentioned in Articles 42–45 and 48--53 and under ss. 1 and 2 of the Evidence Act, 1938.

3. Clause 2 will cease to apply when part 1 of the Civil Evidence Act 1968 is applied to proceedings in Magistrates' Courts. Hearsay in civil proceedings in those Courts will then be governed by Articles 39–45.

Explanation:

(1) *Criminal cases*

Certain statutory provisions relating to hearsay statements are in the nature of things exclusively applicable to proceedings either in the Crown Court or in Magistrates' Courts. Article 47 cannot apply to trials in the latter Courts because the common law exception to the hearsay rule with which it deals is confined to charges of homicide, but dying declarations as to the cause of death in homicide cases are of course admissible at committal proceedings.

(2) *Civil cases*

The civil proceedings in Magistrates' Courts in which hearsay statements are most likely to be tendered are affiliation proceedings and domestic proceedings. The reception of such statements is governed by the same amalgam of common law and statutory exceptions as that which applies to criminal cases with the exception, of course, of the common law exception mentioned in Article 47. There is, however, an important

---

[10] *R.* v. *Pettigrew* (1980), *Times,* 22nd January.

general statutory exception confined to civil cases, the Evidence Act 1938. This is not the place for a detailed account of the provisions of that statute. The effect of ss. 1 and 2 is that statements contained in a document, duly authenticated by the maker, are admissible as evidence of any fact of which direct oral evidence would be admissible, provided the maker had personal knowledge of such fact or provided the document is or forms part of a record compiled from information supplied by someone who may reasonably be supposed to have had personal knowledge of the matters dealt with in the information. The maker of the statement must be called as a witness unless he is unavailable through death, illness, or absence beyond the seas, or if all reasonable efforts to find him have proved fruitless. The 1938 Act is narrower than that of 1968 because it does not extend to oral hearsay statements. There is moreover a restrictive provision in s. 1 (3) which prohibits the reception of statements by persons interested when proceedings are pending or anticipated involving any disputed fact which the statement would tend to prove. But there is no requirement of the service of notice of desire to rely on the statement, and, if the maker is called as a witness, the leave of the court for the reception of the statement in evidence is not required. The greater simplicity of the Act may mean that it is more suited to magisterial proceedings than the Act of 1968.

(3) *The Civil Evidence Act 1968*

When that Act is applied to Magistrates' Courts, the reception of hearsay statements in civil proceedings in those courts will be primarily dependent on the provisions mentioned in Articles 39–41, incorporating as they do the provisions of Articles 42–3. This will mean that almost all of the statements admitted or rejected in cases mentioned in Articles 48–53 could, on similar facts, be rendered admissible under s. 2 or s. 4 of the 1968 Act, or would be admissible by virtue of s. 9 of that Act.

CHAPTER 7

Original Evidence and Res Gestae

ART. 56.—**Statements proved as original evidence**

Statements other than those made by a witness while testifying in the proceedings may be proved as original evidence when the fact that they were made, as distinct from their truth, (1) is in issue; (2) is relevant to an issue; or (3) affects the credit of a witness.

Explanation: The distinction between hearsay and original evidence has already been mentioned in Chapter 1. It is nowhere better stated than in the case of *Subramaniam* v. *Public Prosecutor*[1], where it was said that:—

> "Evidence of a statement made to a witness by a person who is not himself called as a witness may or may not be hearsay. It is hearsay and inadmissible when the object of the evidence is to establish the truth of what is contained in the statement. It is not hearsay and is admissible when it is proposed to establish by the evidence, not the truth of the statement, but the fact that it was made."

Though of less importance, the distinction holds good in cases in which the maker of the statement is called as a witness.

A few examples of the proof of statements as original evidence may be given as an introduction to the proof of statements as part of the *res gestae*. The Civil Evidence Act 1968 has no application to statements tendered as original evidence.

---

[1] [1956] 1 W.L.R. 965, at p.969.

(1) *Statements as facts in issue*

In an action for slander, the plaintiff frequently calls a witness to prove the speaking of the defamatory words by the defendant. The witness does not narrate the statement in order that the court may treat it as evidence of the truth of its contents. That is the very last thing the plaintiff wants. The statement is narrated by the witness because the question whether it was made is in issue between the parties.

In some cases, where a witness is allowed to narrate a statement because the fact that it was made is a fact in issue, there is no question of the possible application of the rule against hearsay. In an action on a contract, for example, witnesses may be called to depose to the speaking of words of offer and acceptance by the plaintiff and defendant. At a criminal trial, where duress is pleaded, it would be quite wrong for the judge to refuse to hear evidence of the utterance of menacing words by terrorists to the accused[2].

(2) *Statements as relevant facts*

There are many situations in which a statement of fact made to a witness may be relevant, whether it is true or false. If it becomes material to know what a testator believed to be the contents of the will he was executing[3], or the nature of a husband's belief concerning the destination of his wife on leaving him[4], evidence of what was said to them may be crucial, and the court is not concerned with the truth of the words used. In *R.* v. *Willis*[5], W was charged with having assisted N to commit larceny. W told the police that he had no reason to suppose that the goods in question had been stolen by N, and the Court of Criminal Appeal held that the trial judge should have allowed him to depose to N's assertion of innocence made to him at an interview which took place after N's apprehension. The Court recognised that what is said by someone else to a witness may often be relevant to that witness's state of mind whether what is said is true or false. In *Mawaz Khan* v. *R.*[6], each appellant made a statement in the absence of the other setting up the same demonstrably false alibi. It was held that these statements were admissible, not of course in order to establish

---

[2] *Subramaniam* v. *Public Prosecutor, supra.*
[3] *Doe d. Small* v. *Allen* (1799), 8 Term Rep. 147.
[4] *Hoare* v. *Allen* (1801), 3 Esp. 276.
[5] [1960] 1 All E.R. 331.
[6] [1967] 1 A.C. 454; [1967] 1 All E.R. 80.

their truth, but in furtherance of the Crown's contention that the appellants were conspiring to fabricate evidence.

The fact that a preposterous or demonstrably false statement was made may sometimes be relevant to the issue. If the question concerns A's sanity at a particular time, the fact that he was heard to say, about that time, that pink elephants were approaching would be highly relevant. In *A-G.* v. *Good*[7], a fact in issue was whether a man was endeavouring to evade his creditors. A witness was allowed to prove a statement made to him by the man's wife to the effect that her husband was away from home. GARROW, B., said:

> "The doubt on the present occasion has originated in calling that hearsay evidence which has no approximation to it. The answer is received as a distinct fact in itself, to be compared and combined with other facts."

Reference was made on p. 16, *ante,* to the two senses in which the word "hearsay" is used. In the non-technical sense, it means anything that someone else was heard to say, and, in that sense, the witness's repetition of the wife's statement was hearsay; but it was not hearsay in the technical sense of the narration of someone else's statement as evidence of its truth. In the above quotation, GARROW, B., was using the word in its technical sense.

(3) *Statements affecting the credit of a witness*

Reference was made in Article 22 to the general rule that the previous consistent statements of a witness may not be proved in order to establish consistency. Whenever such statements are allowed to be proved under exceptions to the rule, they are received as original and not as hearsay evidence. The object is to enhance the credibility of what the witness said in court, not to prove the truth of what he said out of court.

In Article 25, reference was made to the possibility of proving the fact that a witness has previously made a statement inconsistent with his evidence in court. It was pointed out that, when proved, such a statement could not be treated as evidence of the facts stated in a criminal case. It simply neutralises the effect of the witness's testimony, and thus amounts to original as opposed to hearsay evidence.

---

[7] (1825), M'Cle. & Yo. 286.

ART. 57.—Res gestae

1. Statements connected with and made substantially contemporaneously with the occurrence of the facts to which they relate are often said to be received as part of the *res gestae* (part of the happenings or part of the story). Statements received as part of the *res gestae* are sometimes received by way of exception to the rule against hearsay, but they can now only be so received in criminal cases; on other occasions they constitute original evidence, i.e. they are not proved in order to establish the truth of that which was asserted.

2. Statements proved as conduct are sometimes said to form part of the *res gestae*.

3. Facts forming part of the transaction under investigation are also said to form part of the *res gestae*.

4. The doctrine of the *res gestae* is inclusionary, allowing for the reception of evidence by way of exception to a number of exclusionary rules.

Explanation: "*Res gestae*" is a blanket phrase, covering the reception of a variety of items of evidence for a variety of purposes. If there is any feature common to all the cases in which evidence has been said to have been received as part of the *res gestae,* it is that of relevance via contemporaneity. A statement is received because it was made contemporaneously with the event to which it relates, or a fact is allowed to be proved because it is inextricably connected with a fact in issue. Evidence which would otherwise be excluded as irrelevant, hearsay, opinion, or as tending merely to show bad disposition, may be received as part of the *res gestae*.

(1) *Statements*

It is unnecessary to say much more about the reception of statements as part of the *res gestae*. *R.* v. *Fowkes*[8] and *R.* v. *Foster*[9] respectively show how a spontaneous statement relating to an event in issue and made contemporaneously with it may be proved as part of the *res gestae*. Statements of contemporaneous physical or mental states are sometimes said to be received as part of the *res gestae,* and we have already dealt with them as exceptions to the rule against hearsay applicable only to

[8] See p. 80, *ante*.
[9] See p. 184, *ante*.

criminal cases since the coming into force of the Civil Evidence Act 1968. What a patient says to his doctor will usually be received under an exception to the hearsay rule, but the doctor's reply may constitute relevant original evidence[10].

Statements are sometimes received in evidence because they accompany a relevant act, and they are then often said to form part of the *res gestae*. They must have been made contemporaneously with the act and be relevant as qualifying or explaining it. For example, in *Hayslep* v. *Gymer*[11], a man asked his deceased father's housekeeper, who had just delivered some of her late master's belongings to him, whether she had any more of the deceased's property. She then handed over some banknotes, remarking that she had received them as a gift from the deceased. This statement was held to be admissible because it qualified the act of handing over the notes. Had no such statement been made, that act might have been construed as an admission by the housekeeper that she had no right to the notes.

In the above instance the statement constituted original evidence for it was not received as evidence of the gift of the notes to the housekeeper by her former employer, but statements accompanying acts were sometimes received as exceptions to the hearsay rule in civil cases at common law, as when a bankrupt's declarations of intention in going or remaining abroad were allowed to be proved as evidence of intention[12]. The overlap with the reception of a person's contemporaneous statement as evidence of his mental state is obvious, but it is impossible to achieve precision in any attempt to formulate the effects of the *res gestae* doctrine. It should simply be borne in mind that statements accompanying acts may sometimes be received under exceptions to the hearsay rule in criminal cases.

(2) *Statements proved as conduct*

A statement often has a dual aspect. From one point of view, it may be regarded simply as the utterance of words; from another point of view, it may be regarded as conduct—the making of some arrangement, or the entering into some transaction, for example. When statements are allowed to be

---

[10] *Tickle* v. *Tickle,* [1968] 2 All E.R. 154. *Cf. Aveson* v. *Kinnaird (Lord)* (1805), 6 East 188.

[11] (1834), 1 Ad. & El. 162.

[12] *Rouch* v. *Great Western Rail. Co.* (1841), 1 Q.B. 51.

proved as conduct, they are sometimes said to be received as part of the *res gestae*. Thus, at the hearing of the *Aylesford Peerage* claim[13], the question was whether the claimant was the legitimate son of Lady Aylesford and her husband. Evidence was received in support of the contention that he was illegitimate in the form of statements by Lady Aylesford and communications passing between her and her paramour, in which the claimant was treated as the son of Lady Aylesford and her paramour. Similarly, at the hearing of the *Dysart Peerage* claim[14], the question was whether the claimant's mother was validly married to his father. There was some evidence of a marriage in Scotland in 1845, and witnesses were prepared to swear that the father referred to the woman as his wife, although he went through a ceremony of marriage with another woman in England in 1851. When speaking of the evidence of the marriage in 1845, Lord BLACKBURN said:

> "Where there has been such evidence given, and you are to see whether or not it is true, you look at what the parties did; what is technically called the res gestae, viz., their conduct at the time, their conduct before, their conduct afterwards, and all that they may do and say, as tending to show that they did really enter into this contract, or as tending on the other side to show that they did not enter into this contract."

In *Lloyd* v. *Powell Duffryn Steam Coal Co. Ltd.*[15], a woman claimed workmen's compensation on behalf of her illegitimate child, who was, she alleged, the posthumous son of a deceased employee of the defendants. As there was no doubt that the deceased was killed in the course of his employment, the claim succeeded if it could be proved that the child was the workman's son, and that the workman would have supported him. The woman gave evidence that she had had intercourse with the deceased, and with no one else. She then deposed to a conversation in which the deceased had promised to marry her immediately after she had informed him of her pregnancy. Two other witnesses gave evidence of conversations which they had had with the deceased a short while after, and said that he had intimated that he intended to marry the woman. In the

---

[13] (1885), 11 App. Cas. I.
[14] (1881), 6 App. Cas. 489.
[15] [1914] A.C. 733.

Court of Appeal it was argued that the evidence of what the deceased had said ought to be received under the exception to the hearsay rule, then applicable to civil as well as criminal cases, relating to declarations against pecuniary interest. As we saw when discussing the same case under the name of *Ward* v. *Pitt* on p. 174, it was held in the Court of Appeal that the evidence should have been rejected as a declaration against interest because the deceased had not got personal knowledge of his paternity of the child. In the House of Lords, it was argued that the evidence formed part of the *res gestae* and this argument was accepted:

> "To treat the statements made by the deceased as statements made by a deceased person against his pecuniary interest, is wholly to mistake their true character and significance. This significance consists in the improbability that any man would make these statements, true or false, unless he believed himself to be the father of the child of whom Alice Lloyd was pregnant."[16]

The workman's promise to marry was conduct. His ensuing conversations were treated as part of that conduct. They showed that he regarded the woman as his fiancée.

The Civil Evidence Act 1968 has no application to statements proved as conduct. Were the facts of the *Aylesford Peerage* case, the *Dysart Peerage* case or *Lloyd* v. *Powell Duffryn Steam Coal Co. Ltd.* to recur, the statements with which those cases were concerned could be proved without the necessity of serving any notice on opposite parties.

(3) *Facts forming part of the same transaction*

It is sometimes said that facts may be proved as part of the *res gestae* when they form part of the same transaction as that under investigation. For example, a man is charged with murder, and it is proved that the culprit stole a car immediately after the incident in order to effect his escape. Evidence tending to show that the accused stole the car would be admissible, and it might be spoken of as part of the *res gestae*. As we shall see in Chapter 12, evidence of other crimes is inadmissible if it merely shows that the accused is the kind of man who would commit the crime under investigation, but when the other crime is closely connected with that under investigation, the fact that

---

[16]Lord ATKINSON.

the accused committed it becomes relevant for a further and more specific reason than its tendency to show bad disposition.

(4) *The inclusionary nature of the res gestae doctrine*

Facts may thus be received as part of the *res gestae* although they would be irrelevant and inadmissible if not connected and contemporaneous with some other fact which is either in issue or relevant to the issue. Statements may be received as part of the *res gestae* by way of exception to the rule against hearsay, and they may also be received as part of the *res gestae* although they would be inadmissible as a witness's testimony given some time after the event to which they relate on account of the exclusion of evidence of opinion. For instance, there is a loud crash as two motor cars collide on a busy road. A, a bystander who is called as a witness and was looking the other way at the time of the crash, heard B, another bystander not called as a witness, exclaim "I saw it all, the driver of the Morris Minor was criminally negligent". A's narration of B's statement is hearsay evidence of opinion, but it might be admissible on account of its spontaneity at a prosecution for reckless driving[17]

[17] *Milne* v. *Leisler* (1862), 7 H. & N. 786, at p. 796.

CHAPTER 8

Documents, Things and Facts

ART. 58.—**Documentary evidence generally**

1. In the case of private documents, proof of due execution and production of the original is usually necessary, subject to the exceptions mentioned in Articles 61 and 62.

2. Public documents may be proved in the manner specified in Article 63.

Explanation: A party to litigation may wish the judge or jury to read a document for a variety of reasons. The terms of the document may be among the facts in issue. Reliance may be placed on the contents of a document as evidence of the facts stated under an exception to the rule against hearsay. The fact that a particular kind of document was executed by a particular person may be an item of circumstantial evidence. For example, the fact that someone proved to have been in possession of land executed leases may be tendered as evidence of that person's ownership of the piece of land[1]. In all these cases, and others that could be imagined, it is not enough that

[1] *Malcomson* v. *O'Dea* (1863), 10 H.L. Cas. 593, at p. 614.

a document should simply be produced by one party, his counsel, or solicitor. The judge will require to be satisfied that the document was properly executed, i.e. signed or sealed by the person whose signature or seal it purports to bear, and that the document is the original.

The due execution of the original and the accuracy of a copy are usually admitted in civil cases. When this is not so, execution must be proved. This is almost invariably done by proving the handwriting of the signatory, or by proof of attestation. These matters are discussed in Articles 59 and 60. Proof of execution by other means is so rare that it does not call for discussion.

Proof of due execution is assisted by various presumptions discussed in Article 61.

In the absence of an admission, the original of a private document must be produced to the court unless the case comes within one of the exceptions mentioned in Article 62.

Proof of due execution and production of the original would have been impossibly irksome in the case of such public documents as statutes, judicial records and registers of births, deaths or marriages. Accordingly, the common law recognised a number of public documents of which copies might be produced to the court. Proof of due execution was unnecessary, and the mere production of the appropriate kind of copy would suffice. The number of documents which may be brought before the court in this way has been greatly increased by statute, and, in many instances, the nature of the copy to be produced has been indicated. In the case of public documents, therefore, it is frequently sufficient simply to produce a copy. This may be handed to the court by the party relying on it, his counsel or solicitor, and the court will receive the document in evidence without any further requirement. No witness is required to produce the document or to say anything about it. Public documents, as it is sometimes put, prove themselves. A public document may be defined as any document brought into existence in order that the public might make use of it, and be able to refer to it. The different kinds of copies of public documents which may be produced to the court by those wishing to rely on them are discussed in Article 63. We saw in Article 43 that the contents of public documents are admissible as evidence of the facts stated under an important exception to the rule against hearsay.

ART. 59.—Proof of handwriting

Handwriting may be proved:

1. by direct evidence which may consist of:

   (a) the testimony of the writer or of someone who saw him write; or

   (b) the extra-judicial statements of the writer or someone who saw him write, if admissible under exceptions to the rule against hearsay;

2. by evidence of opinion, expert or lay;
3. by comparison.

Explanation:

(1) *Direct evidence of handwriting*

The first two methods of proving handwriting mentioned in the article may be conveniently described as direct evidence. Nothing need be said about the obvious method of calling the writer himself to swear that a particular signature is his, or that he wrote out a particular document. The next best method is to call someone who saw the document signed or written out. If he can speak from his personal knowledge to the identity of the person who executed the document, so much the better; but it will generally be sufficient for him to swear that he saw someone sign a document in a particular name[2]. Unless the evidence is seriously challenged, or the name is a very common one, the name will in itself be sufficient evidence of the identity of the signatory with the person whose handwriting is to be proved.

Statements by the writer himself, or by someone who saw him write, might, in appropriate circumstances, be received as evidence of the facts stated under exceptions to the rule against hearsay, such as the admissions of a party or, in a criminal case, the declaration of a deceased person against his pecuniary or proprietary interest.

(2) *Opinion evidence of handwriting*

An expert may give evidence of his opinion that a particular document is in the handwriting of, or signed by, a particular person. He will usually have compared the writing on the

---

[2] *Roden* v. *Ryde* (1843), 4 Q.B. 626.

document to be proved with the writing on a document which was indubitably written or signed by the person whose handwriting is to be proved. It is immaterial that the witness did not acquire his expertise in handwriting professionally. In *R.* v. *Silverlock*[3], a solicitor who had acquired a knowledge of handwriting as an amateur was allowed to testify as an expert in these matters.

Handwriting may also be proved by a witness who is not an expert, for this is one of the matters on which non-expert opinion may be received in accordance with the principles discussed in Article 34. All that is necessary is that the witness should be familiar with the writing of the person who signed, or wrote, the document which is in issue. He need not actually have seen the person in question write, for it will be sufficient if he has received a reasonable number of documents purporting to be written or signed by him; the capacity in which he has done so is immaterial.

> "The clerk who constantly reads the letters, the broker who was ever consulted upon them, is as competent to judge whether another signature is that of the writer of the letters, as the merchant to whom they were addressed. The servant who has habitually carried letters addressed by me to others has an opportunity of obtaining a knowledge of my writing, though he never saw me write or received a letter from me."[4]

(3) *Comparison*

There is a general sense in which it is true to say that all opinion evidence of handwriting is comparison. Even when a witness identifies a particular signature, he is simply deposing to the belief which he "entertains on comparing the writing in question with an exemplar in his mind, derived from some previous knowledge"[5]. Section 8 of the Criminal Procedure Act 1865 contemplates a more direct kind of comparison. It reads:

> "Comparison of a disputed writing with any writing proved to the satisfaction of the judge to be genuine shall be permitted to be made by witnesses; and such writings, and the evidence of witnesses respecting the same, may be submitted to the court and jury as evidence of the

---

[3][1894] 2 Q.B. 766.

[4]*Doe d. Mudd* v. *Suckermore* (1837), 5 Ad. & El. 703, at p. 750.

[5]*Ibid.*, at p. 739.

genuineness or otherwise of the writing in dispute."

The section applies to civil and criminal cases and, in both instances, the standard of proving that the writing with which comparison is to be made is genuine is the civil one[6]. If he gives evidence, the person whose handwriting is disputed may be asked to write in court in order that an undisputed specimen may be available for comparison[7]. On a literal construction of the section the witnesses by whom the comparison is to be made need not be experts, but, without deciding that experts are always essential, the Court of Criminal Appeal quashed convictions in which the judges let the writings go to the jury without expert guidance[8]. When there is no such guidance, and a disputed signature as well as an authentic one is before the jury, all that can be done is for the judge to warn the jury against making comparisons[9].

ART. 60.—Proof of attestation

1. If it becomes necessary to prove the due execution of a will, it is essential to call one of the attesting witnesses if any are available. Before other evidence of attestation is admissible, it must be shown that all the attesting witnesses are dead, insane, beyond the jurisdiction or untraceable.

2. In the case of other documents to which attestation is necessary as a matter of law, it is not essential for the person, required to prove attestation, to call the attesting witness, even if he is available. Other evidence of attestation will suffice.

Explanation: One means of proving the due execution of a document is to show that it was duly attested. There was an old common law rule that, when a document was attested, whether attestation was necessary as a matter of law or not, one of the witnesses had to be called, or his absence had to be explained, unless the presumption of due execution mentioned in the next

---

[6] *R.* v. *Angeli,* [1978] 3 All E.R. 950.

[7] *Cobbett* v. *Kilminster* (1865), 4 F. & F. 490.

[8] *R.* v. *Tilley,* [1961] 3 All E.R. 406; *R.* v. *Harden,* [1963] 1 Q.B. 8; [1962] 1 All E.R. 286.

[9] *R.* v. *O'Sullivan,* [1969] 2 All E.R. 237.

article, applied to the case. Thanks to s. 7 of the Criminal Procedure Act 1865, and s. 3 of the Evidence Act 1938, the common law rule now only applies to wills. The common law rule applied to civil and criminal cases alike, as do the statutory provisions which have just been mentioned.

(1) *Wills*

Generally speaking, it is only necessary to prove the due execution of a will when its validity is disputed. For the purpose of obtaining probate in common form, the mere production of a will with a proper attestation clause will usually suffice. When due execution has to be proved, one of the attesting witnesses must be called, unless the absence of all of them can be explained on the grounds mentioned in the article. If an attesting witness is called, other evidence of execution may be adduced by the party seeking to prove it should the witness refuse to testify or, when testifying, deny due execution[10].

If it is impossible to call any of the attesting witnesses to a will, steps must be taken to prove the handwriting of one of them. This constitutes secondary evidence of attestation, the theory being that the witness would only have signed if everything had been in order when he did so[11]. If evidence of the handwriting of the attesting witness is unobtainable, execution may be proved by anyone who saw the will executed, or by any other evidence from which due execution can be inferred.

(2) *Other documents requiring attestation as a matter of law*

Apart from wills, which require two witnesses, there are comparatively few documents which must be witnessed as a matter of law, although many are witnessed in practice. When attestation is necessary as a matter of law, execution may be proved by calling one of the subscribing witnesses, as in the case of a will. But it is not essential for the person seeking to prove execution to call one of the witnesses. He may content himself with proof of the witness's handwriting, or rely on any other available evidence of due execution. This is because s. 3 of the Evidence Act 1938 provides that, in any proceedings, whether civil or criminal, an instrument to the validity of which attestation is requisite, may, instead of being proved by an

---

[10] *Bowman* v. *Hodgson* (1867), L.R. 1 P. & D. 362.
[11] *Stobart* v. *Dryden* (1836), 1 M. & W. 615.

attesting witness, be proved in the manner in which it might be proved if no attesting witness were alive. Wills and other testamentary instruments are expressly excluded.

(3) *Other documents*

Section 7 of the Criminal Procedure Act 1865 provides that it shall not be necessary to prove by the attesting witness any instrument to the validity of which attestation is not requisite, and such instrument may be proved as if there had been no attesting witness thereto. This means that, although the execution of such a document may be proved by the attesting witness, it is unnecessary to call him, or to prove attestation at all.

ART. 61.—**Admissions and presumptions relating to private documents**

1. In civil cases the due execution of a private document is generally admitted or deemed to be admitted.
2. Due execution is presumed in the case of a private document not less than twenty years old, coming from the proper custody.
3. Various other presumptions are relevant to the proof of documents.
4. In civil cases documents must be proved or presumed to have been properly stamped.

Explanation: In civil cases, it is frequently unnecessary to prove that a document was properly executed because that fact is, or is deemed to be, the subject of a formal admission for the purposes of the particular litigation. Unless notified to the contrary by their opponents, the parties may assume that documents mentioned in their lists of documents are admitted to have been duly executed[12]. In criminal cases the due execution of a document may be formally admitted under s. 10 of the Criminal Justice Act 1967 if notice requiring it is served on the opposite party and he does not serve a counter-notice requiring proof of execution.

In civil and criminal cases alike, those seeking to rely on a document are greatly assisted by the presumption of due execution, which attaches to all documents not less than twenty

[12] R.S.C. Ord. 27, r. 4 (1).

years old, provided they are produced from proper custody. The period of twenty years was substituted by s. 4 of the Evidence Act 1938 for the thirty years required by the common law presumption. What "proper custody" is depends on the particular document. Expired leases may be expected to be in the custody of lessor or lessee and those claiming under them. A family bible may properly be in the custody of any member of the family. Proper custody in this context does not mean the most appropriate custody possible. Papers relating to a bishopric have been held to come from proper custody when found among the family papers of a deceased bishop, and not, as they should have been, in the possession of the bishop for the time being[13].

Several other useful presumptions in relation to documents may be mentioned. A document is presumed to have been executed on the date it bears[14]; alterations in a deed are presumed to have been made before execution, otherwise the entire deed would be invalidated, but alterations in a will are presumed to have been made after execution, because they would not invalidate the entire testament[15]. They are simply ineffective unless properly attested.

In civil cases, stamp objections are taken by the court and cannot be waived by the parties, who may, however, render the document admissible by making or undertaking to make the appropriate payment. If the original of a document is lost, it is presumed to have been duly stamped. The fact that stamp objections cannot be waived means that the proper stamping of a document cannot be made the subject of a formal admission. Stamp objections are not taken in criminal cases.

ART. 62.—Proof of the contents of private documents and bankers' books

1. The general rule is that the contents of any private document must be proved by primary evidence which usually means the production of the original.

2. The following are the principal exceptions to the general rule; i.e. the contents of the document may be proved by secondary evidence:

---

[13]*Bishop of Meath* v. *Marquess of Winchester* (1836), 3 Bing. N.C. 183.
[14]*Anderson* v. *Weston* (1840), 6 Bing. N.C. 296.
[15]*Doe d. Tatum* v. *Catomore* (1851), 16 Q.B. 745.

(a) when the original is in possession of the opponent, who fails to produce it, after notice when necessary;

(b) when the original is in possession of a stranger, who lawfully refuses to produce it after service, in a civil case, of a *subpoena duces tecum* or, in a criminal case, of a witness summons;

(c) when the original cannot be found after due search;

(d) when production of the original is impossible or impracticable.

3. In all legal proceedings, a copy of an entry in a banker's book is *prima facie* evidence of such entry.

Explanation:

(1) *The general rule*

The rule we are now considering is quite distinct from that requiring proof of the due execution of a private document. Even when the original is produced to the court, so that the rule under consideration is satisfied, the due execution of the document must be proved. Conversely, when the original is not produced, the court will not look at the document although the due execution of the document is proved or admitted. Even when one of the exceptions to the rule under consideration applies, so that the court would treat a copy as evidence of the contents of the document, due execution must first be proved or admitted.

The simplest illustration of the rule mentioned in this article is provided by a case in which a party wishes to put his correspondence with his adversary in evidence. He will normally have the originals of letters received from his adversary, but he will be unable to prove the contents of his replies unless the case comes within one of the exceptions to the rule. The rule may be brought into play in circumstances in which the possibility of its application is not so obvious. In *Augustien* v. *Challis*[16], the plaintiff alleged that the defendant, a sheriff, had negligently caused an execution to be withdrawn. The defendant sought to justify his conduct on the ground that rent was due to the debtor's landlord, whose claim had priority to that of the plaintiff. The defendant called the landlord, who testified to the fact that rent was due to him, but

[16] (1847), 1 Exch. 279.

admitted that it was payable under a lease. This document was not produced, and the landlord's evidence was thus rendered inadmissible because "The moment it appears that there is a lease, you cannot speak about its contents without producing it"[17].

The rule is limited to cases in which direct reliance is placed on the words used in a document. In *R.* v. *Holy Trinity, Kingston-upon-Hull*[18], it was held that the existence of the relationship of landlord and tenant, and the value of the premises let, could be proved without reference to the lease. This case can be distinguished from *Augustien* v. *Challis* because the best evidence of the amount of rent due to the landlord in *Augustien* v. *Challis* was the lease itself; the lease was certainly not the best evidence of the value of the premises in the *Kingston-upon-Hull* case and the existence of the tenancy could be proved without reference to it.

Before considering the exceptions to the general rule, it will be convenient to say what is meant by "primary" and "secondary" evidence in this context.

Primary evidence.—The primary evidence *par excellence* of the contents of a document is the original. Generally speaking, there will be no great difficulty in determining which of several documents is the original; but it is sometimes necessary to have regard to the purpose for which, or the party against whom, the contents are tendered in evidence. A counterpart lease, executed only by the lessee, is the original so far as he, and those claiming under him, are concerned[19], although the other part is the original as against the lessor. If duplicates of a deed are executed by all the parties to it, each duplicate is an original[20].

Certain private documents, notably wills, must be filed in a court or other public office. When they are thus filed, the copy issued by the court or other office may be treated as the original. The probate of a will is conclusive evidence of the words of the will in respect of which the grant was made and, for this purpose, it constitutes primary evidence. On questions of construction, however, the court may examine the original[1].

---

[17]PARKE, B.
[18](1827), 7 B. & C. 611.
[19]*Roe d. West* v. *Davis* (1806), 7 East 363.
[20]*Forbes* v. *Samuel,* [1913] 3 K.B. 706.
[1]*Re Battie-Wrightson,* [1920] 2 Ch. 330.

The clear extra-judicial admission of the contents of a document has been held to constitute primary evidence of its contents as against the party making the admission[2]. We are here referring to informal admissions, received under the exception to the rule against hearsay, discussed in Article 42. This kind of primary evidence of the contents of a document is rare; it is received on the principle that, as against its maker, the admission is as good evidence of the contents of a document as the original.

Secondary Evidence.—Secondary evidence of the contents of a document is constituted by any kind of a copy, and by the oral evidence of those who can recollect what was said in the document. As a general rule there are no degrees of secondary evidence[3]; oral evidence of the contents of a document may be adduced, without accounting for the absence of any copies that may be in existence, and there are no preferences as between the different kinds of copy. It is sometimes said that a copy of a copy is inadmissible evidence of the contents of a document, but there is no reason why such a copy should not be received provided there is evidence that it was checked against the first copy and the first copy checked, in its turn, against the original[4].

(2) *Exceptions to the general rule—Methods of obtaining the production of the original before the court.*—The first two exceptions to the rule requiring production of the original are dependent on every effort having been made to bring it before the court. It will therefore be convenient to refer to the appropriate procedural requirements. These vary slightly according to whether the proceedings are civil or criminal.

In civil cases, if the original is in the possession of the opponent, he could be served with a *subpoena duces tecum* requiring him to produce it. Provided a copy of the document is available, this course is usually unnecessary because, under the Rules of the Supreme Court, he will be deemed to have been served with a notice to produce the original of any document mentioned in his list of documents[5]. The effect of such a notice, which can be served in the case of documents not mentioned in the opponent's list, is that the party requiring

---

[2] *Slatterie* v. *Pooley* (1840), 6 M. & W. 664.
[3] *Doe d. Gilbert* v. *Ross* (1840), 7 M. & W. 102.
[4] *R.* v. *Collins* (1960), 44 Cr. App. Rep. 170.
[5] R.S.C. Ord. 27, r. 4 (3).

production can give secondary evidence of the contents of the document in question.

If the document is in the possession of a stranger to the litigation, the proper course is to serve him with a *subpoena duces tecum*.

In criminal proceedings, the prosecutor should never serve the accused with a witness summons because this might confront the accused with the choice of producing the document or refusing to do so on the ground of possible incrimination as to the offence charged. The accused should be served with notice to produce, compliance with the notice then being optional. If a document is in the possession of the prosecutor, he should be served with a witness summons, as he is technically a stranger to the litigation, and any other stranger having possession of a relevant document should be similarly treated.

In any proceedings, service of notice to produce is unnecessary when the document in question is itself a notice, and when the nature of the case is such as to inform the other party of the necessity of producing the document. Obvious instances are provided by prosecutions for forgery or for a libel contained in a document in the accused's possession.

(a) *Original not produced by party.*—Nothing need be said about the first exception to the general rule mentioned in the article—the case in which the opponent has failed to produce the original.

(b) *Original not produced by stranger.*—So far as the second exception is concerned, it is only necessary to emphasise the point that, in order that secondary evidence of the contents of the document should become admissible, the stranger to the litigation must have lawfully refused to produce the document after service of a *subpoena duces tecum* or witness summons. If the refusal is unlawful, the proper course is to enforce the subpoena. The refusal may be lawful because the document may be privileged, or in the possession of someone enjoying diplomatic immunity.

It has been expressly decided that this exception applies in criminal as well as civil cases[6], and this is no doubt true of the other three mentioned in clause 2 of the article.

---

[6] *R.* v. *Nowaz,* [1976] 3 All E.R. 5.

(c) *Original lost.*—When the document cannot be found after due search, its contents may be proved by secondary evidence. The requirement of due search may be satisfied in different ways according to the differing circumstances of each case[7]. A party may adduce secondary evidence of the contents of a document if his opponent admits to having lost it, or if a stranger served with a *subpoena duces tecum* or witness summons does likewise. The contents of a lost will may be proved by secondary evidence to the same extent as those of any other lost document[8].

(d) *Production impossible.*—The production of the original of a document may be physically impossible in which case secondary evidence of its contents is admissible. It has been said that inscriptions on tombstones and walls are proved by copies every day[9]. Secondary evidence is likewise admissible when the production of the original is legally prohibited by, for example, a foreign court with custody of it[10], or a law requiring it to remain affixed to the walls of a particular place such as a factory[11].

(3) *Bankers' books*

At common law, it was held to be unnecessary for the books of the Bank of England to be produced[12] because of the public inconvenience which would have been occasioned by their production. The common law did not display a similar leniency towards the production of the books of other banks, and this accounts for the passing of the Bankers' Books Evidence Act 1879.

Section 3 provides that a copy of an entry in a banker's book shall, in all legal proceedings, be received as *prima facie* evidence of such entry, and of the matters, transactions, and accounts therein recorded. Four conditions must be satisfied before the copy can be received: (i) the book must have been one of the ordinary books of the bank when the entry was made; (ii) the entry must have been made in the usual course of business; (iii) the book must be in the custody or control of the bank[13];

---

[7] *Brewster* v. *Sewell* (1820), 3 B. & Ald. 296.
[8] *Sugden* v. *Lord St. Leonards* (1876), 1 P.D. 154.
[9] Per ALDERSON, B., in *Mortimer* v. *McCallan* (1840), 6 M. & W. 58.
[10] *Alivon* v. *Furnival* (1834), 1 Cr. M. & R. 277.
[11] *Owner* v. *Bee Hive Spinning Co. Ltd.*, [1914] 1 K.B. 105.
[12] *Mortimer* v. *McCallan* (1840), 6 M. & W. 58.
[13] S. 4.

(iv) the copy must have been examined against the original entry and found to be correct[14]. Proof of the examination must be given by the examiner, and proof of the other matters may be given by a partner or other officer of the bank. In each instance the proof may be by oral evidence or affidavit.

Section 6 provides that, subject to the special order of the judge, a banker shall not be compellable, in proceedings to which the bank is not a party, to produce any banker's book of which the contents can be proved under the Act. Section 7 empowers the court to make orders for the inspection of and the taking of copies from bankers' books. This section is widely phrased. The order may be made on the application of any party to a legal proceeding, with or without the summoning of the bank or the other party. The entries to be inspected may relate to the account of a stranger as well as that of the opposite party. The order must, however, be for the purpose of the legal proceedings in question, and, so far as strangers are concerned, the jurisdiction is exercised cautiously[15]. The order may be made in criminal proceedings, including the preliminary inquiry into an indictable offence before the magistrates[16].

ART. 63.—**Proof of public documents**

1. The contents and due execution of all public documents, not judicially noticed, may be proved by the production of the appropriate copy.

2. Judicial notice is taken of all public Acts of Parliament and of private Acts passed since 1850[17]; hence no particular copy of such Acts need be produced to the court.

3. Proclamations, orders and regulations are usually proved by Queen's Printer's copy, but may also be proved by production of the Gazette containing them or by certified extracts[18].

4. Colonial and Dominion statutes, ordinances and regulations are proved by the appropriate Government Printer's copy[19].

---

[14]S. 5.

[15]*Pollock* v. *Garle*, [1898] 1 Ch. 1.

[16]*R.* v. *Kinghorn*, [1908] 2 K.B. 949; *Williams* v. *Summerfield*, [1972] 2 K.B. 512; [1972] 2 All E.R. 1334.

[17]Interpretation Act 1978, s. 3.

[18]Documentary Evidence Act 1868.

[19]Evidence (Colonial Statutes) Act 1907.

5. Treaties, proclamations and acts of state of any foreign state or British colony, and any judgment, decree or order of any court in such state or copy may be proved by an examined copy or by an authenticated sealed copy[20].

6. English judgments in a civil case are proved as follows: A judgment of the House of Lords, by production of the journal of the House; judgments of the Court of Appeal and High Court by office copy[1].

7. Convictions in an English criminal case are proved by certified extract from the record[2].

8. In the case of all judgments and convictions, oral evidence may be necessary to identify the parties.

9. Byelaws of a local authority are proved by printed copy endorsed with the appropriate certificate[3].

10. Entries in United Kingdom registers are proved by certified copy.

11. Entries in foreign registers to which the Evidence (Foreign, Dominion and Colonial Documents) Act 1933 has been applied by order in council are proved by certified copy.

Explanation: Stationery Office copies are made the equivalent of Government or Queen's Printer's copies by the Documentary Evidence Act 1882. An "examined copy" is one that has been checked against the original; as the examination usually has to be proved by oral evidence, examined copies of public documents are comparatively rarely used in practice. A "certified copy" is one bearing a certificate of its accuracy. An "office copy" is one that has been examined in the court office in which the original is filed.

The article is only concerned with some of the principal types of public document and record that have to be proved. A comprehensive account would be beyond the scope of this work. The matter is governed by a great variety of statutes. When no statute is applicable, the provisions of s. 14 of the Evidence Act 1851 may be found useful. The section allows proof by certified copy of any book or document of such a public nature as to be admissible in evidence upon production from proper custody, when no statute exists which renders the contents of the book or document provable by a copy.

---

[20]Evidence Act 1851, s. 7.

[1]R.S.C. Ord. 38, r. 10.

[2]Evidence Act 1851, s. 13; Criminal Procedure Act 1865, s. 6; Prevention of Crimes Act 1871, s. 17.

[3]Local Government Act 1972, s. 210.

Acts of Parliament

As judicial notice is taken of public Acts of Parliament, and private Acts passed since 1850, the court may be referred to these by means of any book without further ado. In the case of private Acts passed before 1850, it may be necessary to produce a Queen's Printer's copy if the Act does not contain a special provision as to its being judicially noticed.

Proclamations, regulations and orders

The courts vary in the degree of strictness with which they require an Order in Council to be proved, but it is desirable to have a Stationery Office copy available whenever possible, and this is the method of proof of statutory instruments[4]. Proof by the Gazette or a certified extract may be necessary when there is no Stationery Office copy of a proclamation.

Colonial statutes, etc.

There is an overlap in heads 4 and 5 in the article. The Evidence (Colonial Statutes) Act 1907, upon which the fourth head is based, applies to any part of Her Majesty's dominions, exclusive of the United Kingdom.

Judgments and convictions

Although production of the appropriate copy of a judgment or conviction suffices to show, without any further proof, that a judgment was in fact given in the terms indicated, and affecting the parties named, oral evidence will usually be necessary to identify the parties as the persons alleged to have been such parties, and this matter is fully discussed in Chapter 16.

Byelaws

The certificate required to be indorsed on the printed copy of a local authority's byelaw must be signed by the clerk. It must state that the byelaw was made by the authority; that the copy is a true copy; that the byelaw was duly confirmed and the date on which it comes into operation.

Registers

Several special statutes apply to registers. The most common matters to be proved by certified copy, as one link in the chain of evidence, are births, deaths and marriages. Further reference is made to proof of these matters in Chapter 16. The Act of 1933, mentioned in the article, has been applied to a number of countries, including Belgium, Bermuda and Gibraltar.

---

[4] *R.* v. *Clarke,* [1969] 2 Q.B. 91; [1969] 1 All E.R. 924.

ART. 64.—**Things, and real evidence generally**

Things are the principal item of real evidence, but there are others.

Explanation: When discussing the best evidence rule on p. 19 we pointed out that there is no longer any requirement that a thing, the qualities of which are disputed, must be produced to the court. The prosecutor may depose to the defective qualities of a ring with which the accused obtained money without producing, or explaining the absence of the ring[5]. A party's unexplained failure to produce a portable object may, however, be the subject of adverse comment, and, where its value is in issue, prejudice his case[6].

When the object is produced, the court is neither asked to assume that assertions made by witnesses are true, nor required to draw an inference from relevant facts; it is invited to act on its own perception of the thing in question, and that is why real evidence must be treated as belonging to a separate category from testimony and circumstantial evidence.

A document may constitute real evidence, for it may be put in as a chattel—a substance such as paper or parchment bearing an inscription. Usually a document is put in as a statement, the important point being the inscription on the chattel.

The distinction is important because, although a thing does not have to be produced, the original of a document must be produced unless the case can be brought within one of the exceptions mentioned in Article 62. In *R.* v. *Hunt*[7], the prosecution was allowed to give evidence about the inscriptions on banners carried at a meeting, organised by the accused, without producing the banners. There is no reason why the word "thing" should not include a document treated as a thing, but there are a few items of real evidence which can hardly be included in the category of things. For example, a person's physical characteristics may often serve as a valuable means of proof. Whenever an inference is drawn from a witness's demeanour, reliance is placed on real evidence, and a child's resemblance to its parents is some, though slight, evidence of paternity[8].

---

[5] *R.* v. *Francis* (1874), L.R. 2 C.C.R. 128.

[6] *Armory* v. *Delamirie* (1772), 1 Stra. 505.

[7] (1820), 3 B. & Ald. 566.

[8] *Slingsby* v. *A.-G.* (1916), 33 T.L.R. 120.

Fingerprints, blood tests and tracker dogs

There is a type of real evidence relating to physical characteristics which is sometimes called "reported real evidence". It is given when witnesses inform the court of the result of tests and comparisons carried out by them. Examples are provided by evidence of fingerprints and blood tests.

Fingerprints.—A witness informs the court, often with the aid of a photograph, that he took the fingerprints of the accused, and found them to be identical with fingerprints found on some object with which the case is concerned.

The court has a statutory power to take the fingerprints or palm prints of the accused[9]. If, in response to a police officer's request for his fingerprints, a suspect allows them to be taken, they are legally admissible in evidence against him although no caution was given, but the judge probably has a discretion to exclude them if they were obtained by a trick[10].

Blood tests.—The Court has no inherent power to order blood samples to be taken from an adult[11], but there is such a power with regard to children whose paternity is in issue[12] and in a divorce case the court does not have to be satisfied that the test will necessarily be for the benefit of the child[13]. Part 3 of the Family Law Reform Act 1969 governs the making of blood tests in any civil proceedings in which the paternity of any person falls to be determined. The court is empowered to act on the report of the person who makes the test, and adverse inferences may be drawn from a party's refusal to consent to a test. A blood test is evidence of great value from the negative point of view whenever paternity is in issue, for it can eliminate the possibility that a particular person is a child's father.

No special rules of evidence apply to blood tests, except that, when they are taken in cases of suspected driving when unfit or with excessive blood alcohol content, the provisions of ss. 7–9 of the Road Traffic Act 1972 must be scrupulously followed. They do not call for discussion in a book of this nature.

---

[9]Magistrates' Courts Act 1952, s. 40, as amended by s. 33 of the Criminal Justice Act 1967.

[10]*Callis* v. *Gunn,* [1964] 1 Q.B. 495; [1963] 3 All E.R. 677; *cf. R.* v. *Sang,* [1979] 2 All E.R. 1222, p. 305, *infra*.

[11]*W.* v. *W.* (No. 4), [1964] P. 67; [1963] 2 All E.R. 841.

[12]*Re L.,* [1967] 2 All E.R. 1110.

[13]*S.* v. *S., W.* v. *Official Solicitor,* [1970] 3 All E.R. 107.

Tracker dogs.—There is no fully reported English case on the reception of evidence of the behaviour of tracker dogs, but such evidence has been received in other jurisdictions. Thus, in the Northern Irish case of *R.* v. *Montgomery*[14], on a charge of stealing telegraph wire, the evidence of a tracker dog handler was held to have been rightly received. He said that the dog was efficient, and then stated how it had tracked a scent from the base of a telegraph pole to the vehicle in which the accused were seated. Points sought to be made in the course of the argument were (1) that the acceptance of the evidence of the dog's behaviour amounted to the reception of hearsay evidence, and (2) that the evidence was unreliable. The Court refused to equate the dog's behaviour with the statement of a human being not called as a witness, and regarded the handler's evidence as equivalent to reports of tests with scientific instruments. The reliability of the dog's behaviour was treated as something that concerned the weight rather than the admissibility of the evidence.

Tape-recordings

A tape-recording would be real evidence if tendered in order to give the court an idea of the speaker's intonation. In other cases it may be admissible under exceptions to the rule against hearsay or as original evidence.

In *R.* v. *Maqsud Ali*[15], a tape recording of an incriminating conversation between the two accused, taken without their knowledge, after they had been left together in a room by a police officer and a Pakistani liaison officer, was held to have been rightly admitted in evidence. It evidenced an admission and was receivable under an exception to the hearsay rule. The Court of Criminal Appeal stressed the fact that such evidence must be treated with caution, but laid down no fetters on its admissibility. An example of the reception of a tape recording as original evidence would be a case in which the speaking of slanderous words was proved by this means.

Where the authenticity of the tape-recording before the court is disputed at a trial with a jury, the judge must be satisfied by evidence which defines and describes the provenance and history of the recording up to the moment of production in court that there is a *prima facie* case that it is the original before

---

[14][1966] N.I. 120.
[15][1966] 1 Q.B. 688; [1965] 2 All E.R. 464.

leaving the issue to the jury[16].

In *The Statue of Liberty*[17] a shore radar station's cinematograph film strip and recordings of echoes of ships in the Thames was admitted as real evidence. The recording was not monitored but "the law is bound these days to take cognisance of the fact that mechanical means replace human effort" (SIR JOCELYN SIMON, P).

ART. 65.—Facts as evidence of facts in issue—circumstantial evidence

An evidentiary fact is relevant to a fact in issue when, by itself, or together with other facts, it renders the existence of the fact in issue more or less probable. If an attempt is made to give evidence of an irrelevant fact, it ought to be excluded.

Explanation: Facts were the last of the items of judicial evidence mentioned in article 1. In article 2, we saw that the proof of facts in issue by means of other facts was called proof by "circumstantial evidence". The basis of the reception of such evidence is the idea of relevancy, and the object of this article is to refer to the idea of relevancy as a preliminary to distinguishing it in the next article from admissibility. It will also be convenient to show how irrelevant evidence is excluded.

Relevancy

One fact (conveniently called an evidentiary fact) is relevant to another when it renders the existence of that other fact probable or improbable. Relevancy is therefore a matter of common sense and experience rather than law. It would be pointless to give many examples. Obvious instances are provided by the proof of motive in a murder case, the proof of inclination and opportunity when adultery or a sexual offence is in issue, and the so-called presumption of continuance discussed at p. 48.

Problems of relevancy rarely arise in everyday forensic practice because, although it would be going too far to say that irrelevant evidence is seldom tendered, such evidence is not often tendered in such a form or such quantities as to cause the

---

[16] *R.* v. *Robson and Harris*, [1972] 2 All E.R. 699; *cf. R.* v. *Stevenson*, [1971] 1 All E.R. 678, where it was suggested that the standard of proof by which the judge should be satisfied is proof beyond reasonable doubt.

[17] [1968] 2 All E.R. 195.

opponent to object to it. Whenever a problem of relevancy does arise, the best thing to do is first, to ascertain the precise facts in issue, and secondly, to see whether the item of evidence under consideration renders any of the facts in issue probable. This is because there are two reasons why evidence may be irrelevant to an issue. In the first place, the fact which it is sought to establish by the evidence may not be in issue. Secondly, though the fact which it is sought to establish by the evidence is in issue, the evidence may have no real bearing on its probability.

The exclusion of irrelevant evidence

R. v. *Cargill*[18] may be taken as an example of a case in which evidence was excluded because the fact, which it was tendered to prove, was not in issue. A man was charged with unlawful intercourse with a girl between the ages of thirteen and sixteen. The prosecutrix swore that she had been chaste before the accused seduced her. This was irrelevant because it could only go to the issue of consent, and the girl's consent is no defence in such a case. But the reception of the girl's evidence of her virtue did not entitle the accused to call evidence of her behaviour with other men because the Court of Criminal Appeal was not prepared to say that, if the prosecution introduced a matter irrelevant to the issue, the defence was entitled to call evidence with regard to that irrelevant issue.

Hart v. *Lancashire and Yorkshire Railway*[19] may be taken as an example of a case in which evidence was rejected as irrelevant although the fact that it was tendered to prove was in issue. The defendants were sued for damages for negligence in respect of a railway accident. The fact that their method of changing the points was altered after the accident was held to be inadmissible as evidence of negligence. According to BRAMWELL, B.:

> "People do not furnish evidence against themselves simply by adopting a new plan in order to prevent the recurrence of an accident. Because the world gets wiser as it gets older, it was not therefore foolish before."

This case is simply authority for the proposition that the taking of additional precautions after an accident is not, *per se*, evidence that the accident was caused by negligence. If the issue had been whether there were any precautions which the defendants might have taken, their behaviour after the accident would have been very relevant to that question.

---

[18][1913] 2 K.B. 271.
[19](1869), 21 L.T. 261.

PART II

Admissibility

SUMMARY OF PART II

CHAPTER 9

Relevance and Admissibility

ART. 66 The relevance, admissibility and weight of evidence

1. The general rule is that all evidence which is relevant to a fact in issue[1], or to a fact upon which the admissibility of an item of evidence depends[2], or to a fact affecting the credit of a witness[3] is admissible, while all that is irrelevant is excluded. The existence of exceptions to the first part of the general rule necessitates the drawing of a sharp distinction between relevancy and admissibility.

2. It is also necessary to distinguish between the admissibility and weight of evidence.

Explanation: The meaning of relevance was considered in the previous article, and there would be no point in giving further illustrations of the general rule at this stage.

The first part of the general rule is subject to exceptions constituted by the exclusionary rules of evidence to be mentioned shortly. There are no exceptions to the second part of the general rule. Irrelevant evidence may often be tendered without objection, but it is nonetheless legally inadmissible.

Facts in issue are proved by testimonial evidence (testimony and admissible hearsay), as often as they are proved by

---

[1] P. 13, *supra*.
[2] P. 22, *supra*.
[3] See Article 25.

circumstantial evidence. Testimony and admissible hearsay may be said to be relevant to the facts which they are tendered to prove on the ground that a *prima facie* inference from the fact that they were made to their truth is justified by the circumstances in which they were made (liability of a witness to cross-examination, charges of perjury etc., the fact that a hearsay statement was against interest). Facts affecting the admissibility of evidence (e.g. the death of the maker of a hearsay statement) or the credit of a witness (e.g. his previous convictions) are not directly relevant to the facts in issue in any case, but they are indirectly relevant on account of the bearing they have on the means by which such facts may be proved or disproved. If allowance is made for the above points, the most basic of all the rules of evidence was tersely stated by GODDARD, L.J., when he said, "[G]enerally speaking, all evidence that is relevant to an issue is admissible while all that is irrelevant is excluded."[4]

The exclusionary rules

Although there are no circumstances in which irrelevant evidence is admissible, there are many situations in which relevant evidence has to be excluded. This is because rules, considered in the succeeding chapters, prohibit proof of certain facts, although these are in issue or relevant to an issue in a given case. Some of these rules are absolutely exclusionary in their nature, in the sense that they prohibit proof of certain facts altogether. Some of the rules based on public policy discussed in the next chapter are of this kind. Other exclusionary rules are, like those connected with estoppel, discussed in Chapter 11, equally all-embracing, but they can be waived. Yet other exclusionary rules only prohibit the proof of certain facts for certain purposes, as does the rule excluding similar fact evidence discussed in Chapter 12.

Some exclusionary rules, notably those against hearsay and opinion, have already been discussed, but they differ from those about to be mentioned. The primary function of the rules considered in chapters 10 to 14 is to prevent relevant facts from being proved, absolutely or for certain purposes, but the primary function of the rules we have already mentioned is merely to prevent proof of relevant facts by certain means, such as hearsay.

---

[4] *Hollington* v. *Hewthorn and Co., Ltd.*, [1943] K.B. 587, at p. 594.

Relevancy and admissibility

The exclusionary rules make it necessary to distinguish between relevancy and admissibility. "Relevancy" signifies, as we have seen, something which renders the existence of a fact probable or improbable. "Admissibility" signifies compliance with all the exclusionary rules, including that prohibiting the receipt of irrelevant evidence.

If evidence is admissible for one purpose, the fact that it is inadmissible for some other purpose does not affect its over-all admissibility. Thus a sister's informal extra-judicial admission of incest is evidence against her, but it is inadmissible hearsay as far as her co-accused brother is concerned.

Admissibility and weight

Questions concerning the admissibility of evidence must be distinguished from those relating to its weight. Admissibility is a matter of law for the judge (although it may sometimes depend on a preliminary finding of fact by him). The weight of evidence, on the other hand, is a question of fact. There are numerous factors that may affect the weight of evidence. Obvious instances are provided by the age, reliability or demeanour of a witness, the proximity in time of certain facts to those under investigation and the number of possible explanations of a particular event. The distinction between the admissibility and weight of evidence does not require further elaboration, but it is not clear-cut. Weight may affect admissibility, because relevancy is a matter of degree, and evidence of very slight weight will sometimes be excluded altogether. We shall see in Articles 75 and 76 that a very high degree of relevance is necessary before prejudicial evidence of propensity becomes admissible.

ART. 67.—**The exclusion of evidence which is too remote**

Evidence which is only remotely relevant, or liable to raise too many side issues, or which could be easily manufactured, is inadmissible.

Explanation: A legal inquiry is not like an academic investigation. Experience has shown that it is desirable for the court's mind to be focused on as few points as possible. To this end, evidence which is liable to lead to conjecture or a waste of time is excluded, although there may be some tenuous grounds for holding it to be relevant. Evidence which is of little weight, on account of the ease with which it could have been manufactured, is likewise rejected. These points are sometimes stated by saying that insufficiently relevant evidence is inadmissible, or by distinguishing between logical and legal relevancy. Perhaps it is simpler to recognise that, although the general rule is that all relevant evidence is admissible, there is a necessarily vague exclusionary rule covering the types of evidence mentioned in the article.

Remoteness

Cases in which evidence was excluded because it was, at best, only remotely relevant, are *Hollingham* v. *Head* and *Holcombe* v. *Hewson*.

In *Hollingham* v. *Head*[5], the defence to an action for the price of guano was that an express condition in the contract of sale provided that the goods should be equal to Peruvian guano. The defendant wished to call witnesses to swear that the plaintiff had entered into contracts with other customers containing a term similar to that for which he contended, but the Court of Common Pleas held that he was not entitled to do so. The fact that someone entered into contracts containing a particular term in the past may render it a little more probable that he later made another contract containing such terms, but the enhancement of the probability is very slight, and a great many other contracts would have to be proved to give it any real weight.

> "It may often be difficult to decide upon the admissibility of evidence, where it is offered for the purpose of establishing probability, but to be admissible it must at least afford a reasonable inference as to the principal matter in dispute."[6]

In *Holcombe* v. *Hewson*[7] a brewer claimed damages for breach of a publican's convenant to buy beer from him. The defence was that the plaintiff had supplied bad beer. Evidence to the

---

[5] (1858), 27 L.J.C.P. 241.
[6] WILLES, J.
[7] (1810), 2 Camp. 391.

effect that he had supplied other publicans with good beer was rejected. He "might deal well with one and not with others."[8]

Side-issues

Agassiz v. *London Tramway Co.*[9] is a case in which the reason given for the exclusion of evidence was its tendency to produce side-issues. A passenger on a tram claimed damages for injuries caused by a collision, alleged to be due to the negligence of the driver. She said that she heard another passenger tell the conductor that the driver ought to be reported, only to be met by the disconcertingly frank reply, "he has already been reported, for he has been off the lines five or six times today—he is a new driver". The evidence was rejected because it would have given rise to many collateral issues as to whether the driver had been reported, and whether he had been off the points five or six times or was a new driver.

Easily manufactured evidence

The best illustration of the exclusion of evidence on account of the ease with which it might be manufactured is provided by the common law rule (still applicable to criminal cases and only cautiously modified by the Civil Evidence Act 1968, under which the leave of the court is required before the statement can be proved) that a party may not prove his consistency by showing that he has previously made statements consistent with his present testimony. This rule was discussed in Article 22 and the exceptions to it were mentioned in Articles 23 and 24. It was stated as long ago as 1794, in the following cynical words of EYRE, C.J., which are often quoted:

> "[T]he presumption ... is, that no man would declare anything against himself, unless it were true; but that every man, if he was in a difficulty, or in the view to any difficulty, would make declarations for himself."[10]

---

[8] Lord ELLENBOROUGH.

[9] (1872), 21 W.R. 199.

[10] *R.* v. *Hardy* (1794), 24 State Tr. 199, at cols. 1093–4.

CHAPTER 10

Public Policy and Illegally Obtained Evidence

ART. 68.—The exclusion of evidence on the ground of public policy

1. Relevant evidence must be excluded if its reception would be contrary to a public interest held to be of greater importance than the public interest in the adduction of all relevant evidence in the course of the administration of justice. Examples of such interests are the maintenance of secrecy with regard to certain affairs of state and to sources of police information, but there are others which the courts recognise by analogy with them. Such public interests may be overridden by the necessity of disclosing information which could lead to the acquittal of someone accused of crime. In some cases the consent of the individuals affected may mean that the disclosure of the evidence would cease to be contrary to the public interest.

2. The judges of the superior courts cannot be compelled to give evidence concerning cases tried by them, and more or less closely analogous rules exist concerning the evidence of arbitrators, jurors and barristers.

Explanation: Whatever the position may be with regard to other public interest privileges or immunities, that concerned with the maintenance of secrecy with regard to certain affairs of state cannot be waived[1] any more than it can be circumvented by the reception of secondary evidence[2]. In both respects it is to be contrasted with the private interest privileges discussed in Articles 28–32. This is the justification for treating it as an exclusionary rule of evidence. It is not so clear whether the other public interest immunities about to be discussed should be so treated and we saw on p. 99 that the privilege attaching to without prejudice statements might as well have been treated under the present head as in Article 33. The public undoubtedly has an interest in the adduction of all relevant evidence in the course of the administration of justice and, in the event of there being any uncertainty whether this or some other public interest should prevail, there is a presumption in its favour[3].

Affairs of state

The decisions with regard to affairs of state fall under two heads, those in which evidence has been excluded because its disclosure would be injurious to national security and those concerned with some other state interest. The claim to the immunity is made by the appropriate minister or head of department directly if the Crown is a party to the proceedings and indirectly, by means of his instructions to one of the parties, when this is not the case. The claim, which is more often made on applications for discovery than at the trial of an action, is sometimes spoken of as one of "Crown privilege" although the term has been criticised because of the impossibility of waiver[4].

National security. — Items of evidence rejected in the name of national security include a letter from the Admiralty to one of the parties containing information about a campaign in time of war[5], documents concerning the structure of British submarines in time of war[6] and communications passing between the government and the commander-in-chief of our forces abroad[7].

---

[1] See *per* Lord SIMON in *Duncan* v. *Cammell Laird and Co., Ltd.*, [1942] A.C. 624, at pp.641–2.

[2] *Cooke* v. *Maxwell* (1817), 2 Stark. 183, *per* BAILEY, J.

[3] *Per* Lord EDMUND DAVIES in *D.* v. *N.S.P.C.C.*, [1978] A.C. 171, at p.246.

[4] *Duncan* v. *Cammell Laird and Co., Ltd.*, [1942] A.C. 624 at pp. 641–2.

[5] *Asiatic Petroleum Co., Ltd.* v. *Anglo-Persian Oil Co., Ltd.*, [1916] 1 K.B. 822.

[6] *Duncan* v. *Cammell Laird and Co., Ltd.*, [1942] A.C. 624; [1942] 1 All E.R. 587.

[7] *Chatterton* v. *Secretary of State for India in Council*, [1895] 2 Q.B. 189.

Other state interests.—In the name of other state interests the Home Office has successfully objected to the production of reports made by doctors and police officers concerning the mental condition of a prisoner awaiting trial[8] and the Minister of War has successfully objected to the production of a soldier's medical sheets at the hearing of a divorce case[9]. More recently, in *Alfred Crompton Amusement Machines, Ltd.* v. *Commissioners of Customs and Excise*[10], the House of Lords held that internal communications between the Commissioners and their officers concerning the company's purchase tax liability together with their communications with third parties concerning the market value of the company's machines ought not to be disclosed in the public interest, although, as we saw on p. 106, these documents were held not to be the subject of legal professional privilege. In *Burmah Oil Co., Ltd.* v. *Bank of England*[11] the House of Lords upheld a claim to public interest immunity by the Treasury in respect of memoranda relating to meetings between its representatives and those of the Bank held for the purpose of discussing the purchase of the company's holding in British Petroleum. Ministers and government officials were present and the Bank was acting under government instructions with the object of rescuing Burmah Oil from financial difficulties. In all these cases the basis of the claim to immunity is the necessity of maintaining secrecy in the interest of the proper functioning of the government or public service.

Sources of police information

In *Marks* v. *Beyfus*,[12] an action for malicious prosecution, the plaintiff called the Director of Public Prosecutions and wished to ask him the name of the person who gave the information which led to the prosecution for which he had been responsible. The Court of Appeal held that it was a public prosecution; that, in such a case, the information sought by the plaintiff ought to be withheld, and that the trial judge had rightly disallowed the question.

In *Rogers* v. *Secretary of State for the Home Department*[13] witness

---

[8] *Ellis* v. *Home Office*, [1953] 2 Q.B. 135; [1953] 2 All E.R. 149.

[9] *Anthony* v. *Anthony* (1919), 35 T.L.R. 559; *Gain* v. *Gain*, [1962] 1 All E.R. 63.

[10] [1974] A.C. 405; [1973] 2 All E.R. 1169, H.L.

[11] [1979] 3 All E.R. 700.

[12] (1890), 25 Q.B.D. 494.

[13] [1973] A.C. 388; [1972] 2 All E.R. 1057.

summonses served on the secretary of the Gaming Board and the Chief Constable of Sussex requiring them to produce the original and a copy of a letter written by the Deputy Chief Constable to the secretary were set aside. They had been issued on behalf of Rogers, an applicant for a gaming licence, who wished to prosecute the Deputy Chief Constable for libel. The letter contained confidential information supplied by third parties and was written in confidence. The mere fact that a communication was confidential does not support a claim to a public, any more than a private, privilege; but, if the communication was made in furtherance of a public interest to which society attaches importance, the fact that it was confidential may be of considerable significance. Were they to be disclosed without the consent of those making them, such communications would be unlikely to be made in the future. In this instance the relevant public interest was society's wish to insure that gambling is clean.

Other analogical public interests

In *D.* v. *N.S.P.C.C.*[14] the plaintiff was claiming damages for injury to her health occasioned by false allegations that she had maltreated her baby made to her by a representative of the Society acting, as she contended, without due inquiry, on information supplied in confidence. The Society applied for an order exempting them from giving discovery of documents relating to the identity of their informant. After some difference of opinion in the courts below, the House of Lords unanimously held that the order should be made. The public interest concerned was the welfare of children and the House acted on the analogy of the protection afforded to confidentiality with regard to the names of police informers, an analogy strengthened by the fact that the Society, in addition to a constable or local authority, is authorised to bring care proceedings under the Children and Young Persons Act 1969. Some members of the House recognised the possibility that local government communications might be protected by a public interest privilege by analogy with some of the decisions on state secrecy, and no doubt there will be analogical extensions of other decisions with regard to public, or even private interest privileges which the courts will come to recognise. In each instance it will be necessary to balance the

---

[14] [1978] A.C. 171.

interest in question against the public interest in full disclosure in the course of the administration of justice, the presumption in case of doubt being in favour of the latter.

Criminal cases

It was recognised in *Marks* v. *Beyfus* and subsequent cases that questions with regard to the sources of police information must be answered in criminal proceedings if the answer might establish the innocence of an accused person. There is at least one reported case in which disclosure of the name of an informant has been ordered[15]. The accused must show that there is good reason to suppose that the disclosure will be of real assistance to him[16]. There can be little doubt that the analogical public interests which have just been discussed would likewise be overridden by public interest in the disclosure of information which might reasonably be supposed to have a bearing on the innocence of an accused person. It is of course possible to imagine criminal prosecutions in which the disclosure of information which might establish the accused's innocence would be injurious to national security, but there would have to be very good reason for bringing the prosecution before the general interest should be allowed to prevail over that of the particular accused.

Consent to disclose

No one doubts that there are certain state secrets which must not be disclosed in court and, if the claim to public interest immunity were not made by the government, the point should be taken by the judge, but, although there is no decision on the point, it would almost certainly be going too far to say that no public interest privilege can be waived. In *Alfred Crompton Amusement Machines, Ltd.* v. *Customs and Excise Commissioners* the House of Lords upheld the Commissioners' claim to immunity from disclosure of communications passing between themselves and third parties concerning the market value of the company's machines. The information supplied by the third parties was given in confidence, but Lord CROSS of CHELSEA said that, if any of them were willing to give evidence, privilege in respect of any document or information obtained from him would be waived[17]. The same remark would appear to be

[15] *R.* v. *Richardson* (1863), 1 F. & F. 693.
[16] *R.* v. *Hennessey* (1978), 68 Cr. App. Rep. 419.
[17] [1974] A.C. at p.434.

applicable to a case in which the supplier of confidential information to the police or the National Society for the Prevention of Cruelty to Children was willing to testify.

Method of determining claim

Before the decision of the House of Lords in *Conway* v. *Rimmer*[18], there was authority for the views (a) that the Minister's objection to the production of a document or the adduction of evidence was final, and (b) that it might be necessary to distinguish documents belonging to a class the production of which was objectionable (although the contents of the particular document were innocuous) from documents in respect of which the objection was based on their contents.

Both views are contradicted by *Conway* v. *Rimmer*. In an action for malicious prosecution, Crown privilege was claimed, contrary to the wishes of the parties, for reports leading to the dismissal from the force of a police probationer on account of suspected theft. The House of Lords made an order for the production of the reports, perused them and directed their production in the action.

> "Whenever objection is made to the production of a relevant document it is for the court to decide whether to uphold the objection . . . The power of the court must also include a power to examine documents privately . . . I see no difference in principle between the considerations which should govern what have been called contents cases and class cases."[19]

It was of course recognised that, in many cases, the claim of a responsible minister would be upheld without inspection by the court. It was also recognised that the minister should have a right of appeal against an order for production.

Four of the five members of the House of Lords who heard the appeal in *Burmah Oil Co., Ltd* v. *Bank of England*[20] looked at some of the disputed documents before upholding the Treasury's claim to immunity. The House was not satisfied that disclosure would have been of real assistance to Burmah Oil's action to have the sale of their interest in British Petroleum set aside. This is something of which the court must be satisfied

---

[18] [1968] A.C. 910.
[19] Lord MORRIS.
[20] [1979] 3 All E.R. 700.

before it begins to weigh the public interest in respect to which the claim to immunity is made against the public interest in the disclosure of all relevant evidence. Although there is no distinction in principle between cases in which immunity is claimed on account of the class to which the document belongs and those in which the claim relates to its contents, it seems clear that the courts will be much more loth to inspect the document in the latter case.

Judicial matters

The dignity of the judicial office is regarded as such that the judges of the superior courts ought not to be compelled to testify concerning matters occurring in cases tried by them. There is little authority on the subject because the judges do not appear to object to giving evidence, at least from the well of the court, whenever their doing so would assist subsequent litigation. Judges of inferior courts appear to be compellable, like any other witnesses.

Arbitrators can be compelled to give evidence with regard to that which occurred during the arbitration, but they must not be asked questions about the reasons for their award[1].

There is a settled rule that jurors must not give evidence of discussions which took place in the jury box or jury room. The rule is confined to discussions concerning and leading up to the verdict; it does not prevent a new trial from being ordered on the ground that all the jurors were not in court when the verdict was pronounced[2]; but it does prevent the Court of Appeal from considering an appeal or application for a new trial on the ground that the jury misapprehended the effect of its verdict, even though all the jurors swear affidavits that this was the case[3].

ART. 69.—**Illegally obtained evidence**

Evidence is admissible, though it was obtained illegally, provided it does not involve a reference, in a criminal case, to an inadmissible confession of guilt, and subject to the judge's

---

[1] *Duke of Buccleuch* v. *Metropolitan Board of Works* (1872), L.R. 5 H.L. 418.
[2] *Ellis* v. *Deheer*, [1922] 2 K.B. 113.
[3] *Boston* v. *W. S. Bagshaw & Sons*, [1967] 2 All E.R. 87.

discretion in a criminal case to exclude admissible evidence in order to ensure a fair trial for the accused.

Explanation: There is very little authority on the subject of illegally obtained evidence. If such evidence were to be excluded, it would no doubt be under an absolute exclusionary rule, such as that excluding evidence which it would be contrary to the public interest to disclose; but there is very little sign that such a rule is developing in England. So far as the strict law is concerned, the current judicial approach may be summed up in the following remark of CROMPTON, J.[4]

> "It matters not how you get it, if you steal it even, it would be admissible in evidence."

In *Kuruma, Son of Kaniu* v. *R.*[5], the accused had been convicted of being in unlawful possession of ammunition, which had been discovered in consequence of a search of his person by a police officer below the rank of those who were permitted to make such searches. An appeal was brought to the Privy Council from Kenya where the relevant law was the same as English law. The Judicial Committee were of opinion that the evidence had been rightly admitted. Their view was that, if evidence is relevant, it matters not how it was obtained, although they made it plain that they were not qualifying the law with regard to the admissibility of confessions. We have seen, however, that, although there is a rigorous rule excluding confessions which were not made voluntarily, there is no rule of law under which facts discovered in consequence of inadmissible confessions must be excluded[6].

In *King* v. *R.*[7], where drugs had been discovered in consequence of a technically illegal search of the accused's person, Lord HODSON, speaking for the Judicial Committee, said:

> "This is not, in their opinion, a case in which evidence has been obtained by conduct of which the Crown ought not to take advantage, if they had thought otherwise they would

---

[4] *R.* v. *Leatham* (1861), 8 Cox C. C. 498, at p. 503.
[5] [1955] A.C. 197; [1955] 1 All E.R. 236.
[6] Article 46.
[7] [1969] A.C. 304; [1968] 2 All E.R. 610.

have excluded the evidence even though tendered for the suppression of crime."

Discretion

In *Kuruma* v. *R.* and *King* v. *R.* the Judicial Committee affirmed the existence of a discretion to exclude illegally or improperly obtained evidence in a criminal case. Such a discretion was subsequently recognised by a Divisional Court in *Jeffery* v. *Black*[8] when holding that the Justices should have admitted evidence of the discovery of cannabis in the accused's house in consequence of an illegal search by the police, because there had been no unfairness, trickery or oppression. The only reported case in which a conviction has been quashed by an appellate court because the judge should have exercised his discretion appears to be *R.* v. *Payne*[9]. The accused was convicted of driving while unfit. He had been examined by a police doctor in order to ascertain that his condition was not due to illness without having been warned that the results might be used in evidence against him as they were. Although they had no doubt that the results were admissible in law, the Court of Criminal Appeal held that the judge should have excluded them in his discretion because Payne might not have consented to the examination had he known that what was discovered in consequence of it might be proved against him.

The question of the exclusionary discretion in a criminal case was considered by the House of Lords in *R.* v. *Sang*[10] in which it was held that there is no discretion to exclude evidence procured by the police by their entrapment of the accused because, if there were, the rule of substantive law that entrapment is no defence would be evaded. This case is discussed again on p. 305. The most that can be said with certainty is that there is a discretion to exclude evidence if its reception would mean that the accused's trial is unfair because he had been misled into incriminating himself.

---

[8] [1978] Q.B. 490; [1978] 1 All E.R. 555.
[9] [1963] 1 All E.R. 848.
[10] [1979] 2 All E.R. 1222.

CHAPTER 11

Estoppel

ART. 70.—Estoppel in general

1. The party against whom an estoppel is established may not adduce any evidence with regard to facts covered by the estoppel.

2. Estoppels may be by record or, in civil cases, by deed or by conduct.

Explanation: From the point of view of the party against whom they operate, estoppels have the effect of an absolute exclusionary rule. This means that no regard need be had to the purpose for which evidence concerning facts covered by the estoppel is tendered; it is excluded altogether. In this respect the exclusion of evidence as a result of an estoppel resembles the exclusion of evidence on the ground of public policy, but all estoppels, unlike some instances of public policy, may be waived. In fact they must usually be pleaded by the party who proposes to rely on them. They play a much more important role in civil litigation than they do in criminal cases where there is no equivalent to estoppel by deed or estoppel by conduct.

The nature of estoppel

Although many judges have spoken of estoppel as a rule of

evidence[1], others have referred to it as a rule of substantive law[2]. A rule of evidence merely says what facts may or may not be proved in order to establish a legal right, whereas estoppel sometimes gives rise to legal rights. Thus, someone who fails to inform his bank that his wife has been forging his cheques is estopped from claiming repayment from the bank[3]. The bank could be said to have a right to debit the customer's account in such circumstances. Perhaps the difference between the two views is a verbal one. If a party to litigation is absolutely precluded from proving or denying certain facts, the effect may frequently be to confer rights on his adversary. Estoppel is an absolute exclusionary rule of evidence which sometimes has the same effect as a rule of substantive law.

ART. 71.—**Estoppel by record**

1. A judgment is conclusive as against all persons of the existence of the state of things which it actually effects.

2. In civil cases as a result either of cause of action estoppel or of issue estoppel, parties and their privies are estopped from denying any fact expressly or impliedly decided in former litigation, provided the question is raised with regard to the same subject-matter, and provided the parties are litigating in the same capacity.

3. In the Divorce Court, estoppels bind the parties, but do not bind the Court.

4. There is no issue estoppel in criminal law, but allowance must be made for extensions of the plea of *autrefois acquit* to strengthen the protection of the accused against double jeopardy.

Explanation: Estoppels by record have the common feature that they are based on the judgment of a court, and might therefore be better described as estoppels by judgment. In

---

[1]BOWEN, L.J., in *Low* v. *Bouverie*, [1891] 3 Ch. 82, at p. 105; Lord MAUGHAM in *Maritime Electric Co., Ltd.* v. *General Dairies Ltd.*, [1937] A.C. 610, at p. 620; [1937] 1 All E.R. 748, at p. 753.

[2]Lord WRIGHT in *Canada and Dominion Sugar Co., Ltd.* v. *Canadian National (West Indies) Steamships, Ltd.*, [1947] A.C. 46, at p. 56.

[3]*Greenwood* v. *Martins Bank, Ltd.*, [1933] A.C. 51.

order to appreciate the way in which they operate, it is necessary to distinguish between two aspects of a judgment, its effect, and the findings of fact upon which it must necessarily have been based. For example, the effect of a conviction for theft is that the accused becomes a convicted thief; the conviction was based on findings of fact that his conduct came within the definition of stealing. Similarly, the effect of a divorce decree is that the parties are no longer married; if the petition alleged adultery, the decree necessarily involves a finding that that offence was committed. The distinction between the two aspects of a judgment is important because it is only the effect of a judgment that constitutes an estoppel in proceedings between strangers to it, whereas, between parties and their privies there is a further estoppel with regard to the facts on which the judgment must have been based.

(1) *Conclusive effect of judgment*

There would be no point in multiplying examples of the conclusiveness of a judgment with regard to its effect. An obvious instance is provided by a civil action for malicious prosecution. The record of the criminal proceedings in which the plaintiff was prosecuted is conclusive of his acquittal; the defendant is estopped from denying this fact, even if he wishes to do so.

The most important instances of estoppels constituted by the effect of a judgment are provided by judgments affecting status, commonly called "judgments in rem". For example, if, in litigation between A and B, A wishes to establish that C was D's wife at the time of a particular transaction, he will be estopped from asserting this fact by the production of a divorce decree made before the date of the transaction.

(2) *Judgments as estoppels between the parties in civil cases other than matrimonial causes*

When considering the effect of a judgment as between the parties to a civil case, it is necessary to distinguish between "cause of action" estoppel and "issue" estoppel[4].

Cause of action estoppel is based on the idea that the cause of action merges in the judgment which therefore destroys it. If A claims damages from B for a particular assault or breach of

[4]The terminology derives from *Carl-Zeiss Stiftung* v. *Rayner and Keeler, Ltd.* (*No. 2*), [1967] 1 A.C. 853; [1966] 2 All E.R. 536.

contract and recovers a specific sum, he cannot sue for more damages for the same cause, however clearly he would have been entitled to them had subsequent events, such as the deterioration of his health in consequence of the assault, been known at the time of the original claim.

Issue estoppel is wider and less technical. It is based on the desirability of achieving finality in the litigation of certain issues between the parties. If, in June, A claims damages for a breach of contract committed by B in January, and B successfully pleads that the contract is void, A would be met by a successful plea of issue estoppel if, in December, he claimed damages for a further breach of the same contract committed in June. The causes of action would have been different, but a crucial issue would have been decided in B's favour in the first litigation.

(a) *Cause of action estoppel*

In *Workington Harbour and Dock Board* v. *Trade Indemnity Co., Ltd.* (*No. 2*)[5], the defendants guaranteed the plaintiffs against any loss they might sustain through breaches of contract by building contractors who had undertaken to do some work for the plaintiffs. The plaintiffs had previously sued the defendants for such loss, and their action had been dismissed because the loss was only proved by a surveyor's certificate which, on the true construction of the contract between the plaintiffs and the defendants, was held not to be binding on the defendants. It was held that the plaintiffs were estopped from making a further claim for the loss because it was the same loss allegedly caused by the same breach of contract, and the plaintiffs were simply trying to prove it in a different way.

(b) *Issue estoppel*

In *Priestman* v. *Thomas*[6], the plaintiff sought to have a grant of probate set aside in the Probate Division because the will was forged. It was held that the defendant was estopped from denying this fact, because it had previously been held that the will was forged in proceedings between the same parties in the Chancery Division.

The following is one of the clearest formulations of the principal of issue estoppel:

---

[5][1938] 2 All E.R. 101.
[6](1884), 9 P.D. 210.

"A party to civil proceedings is not entitled to make, as against the other party, an assertion, whether of fact or of the legal consequences of facts, the correctness of which is an essential element in his cause of action or defence, if the same assertion was an essential element in his previous cause of action or defence in previous civil proceedings between the same parties or their predecessors in title, and was found by a court of competent jurisdiction in such previous civil proceedings to be incorrect, unless further material which is relevant to the correctness or incorrectness of the assertion by that party in the previous proceedings has since become available to him."[7]

If, in *Priestman* v. *Thomas*, further evidence had become available to the defendant, the decision might have been different.

Conditions

In order that a plea of estoppel by judgment should be successful, the causes of action or particular issue must have been identical in the two sets of proceedings, and the parties must have been the same, suing in the same capacity. The requirement of identity of parties is subject to the rules concerning privity set out below. Most of the cases concern issue estoppel.

Identity of issues.—In *Wood* v. *Luscombe*[8], motorcycles driven by Wood junior and Luscombe respectively were in collision, and Wood senior was a pillion passenger on that driven by Wood junior. Luscombe sued Wood junior for damages for negligence, and the parties were held equally to blame. Wood senior then sued Luscombe and recovered damages from him; Luscombe claimed contribution to these damages from Wood junior. It was held that Wood junior was estopped from denying that he was responsible for half the sum which Luscombe had to pay to Wood senior. The issue of Wood junior's liability to Luscombe, and his liability to Wood senior were substantially the same; but there was a technical distinction turning on the fact that the duties owed by Wood junior in the two cases were not identical because they were owed to different people. In an earlier case[9] which conflicts

---

[7]*Mills* v. *Cooper,* [1967] 2 Q.B. 459, at p. 468, *per* DIPLOCK, L.J.

[8][1966] 1 Q.B. 169; [1964] 3 All E.R. 972.

[9]*Randolf* v. *Tuck,* [1962] 1 Q.B. 175; [1961] 1 All E.R. 814.

with *Wood* v. *Luscombe* this point was held to be crucial against there being an estoppel on the claim to contribution.

Identity and capacity of parties.—Generally speaking, the requirement as to the identity of parties does not give rise to difficulty, but questions are sometimes raised on this point when the same party is suing in different capacities in successive actions. In *Marginson* v. *Blackburn Borough Council*[10], for instance, the defendant's omnibus was involved in a collision with the plaintiff's car driven by his wife. The plaintiff's wife was killed, the plaintiff sustained personal injuries and some houses were damaged. The owners of the houses recovered damages in an action, brought against the Borough Council and Mr. Marginson, when both drivers were held guilty of negligence. In a subsequent action, Mr. Marginson claimed damages for his injuries and sued as his wife's personal representative under the Law Reform (Miscellaneous Provisions) Act 1934, and the Fatal Accidents Acts. It was held that, so far as Mr. Marginson's personal claim was concerned, he was estopped from denying the contributory negligence of his wife, as she was driving the car as his agent, but he was not estopped from doing so in relation to the other claims, because they were brought as his wife's administrator, whereas the previous action had been defended by him in his personal capacity as the owner of a car driven by his wife.

Privity.—A judgment operates as an estoppel, not only as between the parties to it, but also between "privies" to those parties or a privy and one of the parties. In this context "privity" means claiming through the original party. Privies are said to be either "in estate", "in blood" or "in law". Privies in estate include lessor and lessee, and vendor and purchaser. Privies in blood are ancestor and heir on intestacy, privies in law include testator and executor or intestate and administrator.

(3) *Matrimonial causes*

In *Thompson* v. *Thompson*[11] DENNING, L.J., said:

"Once an issue of a matrimonial offence has been raised between the parties and decided by a competent court, neither party can claim as of right to reopen the issue and

---

[10][1939] 2 K.B. 426.

[11][1957] P. 19, at p. 29; [1957] 1 All E.R. 161, at p. 165.

litigate it all over again if the other party objects (that is what is meant by saying that estoppels bind the parties). But the Divorce Court has the right, and indeed the duty in a proper case, to reopen the issue, or to allow either party to reopen it, despite the objection of the other party (that is what is meant by saying that estoppels do not bind the court)."

An illustration of an estoppel binding the parties, but not the court, is provided by *Hayward* v. *Hayward*[12]. The parties were married in 1945. The husband left his wife in 1957, and the wife claimed maintenance before the magistrates. The husband admitted desertion in these proceedings, and this admission impliedly recognised the validity of the marriage. In 1959, it came to be known for certain that the husband's first wife was alive in 1945, with the result that the marriage to Mrs. Hayward was a nullity. The husband petitioned for nullity. In the ordinary case he would have been estopped from alleging the invalidity of the marriage, if he was unable to satisfy the court that fresh evidence which he could not, with due diligence, have adduced earlier was available to him. It was held, however, that, as status was a question of public interest, the divorce court could investigate the matter all over again, and a decree of nullity was pronounced.

Now that divorce is no longer based on a matrimonial offence and the bars to relief have been abolished, the rule that in matrimonial causes estoppels bind the parties but not the court may have to be reconsidered; but recent legislation does not appear to have affected the principle of *Hayward* v. *Hayward*.

(4) *Criminal cases*

Pleas of *autrefois acquit* or *autrefois convict* are the nearest equivalent to cause of action estoppel in criminal cases. They are available whenever the accused is in danger of being convicted of the same or substantially the same offence as one for which he has already been acquitted or convicted, or when he is in danger of being convicted of an offence of which he could have been convicted at a former trial.

After widely differing opinions had been expressed on the subject in earlier cases, the House of Lords unanimously stated in *Director of Public Prosecutions* v. *Humphrys*[13] that there is no

---

[12] [1961] P. 152; [1961] 1 All E.R. 236.
[13] [1977] A.C. 1; [1976] 2 All E.R. 497.

issue estoppel in criminal law. Humphrys had been acquitted on a charge of driving a motor vehicle on 18th July, 1972, while disqualified. The only contested issue at his trial had been whether a constable was correct in identifying him as the man he had stopped after seeing him drive a motor cycle on 18th July. Humphrys gave evidence in the course of which he denied having driven a motor cycle at any time during 1972. He was then charged with perjury in having made this statement. He was convicted after the same constable had given the same evidence as that which he had given in the former proceedings, although there was evidence from other sources that Humphrys had driven a motor cycle on days other than 18th July during 1972. His appeal to the Court of Appeal was allowed on the ground that the constable's evidence was precluded by issue estoppel. The House of Lords restored the conviction, the main reason for the emphatic rejection of issue estoppel in criminal cases being the difficulty of ascertaining the issues that were decided on account of the facts that there are no pleadings and that the jury returns a general verdict unsupported by stated reasons.

Extensions of autrefois acquit.—In *Sambasivam* v. *Malaya Federation Public Prosecutor*[14] the appellant had been charged with two offences, carrying a fire-arm and being in possession of ammunition. He was acquitted on the second but a new trial was ordered on the first. At the second trial the prosecution relied upon a statement in which the appellant said that he was both carrying a fire-arm and in possession of ammunition. He was convicted of carrying a fire-arm but the Judicial Committee advised that his conviction should be quashed because the assessors had not been told that the prosecution had to accept that the part of the statement dealing with the ammunition was untrue, and this might have affected their attitude towards the other part.

In *G. (an Infant)* v. *Coltart*[15], G, a domestic servant was convicted of stealing goods from T, her mistress. Her defence was that she intended to return the goods to T. In order to rebut it the prosecution had adduced evidence that G had taken goods from D, a guest of T, and failed to return them although she knew that D was going to South Africa. G had,

---

[14] [1950] A.C. 458.

[15] [1967] 1 Q.B. 432; [1967] 1 All E.R. 271.

however, been acquitted of stealing D's goods at the instance of the prosecutor who was under the impression that the absence of D was fatal to his case. A Divisional Court held that the conviction of stealing from T must be quashed because it was not open to the prosecutor to invite the court to make an inference that G was guilty of an offence of which she had been acquitted.

Sambasivam v. *Malaya Federation Public Prosecutor* decided that the prosecution may not, in case B, rely on evidence the relevance of which is enhanced by the assumption that the accused was guilty of an offence of which he was acquitted in case A. *G. (an Infant)* v. *Coltart* is an illustration of the same point. The prosecution relied in case B on evidence which was only relevant on the assumption that the accused was guilty of the offence of which she had been acquitted in case A. The decisions are best regarded as extensions of the plea of *autrefois acquit*. In neither case was the accused in danger of being convicted of the offence of which there had been an acquittal, but they were in danger of suffering on the second occasion in consequence of a challenge to their innocence on the first. The decisions are based on a thoroughgoing application of the rule against double jeopardy.

In *Director of Public Prosecutions* v. *Humphrys* the absence of issue estoppel in criminal law favoured the prosecution. It could of course operate favourably to the accused. If A is convicted of causing grievous bodily harm with intent and later charged with the murder of his victim on the same facts, he would, if the criminal law recognised issue estoppel, be estopped from denying the intent to cause grievous bodily harm[16]. Had it not been for the further evidence in Humphrys' case, some of the law lords who decided it would have favoured a judicial discretion to stay the prosecution for perjury on the ground that the Crown would, in effect, then have been seeking a retrial of the driving charge.

ART. 72.—**Estoppel by deed in civil cases**

Subject to the limitations mentioned below, in civil cases "A

---

[16]As happened in *R.* v. *Hogan,* [1974] 2 All E.R. 142, overruled by *Director of Public Prosecutions* v. *Humphrys.*

party who executes a deed is estopped in a court of law from saying that the facts stated in the deed are not truly stated"[17].

Explanation: Estoppel by deed is really a species of estoppel by agreement, mentioned in the next article. This point was made by Lord MAUGHAM in the House of Lords in *Greer* v. *Kettle*[18].

> "Estoppel by deed is a rule of evidence founded on the principle that a solemn and unambiguous statement or engagement in a deed must be taken as binding between the parties and privies and therefore as not admitting any contradictory proof."

It is on this principle that parties have been held to be estopped, not merely by statements in the operative part of a deed, but also by unambiguous statements in the recitals.

Limitations

The requirement that the statement should be unambiguous is the first of three important limitations on the operation of estoppel by deed. The second is that it can only be raised in an action on the deed. In *Carpenter* v. *Buller*[19], the defence to an action for trespass was that the defendant was seised of the land in question and he produced a deed. The deed was made between himself, the plaintiff and a third party and it stated that the defendant was seised of the land in question. But it was held that the plaintiff was not estopped from denying the defendant's seisin because the action was not brought on the deed.

The third limitation is that the doctrine of estoppel by deed does not prevent a party from setting up a plea of illegality or fraud, or from availing himself of any fact giving rise to a right to rescind the deed. This means that a party is not estopped from denying the receipt of the purchase price of land or goods, even though it is acknowledged in the body of a deed.

ART. 73.—Estoppel by conduct in civil cases

Subject to the requirements mentioned below, in civil cases when one person, by words or conduct, has caused another to

---

[17] *Baker* v. *Dewey* (1823), 1 B. & C. 704, at p. 707, *per* BAYLEY, J.
[18] [1938] A.C. 156, at p. 171; [1937] 4 All E.R. 396, at p. 404.
[19] (1841), 8 M. & W. 209.

believe in the existence of a certain state of things, and to act upon that belief to his detriment, he is estopped from denying the existence of that state of things.

Explanation: Two people often agree, expressly or by implication, that their legal relations shall be based on the assumption that a certain state of facts exists; when this has been done, the original parties to the agreement, as well as those claiming through them, are estopped from denying the existence of the assumed state of facts. Estoppel by agreement is a species of estoppel by representation.

Requirements

In order that a representation should operate as an estoppel, it must be one of fact, it must be unambiguous, it must have been made in such circumstances that a reasonable man would have thought that it was intended that he should act on it, and it must have been acted upon to the detriment of the person to whom it was made.

The requirement that the representation must be one of fact means that, at common law, a promise concerning future conduct can never constitute an estoppel[20]. An undertaking not to enforce an existing legal right, such as a claim to higher rent than that received by the landlord, does not produce an estoppel; although it may have some legal effect, this is no concern of the law of evidence[1].

When there is a duty to disclose material facts, deliberate silence with regard to them may be equivalent to a misrepresentation. In *Greenwood* v. *Martins Bank*[2], for instance, a husband's failure to disclose the fact that his wife had been forging his cheques was held to estop him from alleging the forgery in an action to recover the amounts debited to his account. Had the husband been allowed to prove the forgery, he would have succeeded in the action, for banks are normally obliged to recoup their customers for sums paid out of their account on forgeries of the customer's signature.

The requirement that the representation must be unambiguous may be illustrated by *Freeman* v. *Cooke*[3]. The assignee of

---

[20] *Jorden* v. *Money* (1854), 5 H.L. Cas. 185.
[1] *Central London Property Trust, Ltd.* v. *High Trees House Ltd.*, [1947] K.B. 130.
[2] [1933] A.C. 51.
[3] (1848), 2 Exch. 654.

a bankrupt was held not to be estopped from proving the bankrupt's ownership of goods seized by a sheriff because, although the bankrupt had denied that the goods were his, he had made a number of contradictory statements concerning the person who was their owner.

The requirement that the representation should have been made in such circumstances that a reasonable man would have thought that it was intended that it should be acted on may be illustrated by *Carr* v. *London and North Western Rail. Co.*[4] The defendant's agent told the plaintiff that the company held three consignments of goods to his order. In fact only two consignments had been received. The plaintiff purported to sell all three consignments and had to pay damages to the purchaser of one of them. He sought to recover this payment from the defendants in an action for conversion. Had the defendants been estopped from denying that they held three consignments to the order of the plaintiff, he would have succeeded in his action, but it was held that there was no estoppel, because there was no evidence that the defendant's agent realised that the goods would be sold by the plaintiff. The following words of BRETT, L.J., in *Carr's* case show that the defendants would have been liable, if any reasonable man in the position of the plaintiff would have thought that he was intended to act upon the representation:

> "If a man, whatever his real meaning may be, so conducts himself that a reasonable man would take his conduct to mean a certain representation of facts, and that it was a true representation, and that the latter was intended to act upon it in a particular way, and he with such belief does act upon it in that way to his damage, the first is estopped from denying that the facts were as represented."

Is is not essential that the party in whose favour the estoppel operates, or someone through whom he claims, should have been in direct negotiation with the party against whom the estoppel operates, or someone through whom he claims. In *Coventry-Sheppard & Co.* v. *Great Eastern Rail. Co.*[5] the defendants carelessly issued two delivery orders relating to the same consignment of goods, thus enabling the person to whom they were issued to obtain a loan from the plaintiffs on the security

[4](1875), L.R. 10 C.P. 307.
[5](1883), 11 Q.B.D. 776.

of one of the orders. That person was acting fraudulently, as he had previously obtained a loan on the security of the other order, but, when the plaintiffs sued the defendants, it was held that the defendants were estopped from denying that the goods mentioned in the order which had been handed to the plaintiffs were held on behalf of the person mentioned therein.

Reliance can never be placed on an estoppel when the result of giving effect to it would be something which is prohibited by the law. Accordingly, when a statutory undertaking mistakenly charged less for electricity than the amount specified in the relevant enactment, it was held that no estoppel covered the case although the recipients of the electricity had acted to their detriment[6].

[6]*Maritime Electric Co., Ltd.* v. *General Dairies, Ltd.*, [1937] A.C. 610; [1937] 1 All E.R. 748.

CHAPTER 12

Evidence of Disposition

ART. 74.—**Evidence of disposition generally**

In this chapter "disposition" means a person's tendency to act, think or feel in a particular way. It may be proved by conduct on other occasions ("similar fact evidence"), by evidence of character, and, where there are any, by previous convictions. Whatever form the evidence takes, it is affected by exclusionary rules.

Explanation: In this chapter we are concerned with three types of evidence according to whether it relates to a party's misconduct on other occasions, his character or his previous convictions. The unifying factor is the way in which these types of evidence are affected by exclusionary rules. They are all meant to guard against an over-ready acceptance of the argument that the defendant or accused must have committed the civil wrong or crime charged because he is the kind of man who would do that kind of thing. This argument is common enough in everyday life, but it is dangerous in a court of law because it is all too liable to cover up weak points in the evidence concerning the behaviour of the party on the occasion under investigation. The adage "give a dog a bad name and hang him" is a timely reminder of this danger.

Misconduct on other occasions

The main exclusionary rule prohibits proof of misconduct on other occasions if the sole purpose of the evidence is to establish a party's disposition to commit crimes or civil wrongs in general or even the particular crime or civil wrong charged. The rule is confined to misconduct or, to be more accurate, to conduct which tends to show bad disposition: the admissibility of conduct which tends to establish a good, or morally neutral, disposition simply depends on its relevancy. Unlike the exclusionary rules considered in the last two chapters, this one, which is discussed in Article 75, is largely dependent on the purpose for which the evidence is tendered; it is designed "to exclude a particular kind of inference being drawn which might upset the presumption of innocence by introducing more heat than light"[1]. Evidence involving misconduct on other occasions may be given if it is relevant for some further reason than its tendency to show disposition or even because the disposition is specially relevant to an issue in the case, and some of the principal instances are discussed in Article 76. Statutory exceptions to the rule mentioned in Article 75 are considered in Article 79. The misconduct on other occasions which it is sought to prove usually resembles that under investigation; that is why the evidence is spoken of as "evidence of similar facts".

Evidence of character

"Evidence of character" means the statements of witnesses in answer to questions concerning a party's character. The statements are couched in general terms, such as "he has a good character for honesty", and it is this feature which distinguishes them from evidence of specific acts considered in Articles 75–76.

---

[1] *Per* Lord HAILSHAM in *Boardman* v. *Director of Public Prosecutions*, [1975] A.C. 421, at p. 454.

Previous convictions

To admit evidence of the previous convictions of the accused would obviously be prejudicial and previous convictions may only be proved in-chief when they are in issue and in the exceptional cases mentioned in Article 79.

ART. 75.—The inadmissibility of conduct on other occasions which is of no particular relevance apart from its tendency to show bad disposition

Subject to the statutory exceptions mentioned in Article 79, evidence of the conduct of a party on other occasions cannot be given, or elicited in cross-examination, by the prosecution if it is of no particular relevance apart from its tendency to show a disposition towards wrongdoing in general, or towards the commission of the particular crime or civil wrong with which such party is charged. When such evidence is given or elicited in cross-examination by a co-accused or co-defendant its admissibility depends upon its relevance.

Explanation: The rule stated in the article is said to apply to civil and criminal cases alike, but it is most frequently applied in criminal cases, and it is possible that in civil proceedings, all that is required is that the evidence of disposition should be relevant and not unfair or oppressive[2].

The most commonly cited judicial statement of the rule is that of Lord HERSCHELL in *Makin* v. *A.-G. for New South Wales*[3].

> "It is undoubtedly not competent for the prosecution to adduce evidence tending to show that the accused has been guilty of criminal acts other than those covered by the indictment for the purpose of leading to the conclusion that the accused is a person likely from his criminal conduct or character to have committed the offence for which he is being tried."

The strongest illustration of the rule is provided by the almost universal inadmissibility of the accused's previous convictions as evidence-in-chief for the prosecution at a criminal trial. Suppose A is charged with having committed

---

[2] P. 266, *infra*.

[3] [1894] A.C. 57, at p. 65.

theft in 1975. The prosecution cannot prove in-chief that he was convicted of theft on a number of occasions between 1955 and 1975. The only relevance of the convictions would be to support a general argument to the effect that the accused probably committed the theft charged in 1975 because they showed that he was the kind of man who would commit theft. This is precisely the argument which is prohibited by the rule; some more specific line of reasoning is essential to render evidence of bad disposition admissible.

In *Noor Mohamed* v. *R.*[4], the accused was charged with murdering A, a woman with whom he had been living, by poisoning her with cyanide. There was evidence of quarrels between the accused and A, and A certainly met her death through cyanide poisoning. The accused was a goldsmith and had possession of cyanide for lawful business purposes, and there was no evidence of the administration of poison by the accused. The trial judge admitted evidence tending to show that the accused had previously killed his wife by tricking her into taking cyanide as a cure for tooth-ache. The accused was convicted, but his conviction was quashed on the advice of the Privy Council because the evidence with regard to his wife ought not to have been received. When speaking of this evidence, Lord DU PARCQ said:

> "If an examination of it shows that it is impressive just because it appears to demonstrate in the words of Lord HERSCHELL in *Makin's* case 'that the accused is a person likely from his criminal conduct or character to have committed the offence for which he is being tried', and if it is otherwise of no real substance then it was certainly wrongly admitted."

The only issue in the case was whether the accused administered the poison to A and the only relevance to that issue of the accused's conduct toward his wife was that it tended to show that he was the kind of man who might use poison to get rid of women with whom he had quarrelled. Had the issue been whether the accused accidentally administered poison to A when giving her a drink, the evidence with regard to his wife might well have been admissible to negative accident on principles mentioned in the next article.

In *R.* v. *Fisher*[5], the accused was charged with obtaining a pony and cart by false pretences concerning the state of his

---

[4] [1949] A.C. 182; [1949] 1 All E.R. 365.

[5] [1910] 1 K.B. 149.

family and the state of his bank account. Evidence was admitted which tended to show that he had obtained provender by false pretences concerning his business. The ensuing conviction was quashed by the Court of Criminal Appeal because the pretences were dissimilar, and the evidence could only be relevant as showing that the accused was a man of generally fraudulent disposition.

> "If a man is charged with swindling in a particular manner, his guilt cannot be proved by showing that he has also swindled in some other manner."[6]

The evidence concerning the provender was plainly relevant to the issue whether the false pretences charged were made with intent to defraud; though considerable, its relevance to this issue was only the general relevance of the support it lent to an argument that the accused probably intended to defraud when he made the pretences charged, because the fact that he had made other false pretences tended to suggest that he was a fraudulent man. Had the two sets of pretences been similar, those by which the provender was obtained would have been admissible on principles discussed in the next article as tending to show that the accused was given to obtaining goods by the same fraudulent technique.

Evidence of co-accused

In *Lowery* v. *R.*[7] Lowery and King were convicted of a murder in circumstances in which the crime must have been committed by one or both of them. The appeal to the Privy Council turned on the question whether the judge had acted correctly in allowing King to call a psychiatrist to swear that he was immature, frightened and less likely to have committed the crime than Lowery, who had been examined and subjected to tests by the witness. In the course of delivering the opinion of the Judicial Committee in favour of dismissing the appeal Lord MORRIS OF BORTH-Y-GEST cited with approval the following statement of the Court of Criminal Appeal of Victoria:

> "It is, we think, one thing to say that such evidence is excluded when tendered by the Crown as proof of guilt, but quite another to say that it is excluded when tendered by the accused in disproof of his own guilt. We see no reason of

---

[6] CHANNELL, J.

[7] [1974] A.C. 85; [1973] 3 All E.R. 662.

policy or fairness which justifies or requires the exclusion of evidence relevant to prove the innocence of an accused person".

Lowery had put his character in issue by saying that he had never been charged with a serious crime and generally indicating that he was unlikely to have committed the offence, but Lord MORRIS seems to have regarded this fact simply as adding strength to his views about the admissibility of the evidence. In *R.* v. *Miller*[8], where two men were charged with customs offences, it was held that the trial judge had rightly allowed Miller's counsel to ask a Crown witness if he knew that the illegal importations stopped while the co-accused was in prison.

It seems to follow that the admissibility of evidence tending to show bad disposition on the part of the accused depends, when tendered or elicited by a co-accused, on its relevance. A tendency to commit domestic violence may not be sufficiently relevant when the issue is which of two burglars resorted to violence against the elderly occupier of the burgled house[9], and the fact that one of two people accused of arson had committed similar offences in the past is irrelevant to the other's defence that he was in bed at the material time[10].

ART. 76.—The admissibility of evidence of conduct on other occasions which is of particular relevance in spite of its tendency to show bad disposition

1. Evidence of the conduct of a party on other occasions may be given if it is relevant for some further reason wholly independent of its tendency to show in him a disposition towards wrong-doing in general or the commission of the kind of crime or civil wrong with which he is charged; or if, notwithstanding the fact that it does no more than show in him a disposition to commit the kind of crime or civil wrong with which he is charged, it is of particular relevance on account either of its similarity in significant respects to the conduct

---

[8] [1952] 2 All E.R. 667.

[9] *R.* v. *Westwell* (1976), 68 Cr. App. Rep. 44.

[10] *R.* v. *Neale* (1977), 65 Cr. App. Rep. 304.

charged, or of some further item of evidence in the case, or o its tendency to rebut a defence available to the ac cused.

2. The operation of the above rules is subject to the discretion of the judge to exclude evidence if, in his opinion, its prejudicial effect outweighs its probative value.

Explanation: In *Makin* v. *A.-G. for New South Wales*[11] Lord HERSCHELL said that:

> "The mere fact that the evidence adduced tends to show the commission of other crimes does not render it inadmissible if it be relevant to an issue before the jury; and it may be so relevant if it bears upon the question whether the acts alleged to constitute the crime charged in the indictment were designed or accidental, or to rebut a defence which would otherwise be open to the accused."

Lord HERSCHELL must be taken to have been using the word "relevant" in this passage in the sense of "specially relevant", "highly relevant" or "particularly relevant", because cases such as *R.* v. *Fisher*[12] show that evidence which is undoubtedly relevant to an issue before the jury may have to be excluded because it does no more than show a disposition to commit the kind of crime charged.

Relevant for a further wholly independent reason

No special difficulty is presented by cases in which evidence which incidentally shows bad disposition is admissible for some wholly independent reason, as where it is proved that a robber made a "get away" in a car and evidence is adduced to show that the person charged with the robbery had previously stolen the car.

In *R.* v. *Lovegrove*[13] the accused was convicted of manslaughter by performing an illegal operation on Mrs. P. Mr. P said that he had been given the accused's address by a woman who told him that the accused had performed an illegal operation on her. Lovegrove's defence was that the only time she had seen P was when he called at her flat to inquire about accommodation. It was held that the other woman had been

---

[11] [1894] A.C. 57, at p. 65.

[12] *Supra.*

[13] [1920] 3 K.B. 643.

properly allowed to give evidence about the operation performed on her by Lovegrove because it tended to confirm P's account of what was said at his first meeting with the accused.

In *R.* v. *Armstrong*[14] a solicitor was charged with murdering his wife by arsenical poisoning. The defence was that she had committed suicide. On arrest the accused was found to be in possession of a considerable quantity of arsenic. He said that he had bought it for the purpose of killing dandelions. Evidence that Armstrong had attempted to poison a man with arsenic some eight months after his wife's death was held to have been rightly admitted because it suggested that he was lying when he said that he had purchased the poison for an innocent purpose.

The evidence received over objections in the above two cases certainly showed a disposition on the part of the accused to commit the crimes charged, but, by means of an argument which had nothing to do with disposition, it tended to confirm P's testimony in *R.* v. *Lovegrove*, and to cast doubt on the accused's statement in *R.* v. *Armstrong*.

Disposition of particular relevance

What has given rise to difficulty is the existence of a number of cases in which evidence tending to show a disposition to commit the kind of crime charged has been admitted although it was not relevant for a wholly independent reason, but was particularly relevant either because it showed a disposition to commit the kind of crime charged in a particular way (i.e. according to a particular *modus operandi*), or because it showed a disposition to commit the crime charged against a particular person (e.g. sex offences against the same girl or boy), or on account of some other item of evidence in the case, or because of its tendency to rebut a defence available to the accused. In most instances there is a further reason for admitting the evidence. The argument is not the direct one "A is guilty of the crime charged because he is the kind of man who would commit that offence in this kind of way", but the accused's disposition always forms a link in the chain of inference. An example is "A alleges that he accidentally stumbled against his wife with the result that she fell into the water and was drowned; the similar fact evidence suggests that A is prone to fake 'accidents' of this sort; therefore Mrs. A's death was not accidental".

---

[14] [1922] 2 K.B. 555.

It has become customary to group these decisions together under specific headings based upon the particular issue to which the evidence of conduct on other occasions was relevant. We propose to follow this course, subject to the caveat that it must not be supposed that there is a closed list of the issues on which, or the situations in which, similar fact evidence is admissible.

Of course there must always be some evidence other than the similar fact evidence connecting the accused with the crime charged. This other evidence may take the form of direct testimony concerning his participation in the events in issue, or of circumstantial evidence showing opportunity, preparation, motive and the like. When the similar fact evidence takes the form of a *modus operandi* it must resemble that alleged against the accused on the occasion under investigation in respects which are significant in the sense that they are unusual, suggesting a particular technique or, as it is sometimes put, a "hall mark".

> "For instance, while it would certainly not be enough to identify the culprit in a series of burglaries that he climbed in through a ground floor window, the fact that he left the same humorous limerick on the walls of the sitting room, or an esoteric symbol written in lipstick on the mirror, might well be enough.[15]"

A propensity to take girls for a drive in a car after a dance and the fact that each alleges that improper advances were made to her in the car are not sufficiently unusual matters to justify the reception of the evidence of one girl concerning an indecent assault or a charge of rape of the other or *vice versa*[16]. The argument justifying the reception of the similar fact evidence in the cases mentioned below is not merely that coincidences are rare, but also that a very rare coincidence must be assumed before the accused can be acquitted if the similar fact evidence is accepted.

In some of these cases the indictment contained a number of counts. When this happens, the fact that the evidence on each count is inadmissible on the others may be a ground for the exercise of the judge's discretion in favour of separate trials, but it is sometimes thought to be sufficient to direct the jury to

---

[15] Lord HAILSHAM in *Boardman* v. *Director of Public Prosecutions*, [1975] A.C. 421, at p. 454.

[16] *R.* v. *Wilson* (1973), 58 Cr. App. Rep. 169.

disregard the evidence on the other counts when considering each of them. Even when the evidence on each count is admissible on the others, the jury must be instructed to consider each count separately, and it will often be necessary for the judge to tell them that, when considering later counts, they should only have regard to the evidence on the earlier ones on which they have found the accused guilty[17].

Negativing accident

In *Makin* v. *A.-G. for New South Wales*[18], a husband and wife were charged with the murder of a baby. They received it from its parents for a small sum of money, stating that they wished to bring it up because they had lost their own child. The body of the baby was found buried in the back yard of a house occupied by the accused. Had the evidence gone no further, it is very doubtful whether there would have been sufficient material before the jury to negative the hypothesis that the baby met its death through natural causes, and that the accused had done nothing more heinous than to bury it irregularly. There was, however, evidence that the bodies of other babies, formerly taken in for small premiums, were found buried in the yards of houses occupied by the accused; this evidence was held to be admissible, and the accused were convicted. The convictions were upheld by the Privy Council, on the ground that the evidence had been rightly admitted to rebut the suggestion that the child's death was accidental, in the sense that it was not caused by the conduct of the Makins. This case can be regarded either as one in which the conduct on other occasions was admitted for a reason wholly independent of its tendency to show bad disposition, i.e. the improbability of so many babies dying from natural causes and being buried in houses occupied at different times by the Makins, or else as one in which the evidence was relevant because of the similarity of the technique it suggested to that alleged against the Makins in respect of the crime charged.

In *R.* v. *Smith*[19], the accused was charged with murdering Bessie Munday, a woman with whom he had gone through a bigamous ceremony of marriage. She had died in a bath after insuring her life in his favour. The circumstances in which her

---

[17] *Harris* v. *Director of Public Prosecutions,* [1952] A.C. 694; [1952] 1 All E.R. 1044; *cf. R.* v. *Robinson,* [1953] 2 All E.R. 334.

[18] [1894] A.C. 57.

[19] (1914), 11 Cr. App. Rep. 229.

body was found were consistent with death in consequence of an epileptic fit—a hypothesis which Smith did much to foster. The prosecution was able to prove that he had gone through ceremonies of marriage with two other women, who had also died in their baths in circumstances consistent with epilepsy, and that, in their cases too, he stood to gain financially from their deaths. This evidence was admitted and Smith was convicted. The conviction was affirmed by the Court of Criminal Appeal.

> "That the same accident should repeatedly occur to the same person is unusual, especially so when it confers a benefit on him."[20]

Negativing ignorance or mistake

In *R.* v. *Francis*[1], the accused had been convicted of obtaining an advance from a pawnbroker by false pretences concerning the quality of a ring. His defence was that he did not know that the ring was worthless. The Court for Crown Cases Reserved held that evidence had been rightly received concerning the obtaining of advances by similar means from other pawnbrokers shortly before the occasion covered by the indictment.

> "It is not conclusive, for a man may be many times under a similar mistake, or may many times be the dupe of another; but it is less likely that he should be so often, than once, and every circumstance which shows that he was not under a mistake on any of these occasions strengthens the presumption that he was not on the last."[2]

Negativing innocent association

A common defence to a criminal charge, especially if it is a charge of a sexual crime, is innocent association. The contention is that, although the opportunity of committing the offence existed, advantage was not taken of that opportunity.

In *R.* v. *Ball*[3], a brother and sister were charged with incest during various periods in 1910. It was proved that they occupied the same bedroom at the material times, but the house was a small one and it is possible that, if there had been no further evidence, the jury would not have considered that incest had been proved beyond reasonable doubt. The trial

---

[20] *Per* A. T. LAWRENCE, J., in *R.* v. *Bond,* [1906] 2 K.B. 389, at pp. 420–1.

[1] (1874), L.R. 2 C.C.R. 128.

[2] COLERIDGE, J.

[3] [1911] A.C. 47.

judge admitted evidence showing that the accused had cohabited as man and wife at an earlier period when they had had a child. The House of Lords held that the judge acted rightly because the evidence tended to "establish the guilty relations between the parties and the existence of a sexual passion between them as elements in proving that they had illicit connection in fact on or between the dates charged."[4]

Evidence of inclination is used to supplement evidence of opportunity in many cases of sexual or homosexual offences alleged to have been committed by the accused with a particular girl or boy; it is also frequently employed on the issue of adultery in the divorce court.

In *R.* v. *Sims*[5], the accused was charged with sodomy and gross indecency with four men. It was held that the evidence of each accuser was admissible on the counts concerning the others.

> "The judge was right to try all the four cases together, because the fact was that not one, but four men, who admittedly had gone to the prisoner's house to spend the evening on different occasions, all said exactly the same advances had been made to them by the prisoner, and that exactly the same acts had been committed on them, which tended to show that the association which the prisoner had with these men was a guilty one and not an innocent one. His defence was that he used to invite these young men to have a game of cards and to sit with him in his cottage. The answer that the prosecution made was that in every one of these cases, although the prisoner said that each young man came to him innocently, each young man alleged that the prisoner had committed offences on him. On these grounds the Court held that the evidence was admissible."[6]

Proof of identity where evidence is circumstantial

In *R.* v. *Straffen*[7], the accused was charged with the murder of Linda Bowyer, a little girl who had undoubtedly been strangled. Her body had been left near a road where it would soon be found, and there had been no sexual interference. Straffen had escaped from Broadmoor, and there was no doubt

---

[4] Lord LOREBURN.

[5] [1946] K.B. 531; [1946] 1 All E.R. 697.

[6] Lord GODDARD, C.J., in *R.* v. *Hall,* [1952] 1 K.B. 302, at pp. 305–6; [1952] 1 All E.R. 66, at p. 68.

[7] [1952] 2 Q.B. 911; see also *R.* v. *Morris* (1970), 54 Cr. App. Rep. 69.

that he could have been the culprit, as he was seen to pass near the spot where the body was found. This was, however, true of several other people. Straffen had previously confessed to the murder by strangulation of two other little girls, although he had not been convicted of these offences because he was found to be unfit to plead when put up for trial. The circumstances in which Linda Bowyer met her death were strikingly similar to those in which the other little girls were killed, and the trial judge held that evidence of the other killings was admissible. Straffen was convicted, and the judge's decision to admit the evidence was upheld by the Court of Criminal Appeal.

In this case, as in all those in which similar fact evidence is used circumstantially to single out the accused from others who might have committed the offence, the argument is a direct one from such evidence, via the disposition to the facts and the accused's guilt of the crime charged.

Negativing mistaken identification

Evidence of obtaining by false pretences by a technique similar to the pretence charged has been admitted to confirm the prosecutor's identification of the accused as one of the people who made the pretence to him[8]. But the most controversial case on the subject of the admissibility of evidence of disposition to negative mistaken identification is *Thompson* v. *R.*[9] Thompson was convicted of gross indecency with two boys. The acts of which complaint was made were alleged to have occurred on 16th March, and the person who committed them was alleged to have made a further appointment with the boys for the 19th. The police were informed in the meantime, and they kept watch with one of the boys at the meeting place—a public lavatory. The boys pointed Thompson out to the police and, from the first, the only defence raised was an alibi: "You have got the wrong man." It was held that, having regard to the special nature of the defence, evidence had been rightly admitted of the discovery of powder puffs on the accused's person and of indecent photographs in his lodging. To quote from the speech of Lord FINLAY:

> "The whole question is as to the identity of the person who came to the spot on the 19th with the person who committed the acts on the 16th. What was done on the 16th

[8] *R.* v. *Giovannone* (1960), 45 Cr. App. Rep. 31.
[9] [1918] A.C. 221.

shows that the person who did it was a person with abnormal propensities of this kind. The possession of the articles tends to show that the person who came on the 19th, the prisoner, had abnormal propensities of the same kind. The criminal of the 16th and the prisoner had this feature in common, and it appears to me that the evidence which is objected to afforded some evidence tending to show the probability of the truth of the boy's story as to identity."[10]

Two of the Law Lords appear to have regarded the fact that the boys deposed to the appointment of the 19th as crucial to their decision, and it certainly added considerably to the strength of the evidence of the finding of the powder puffs and photographs. A considerable coincidence had to be supposed if the boys' identification of Thompson as the criminal of the 16th were to be regarded as mistaken for homosexuals are probably not a particularly large class, and, if the boys were mistaken, it would be necessary to assume that a second homosexual appeared at the same time and place where the criminal had said he would be. It has, however, since been suggested in the Court of Appeal that the actual conclusion in *Thompson's* case might be different to-day on account of the change of attitude towards homosexuality[11]; but the relevance of this fact to the coincidence which would have to be assumed if the boys had "got the wrong man" is not obvious. Perhaps the Court of Appeal had in mind the following observations of Lord SUMNER in *Thompson's* case:

> "Persons who commit the offences now under consideration seek the habitual gratification of a particular perverted lust, which not only takes them out of the class of ordinary men gone wrong, but stamps them with the hall-mark of a specialised and extraordinary class as much as if they carried on their bodies some physical peculiarity."

Having been used to support a very broad alternative *ratio decidendi* in *R.* v. *Sims*[12], to the effect that, regardless of any question of similarity of technique, evidence that the accused is a homosexual is always admissible on a charge of homosexuality, these observations were treated as obsolete by the House

---

[10] [1918] A.C. 221, at pp. 225–6.

[11] *R.* v. *Morris* (1970), 54 Cr. App. Rep. 69, at p. 79.

[12] p.259, *ante*.

of Lords in *Boardman* v. *Director of Public Prosecutions*[13], a decision which had, to a large extent, been anticipated by that in *Director of Public Prosecutions* v. *Kilbourne*[14].

Supporting the testimony of a prosecution witness in the case of a bare denial

Boardman, the head of a language school, was convicted of attempted buggery with S, a pupil, and of inciting H, another pupil, to commit buggery. In each case his defence consisted of a denial that the alleged incidents took place. There was no question of mistaken identification, innocent association or alibi. Nonetheless the trial judge had held that H's evidence was admissible on the count concerning S, and *vice versa*. This was because the evidence of each resembled that of the other in that it alleged an invitation by a middle aged man to an adolescent to play the active role in buggery. Boardman appealed unsuccessfully to the Court of Appeal and House of Lords. In the House of Lords stress was laid on the fact that there were other striking similarities in the evidence of S and H concerning the time at which, and the methods by which (quiet nocturnal rousing in the dormitory) advances were made to them.

Having disapproved the broad *radio decidendi* of *R*. v. *Sims*, the House of Lords upheld that decision, not only as a case in which the similar fact evidence had been rightly admitted to rebut the defence of innocent association, but also as a decision based on the following ground stated in the judgment of Lord GODDARD, C.J.:

> "The probative force of all the acts together is much greater than one alone; for whereas the jury might think one man might be telling an untruth, three or four are hardly likely to tell the same untruth unless they were conspiring together."[15]

Provided there is the requisite degree of similarity, similar fact evidence is admissible for the purpose of corroborating or confirming the testimony of a prosecution witness whatever the nature of the defence may be.

---

13 [1975] A.C. 421; [1974] 3 All E.R. 887.

14 P. 119, *ante*.

15 [1946] K.B. 531, at p. 540.

The proviso is important for, to quote Lord WILBERFORCE:

> "The basic principle must be that the admission of similar fact evidence (of the kind now in question) is exceptional and requires a strong degree of probative force. This probative force is derived, if at all, from the circumstance that the facts testified to by the several witnesses bear to each other such a striking similarity that they must, when judged by experience and common sense, either all be true, or have arisen from a cause common to the witnesses or be pure coincidence."[16]

The jury had been warned about the danger of a conspiracy between the prosecution witnesses and the House of Lords rejected the hypothesis of a coincidence.

Effect on previous cases

The repudiation by the House of Lords of Lord SUMNER's observations about homosexuals and the recognition that similar fact evidence may be admissible to support or corroborate the testimony of a prosecution witness when the defence consists of a bare denial, suggest that at least one decision is questionable, and that at least one dictum may require consideration.

In *R.* v. *King*[17] convictions of sexual offences against boys were upheld by the Court of Appeal in spite of the fact that the accused had been asked in cross-examination whether he was a homosexual, a question which received an affirmative answer. The evidence of homosexuality to confirm the Crown witnesses' testimony was thus merely general.

In *R.* v. *Chandor*[18] a Croydon schoolmaster was charged with gross indecency with three of his pupils, A, B and C. C alleged that the incident in which he was concerned took place in the Lake District, and the accused denied that he met C on the occasion in question. A and B testified to incidents in Croydon; so far as these were concerned, the defence was that, though the meetings occurred, nothing improper took place at them. The accused was convicted, but the convictions were quashed by the Court of Criminal Appeal because the jury had not been

---

[16] [1975] A.C. 421, at p. 444.

[17] [1967] 2 Q.B. 338; [1967] 1 All E.R. 379; *cf. R.* v. *Horwood,* [1970] 1 Q.B. 133; [1969] 3 All E.R. 1156.

[18] [1959] 1 Q.B. 545; [1959] 1 All E.R. 702; see also *R.* v. *Flack,* [1969] 2 All E.R. 784.

directed that the evidence of A and B was irrelevant to the question whether C was telling the truth about the meeting in the Lake District. The actual decision may well have been right because there is nothing in the report suggesting striking similarities in the evidence of A, B and C; but the judgment of the Court of Appeal stated in general terms that "Evidence that an offence was committed by the appellant against one boy in Croydon could not be evidence that he met another boy in the Lake District and committed an offence there." What, it may be asked, would have been the position if the evidence of the three boys had been that the accused wore the ceremonial head-dress of a Red Indian chief on each occasion[19]? Even then a pedant might urge that, although, provided there was no question of a conspiracy between them, the evidence would show that offences were committed against A, B and C, it would not tend to show that the offence against C was committed in the Lake District.

Subsequent cases

Director of Public Prosecutions v. *Boardman* decided that, given the requisite degree of "striking similarity", similar fact evidence is admissible to confirm the testimony of a Crown witness irrespective of considerations of the nature of the defence. The question naturally arises whether striking similarity may not suffice whatever the purpose of adducing the evidence may be, and the answer given by SCARMAN, L.J., was that it does.[20] This means that we may hear less in the future of the separate heads of admissibility of similar fact evidence such as those discussed above. If there is striking similarity, properly understood to mean similarity of a kind showing an underlying unity in, or nexus between, the similar fact evidence and the facts charged, it may be unnecessary to have regard to the particular defences available to the accused. Yet it would be premature to dismiss the heads of admissibility because they draw attention to the fact that, though striking similarity is always a sufficient condition of admissibility, it is not always a necessary one. Something less may suffice to make evidence of disposition admissible as in *Thompson* v. *R.*[1], where the

---

[19] Per Lord HAILSHAM in *Boardman* v. *Director of Public Prosecutions,* [1975] A.C. 421, at p. 454.

[20] *R.* v. *Scarrott,* [1978] Q.B. 1016, at p. 1021.

[1] P. 260, *supra*.

accused's general disposition was highly relevant to negative mistaken identification on the particular facts.

Six of the decisions of the Court of Appeal on the subject since *Director of Public Prosecutions* v. *Boardman*, and up to the end of 1979, were concerned with sexual offences in which the question was whether the evidence was admissible to confirm the testimony of a Crown witness[2]. A reminder of the need for realism in the application of the requirement of striking similarity, indicating that it means similarity in significant or unusual respects, has had to be given on several occasions:

> "We cannot think that two or more alleged offences of buggery or attempted buggery committed in bed at the residence of the alleged offender with boys to whom he had offered shelter can be said to have been committed in a uniquely or strikingly similar manner."[3]

Of the other post-Boardman decisions up to the end of 1979, one was concerned with proof of identity by circumstantial evidence[4], one with proof of corruption by such means[5], and one with negativing accident or mistake in a shoplifting case where the goods for which the accused did not pay had found their way from the wire basket provided by the shop into his own bag[6]. Only in the last of these was the old terminology used.

Possession of the instruments of crime

On charges of gross indecency with boys proof has been permitted of the accused's possession of indecent photographs on the ground that they might have been used as a means of incitement[7]. Similarly evidence has been admitted of the accused's possession of apparatus which might have been used in the robbery charged[8], and, since *Boardman's* case the

---

[2] *R.* v. *Tricoglus* (1976), 65 Cr. App. Rep. 16; *R.* v. *Johannsen* (1977), 65 Cr. App. Rep. 101; *R.* v. *Novak* (1976), 65 Cr. App. Rep. 107; *R.* v. *Scarrott,* [1978] Q.B. 1016; *R.* v. *Inder* (1978), 67 Cr. App. Rep. 143; *R.* v. *Clarke* (1978), 67 Cr. App. Rep. 398.

[3] BRIDGE, L.J. in *R.* v. *Novak, supra* at p. 111. See also *R.* v. *Inder, supra.*

[4] *R.* v. *Mansfield,* [1978] 1 All E.R. 134.

[5] *R.* v. *Rance* and *Herron* (1975), 62 Cr. App. Rep. 118.

[6] *R.* v. *Seaman* (1978), 67 Cr. App. Rep. 234.

[7] *R.* v. *Twiss,* [1918] 2 K.B. 853; *R.* v. *Gillingham,* [1939] 4 All E.R. 122.

[8] *R.* v. *Reading,* [1966] 1 All E.R. 521.

accused's possession of a stolen Access card has been held to have been rightly proved because it was the kind of document used by him in the course of obtaining goods by deception[9].

Judicial discretion

The existence of a discretion to exclude evidence on the ground that, though legally admissible, its probative value is outweighed by its prejudicial propensity, recognised for some time in similar fact cases[10], was reaffirmed by the House of Lords in *R.* v. *Sang*[11]. A case in which the Court of Criminal Appeal held that it should have been exercised was one in which the accused was charged with indecent assault upon a boy of five and indecent exposure. Ordinarily the evidence of the one would be inadmissible on the charge of the other, but the alleged offences occurred within a quarter of an hour, or less, of each other and the evidence of each may have been admissible on the charge of the other because the accused was acting under a continuous impulse or sexual excitement[12].

Civil Cases

There are undeniably dicta favouring the view that the rules of law considered in this and the preceding article apply to civil as well as criminal cases[13], but the point has never been fully argued, and it is possible that there is no special rule governing the admissibility of similar fact evidence in civil proceedings. Civil trials are not dominated, as criminal trials are very properly dominated, by the need to guard against prejudice to the accused. In *Mood Music Publications, Ltd.* v. *De Wolfe Ltd*[14], a copyright case in which the plaintiffs were held entitled to adduce evidence of other infringements by the defendants similar to that alleged, Lord DENNING expressed the view that all that was required in a civil case was that the similar fact evidence should be relevant and not oppressive or unfair to the other side. Evidence of this kind is liable to produce side issues and it is possible that this was the point which his Lordship had in mind when stating these concluding qualifications.

---

[9] *R.* v. *Mustafa* (1976), 65 Cr. App. Rep. 26.
[10] *See Noor Mohamed* v. *R.*, [1949] A.C. 182, at p. 192.
[11] [1979] 2 All E.R. 1222.
[12] *R.* v. *Fitzpatrick*, [1972] 3 All E.R. 840.
[13] *Blake* v. *Albion Life Assurance Society* (1878), 4 C.P.D. 94, at p. 102.
[14] [1976] Ch. 119; [1976] 1 All E.R. 463.

ART. 77.—Evidence of character at common law

1. When evidence of character is given in a criminal case, it must usually relate to the general reputation of the person whose character is in question, and not to the witness's opinion of that person's disposition.

2. In criminal cases, although the prosecution may not adduce evidence in-chief of the accused's bad character for the purpose of proving his bad disposition, and hence that he is probably guilty of the crime charged, the accused may adduce evidence in-chief of his good character for the purpose of proving his good disposition and hence that he is probably innocent; it then becomes possible for the prosecution to rebut the evidence of good character with evidence of bad character.

3. In criminal cases the admissibility of the evidence of the character of third parties (including the prosecutor) generally depends on relevancy.

4. In civil cases, evidence of the defendant's character may not be given in-chief so as to support an argument that he either did or did not do the act in respect of which he is being sued.

5. Evidence of the character of the plaintiff or a third party may be adduced in-chief by the defendant in a civil case whenever their characters are in issue.

Explanation:

(1) *Character as meaning reputation in criminal cases*

The leading case on evidence of character at a criminal trial is *R.* v. *Rowton*[15]. Rowton was charged with an indecent assault upon a man. He called a witness to speak to his good moral character, and the prosecution called a witness to give evidence in rebuttal. In reply to a question concerning Rowton's character for decency and morality of conduct, the witness called by the prosecution said:

> "I know nothing of the neighbourhood's opinion because I was only a boy at school when I knew him; but my own opinion, and that of my brothers who were also pupils of his, is that his character is that of a man capable of the grossest indecency and the most flagrant immorality."

[15] (1865), Le & Ca. 520.

Rowton was convicted, but his conviction was quashed by the Court for Crown Cases Reserved because the prosecution's evidence of character had been given in the wrong form. The witness should have been asked about the accused's reputation for morality and it would at once have become plain that he was not competent to speak on that subject.

One way of stating the effect of this decision is to say that in the law of evidence, "character" usually means reputation. When a witness is asked about a person's character with regard to such matters as honesty and morality, it must be made plain to him that he is being asked for what he knows about that person's reputation with regard to these matters, not for his opinion concerning that person's disposition to act honestly or morally.

(2) *The basic rules governing evidence of character in criminal cases*

The general rule mentioned in this article that the prosecution cannot open with evidence in-chief of the accused's bad character follows from the rule with regard to similar fact evidence mentioned in Article 75. If a Crown witness were allowed to testify to the accused's reputation as a man likely to have committed the offence charged, the purpose of the evidence could only be to support an argument that the accused is probably guilty because he is that kind of man; if evidence of specific misconduct is inadmissible in support of such an argument, it would be absurd to allow the much less cogent evidence of character in support of the same contention.

The accused's evidence of character will usually take the form of the evidence of witnesses called by him, but it may include his own testimony. When the accused's character evidence takes this latter form, it is difficult to see how it can relate to his reputation, because a person's reputation is essentially what people say about him when he isn't there. The accused's evidence of his own character usually refers to the fact that he has led a good life, never been in trouble, and done a number of good acts. As the accused could not give evidence on his own behalf when *R.* v. *Rowton* was decided, it is hardly surprising that the Court for Crown Cases Reserved did not consider the applicability of their decision to such evidence.

The prosecution's right to give evidence in rebuttal was recognised in Rowton's case. It may include evidence of the accused's previous convictions[16].

Further rules.—The character of the accused is deemed to be indivisible. This means that, if he is charged with an indecent assault upon a woman, evidence of his previous convictions for offences involving dishonesty may be given in answer to his evidence (or that of one of his witnesses) of a good character for chastity[17].

The prosecution can only give evidence of the accused's bad character in order to rebut evidence of good character. The fact that the accused attacks the character of the prosecutor and his witnesses does not entitle the prosecutor to retaliate with evidence of the accused's criminal record. Thus in *R.* v. *Butterwasser*[18], the accused was charged and convicted of wounding with intent to do grievous bodily harm. He did not give evidence himself, but caused the Crown witnesses to be cross-examined on their bad records for crimes of violence. Counsel for the prosecution then read out a list of the accused's previous convictions for similar offences. Butterwasser successfully appealed to the Court of Criminal Appeal because he had not put his character in issue, he had simply put the character of the Crown witnesses in issue. Had he given evidence himself, he would have been liable to be cross-examined about his previous convictions, because he had thrown his shield away under the provisions of the Criminal Evidence Act 1898, discussed in Article 80, but Butterwasser did not give evidence.

It has been said that

> ". . . Evidence of character, when properly admitted, goes to the credit of the witness concerned, whether the evidence disclosed good character or bad character, if the accused calls evidence of good character, and is shown by cross-examination to have a bad character, the jury may give this fact such weight as they think fit when assessing the general credibility of the accused."[19]

But, if the accused does not testify, his witnesses' evidence of his character must go directly to the probability of his innocence, and it has also been said that, when the accused does give

---

[16] *R.* v. *Redd,* [1923] 1 K.B. 104.

[17] *R.* v. *Winfield,* (1939) 4 All E.R. 164.

[18] [1947] K.B. 4; [1947] 2 All E.R. 415.

[19] *R.* v. *Richardson and Longman,* [1969] 1 Q.B. 299, at p. 311.

evidence of his own good character for the purpose of showing that it is unlikely that he committed the offence charged, he raises by way of defence an issue as to his character[20]. It seems that, when the accused testifies, evidence of his character goes both to his credibility and to his liability.

(3) *Evidence of the character of the prosecutor and other third parties in criminal cases*

When he testifies the prosecutor, like other Crown witnesses, cannot give evidence of his good character because it is irrelevant. Like all Crown witnesses he is liable to cross-examination to credit, and, subject to the exceptions mentioned on p. 91, his denial of imputations on his characters is final.

Generally speaking the accused cannot give or adduce evidence of the bad character of the prosecutor, but, at common law, the accused may give or adduce evidence of the prosecutrix's bad general reputation for chastity on charges of rape or indecent assault when consent is in issue[1]. The common law is now subject to s.2 of the Sexual Offences (Amendment) Act 1976 under which a person charged with rape and kindred offences can only give or adduce evidence of the complainant's sexual experience with other men with the leave of the judge and such leave may only be given on the ground of fairness to the defendant. Similar restrictions apply to the questioning of the complainant in cross-examination.

The character of third parties, including the prosecutor, may become relevant as the facts of a case are unfolded. Evidence of the deceased's bad character for violence may be given on a murder charge in which self-defence or provocation is pleaded, and, provided it is relevant, there seems to be no reason why the evidence should not consist of specific instances as well as reputation. In *R.* v. *Wood*[2] it was held that where the defendant to a charge of robbery alleged that the prosecutor had made indecent overtures to him, a witness could not be called to prove the prosecutor's good reputation for decency. No reasons were given for the decision. In the circumstances the evidence of reputation would appear to have been relevant.

---

[20] *Maxwell* v. *Director of Public Prosecutions,* [1935] A.C. 309, at p. 319; *R.* v. *Bryant* and *Oxley,* [1979] Q.B. 108; [1978] 2 All E.R. 689.

[1] *R.* v. *Clarke* (1817), 2 Stark. 241.

[2] [1951] 2 All E.R. 112.

(4) *Evidence of the defendant's character in civil cases*

In civil cases the plaintiff may not lead evidence of the defendant's character for the purpose of supporting an argument that he is the kind of man who would do a certain act. This is on account of the rule stated in Article 75 if it applies to civil cases. If it does not apply, the adduction of the evidence would be unfair or oppressive[3]. There is a difference between civil and criminal cases so far as evidence of the defendant's character is concerned, because in the former the defendant may not adduce evidence in-chief of his good character[4].

(5) *Evidence of the character of the plaintiff and third parties in civil cases*

Evidence of the plaintiff's character may be given when it is in issue, and when it affects either liability or the measure of damages. The plaintiff's character is in issue at several different stages of a libel action. If justification is pleaded, his character is in issue on the question of liability, and the type of evidence which may be given depends on the terms of the alleged libel. The plaintiff's character is always in issue in a libel action on the question of damages. The defendant may seek to have the damages reduced by tendering evidence to the effect that the plaintiff's reputation is not worth heavy damages. In such a case, the defendant's evidence concerning the plaintiff's character must be confined to reputation; he cannot give evidence of rumours about the plaintiff, or of specific acts of misconduct on the part of the plaintiff[5], but he can prove the plaintiff's relevant previous convictions[6] provided they are not "spent" within the meaning of the Rehabilitation of Offenders Act 1974 discussed in the next article. When justification is not pleaded, the defendant is required to give the plaintiff particulars of the matters on which he intends to call evidence of character[7]. If such particulars are not furnished seven days before trial, the plaintiff may not call the evidence without the leave of the judge. When the particulars have not been given, he may not cross-examine in order to mitigate damages on the

---

[3] P. 266, *supra*.

[4] *A.-G.* v. *Bowman* (1791), 2 Bos. & P. 532 n.

[5] *Scott* v. *Sampson* (1882), 8 Q.B.D. 491; *Plato Films, Ltd.* v. *Speidel*, [1961] A.C. 1090; [1961] 1 All E.R. 876.

[6] *Goody* v. *Odhams Press, Ltd.*, [1967] 1 Q.B. 333; [1966] 3 All E.R. 369.

[7] R.S.C. Ord. 82, r. 7.

matters not mentioned in the particulars, but the questions may, nonetheless, be admissible as part of the cross-examination of the plaintiff as to credit[8].

The character of a third party may occasionally be in issue in a civil case, as where the defendant to an action under the Law Reform Act 1934 contends that the deceased's damages for loss of expectation of life should be reduced because he was a criminal with the result that his life was not a happy one[9]; but there is no point in going into detail because no special rules of evidence are involved.

ART. 78.—The previous convictions of the parties at common law

1. In civil and criminal cases, the fact that a party has been convicted may be proved in-chief whenever it is in issue or, subject to the rule stated in Article 75, relevant to the issue.
2. In civil cases, either party may be asked about his convictions in cross-examination to credit.
3. In criminal cases, evidence of the accused's previous convictions may always be given after verdict as a matter affecting sentence.
4. The rules concerning the admissibility of convictions in civil cases are subject to the provisions of the Rehabilitation of Offenders Act 1974 about spent convictions.

Explanation: An example of a civil case in which a conviction would be in issue would be a libel action alleging that the plaintiff had been convicted. A conviction could also be in issue in an action for malicious prosecution. In *R.* v. *B.*, *R.* v. *A.*[10] it was held that the previous convictions of a boy under 14 at the time of the offence might be proved in order to rebut the presumption that he lacked criminal capacity as it was relevant to the issue of his ability to distinguish good from evil.

In civil cases, a party may be cross-examined about his convictions, not only when they are in issue, but also as a matter affecting his credit. If denied in cross-examination to credit, the convictions may be proved in rebuttal. As the

---

[8] *Hobbs* v. *Tinling*, [1929] 2 K.B. 1.
[9] *Burns* v. *Edman*, [1970] 1 All E.R. 886.
[10] [1979] 3 All E.R. 460.

accused was an incompetent witness at common law in a criminal case, his liability to cross-examination on previous convictions is entirely statutory.

It is the duty of a police officer to prepare a proof of evidence concerning the accused's record to be given in the event of a conviction. The proof should contain information concerning the accused's age, education, employment and character as known personally to the officer, and should have attached to it details of previous convictions, if any[11]. The convictions need not be formally proved, but, if they are denied by the accused, the judge may require strict proof.

Once a conviction is "spent" within the meaning of the Rehabilitation of Offenders Act 1974, no evidence is admissible in civil proceedings, and no question may be put in such proceedings, to show that the rehabilitated person has been charged with, or has been convicted of the offence which was the subject of the conviction, unless permitted by the judge on the ground that justice cannot otherwise be done. Convictions resulting in imprisonment for life or more than thirty months are outside the Act. In other cases a conviction becomes spent after a specified period from its date, ten years when the sentence is one of imprisonment for thirty months or more than six months, seven years when there is a prison sentence of six months or less, five years when a fine is imposed and one year in a case where there has been a discharge. A spent conviction may, where relevant, be pleaded in justification of a libel, or in support of a plea of privilege or fair comment, but the plea of justification may, like the other pleas, be defeated by proof of malice.

The above provisions do not apply to criminal proceedings, but a practice direction requires reference to spent convictions to be as minimal as possible.

ART. 79.—Statutes permitting evidence in-chief in criminal cases of the accused's misconduct on other occasions, bad character and previous convictions

Under exceptional statutory provisions, applying only to criminal cases, evidence may be given in-chief of the accused's

[11] Practice Direction, [1966] 2 All E.R. 929.

misconduct on other occasions, his bad character and previous convictions, although it does no more than show bad disposition.

Explanation: The most important statutory provision concerning evidence in-chief is s. 27 (3) of the Theft Act 1968. It relates to charges of handling stolen goods, but does not apply where the accused is charged with any other offence. In order to prove guilty knowledge or belief, the prosecution may

(a) prove that the accused had in his possession, or had undertaken or assisted in the detention, removal, disposal or realisation of stolen goods from any theft which took place within a year of the offence charged; or

(b) prove that the accused has, within five years of the offence charged, been convicted of theft or handling stolen goods.

A condition precedent to the admissibility of the evidence under either head is that evidence should have been given that the accused had or arranged to have in his possession the goods which are the subject-matter of the charge, or that he undertook or assisted in, or arranged to undertake or assist in, the retention, removal, disposal or realisation of those goods.

In order that evidence of the previous convictions for theft or handling should be given under head (b) above, the prosecution must have given seven days written notice of intention to prove them.

The court has a discretion to reject evidence under either of the above heads although it is technically admissible[12].

Under s. 1 (2) of the Official Secrets Act 1911, evidence of the accused's "known character as proved" may be given in order to prove a purpose prejudicial to the state. There is not much authority on the subject, but it seems that the prosecution might lead evidence of the accused's misconduct on other occasions in cases falling within the statute. The section plainly allows evidence of the accused's bad character to be given in-chief, and it is possible that the evidence may take the form of a statement of the witness's opinion of the accused's disposition, based on observed facts, as well as a statement by the witness concerning the accused's reputation. Evidence of the accused's

[12] *R.* v. *Herron,* [1967] 1 Q.B. 107; [1966] 2 All E.R. 26.

previous convictions may also be given in-chief under this section.

Section 15 of the Prevention of Crimes Act 1871 provides that the accused's "known character as proved" may be used as evidence of intent on charges of loitering with intent to commit an arrestable offence. Everything said in the previous paragraph with regard to s. 1 (2) of the Official Secrets Act 1911 applies to this provision.

ART. 80.—**The cross-examination of the accused under the Criminal Evidence Act 1898**

In criminal cases, if the accused gives evidence, he may not be cross-examined about his other offences, previous convictions, or bad character, unless evidence of the previous offences or convictions about which he is asked would have been admissible in-chief, or unless he has thrown his shield away by putting his character in issue, by casting imputations on the character of the prosecutor or the witnesses for the prosecution, or by giving evidence against another person charged in the same proceedings[13].

Explanation: We saw in Article 25 how s. 1 (f) of the Criminal Evidence Act 1898 gives the accused a shield against cross-examination to credit which is particularly valuable to an accused with a criminal record. We also saw in Article 29 how s. 1 (e) of the Act prevents the accused from refusing to answer questions on the ground that the answer would incriminate him as to the offence charged.

It is now necessary to consider the interpretation of s. 1 (f). The subsection reads as follows:

> "When giving evidence, an accused person shall not be asked, and if asked shall not be required to answer, any question tending to show that he has committed or been convicted of or been charged with any offence other than that wherewith he is then charged, or is of bad character unless:

---

[13] The last four words were substituted for "with the same offence" by the Criminal Evidence Act 1979.

(i) the proof that he has committed or been convicted of such other offence is admissible evidence to show that he is guilty of the offence wherewith he is then charged;

(ii) he has personally or by his advocate asked questions of the witnesses for the prosecution with a view to establish his own good character, or has given evidence of his good character, or the nature or conduct of the defence is such as to involve imputations on the character of the prosecutor or the witnesses for the prosecution;

(iii) he has given evidence against any other person charged with the same offence."

It will be convenient to make some general observations before considering the situations in which the accused is liable to be cross-examined about his past offences and convictions. These observations concern the meaning of the words "tending to show", the meaning of "charged", the impropriety of questions concerning acquittals, even when the accused has thrown his shield away, and the existence of a judicial discretion to disallow cross-examination under s. 1 (f).

"Tending to show"

Section 1 (f) prohibits questions "tending to show" other offences or bad character. The word "show" means "make known to the tribunal of fact for the first time"; accordingly, if the accused has volunteered information in the course of his evidence in-chief which suggests that he has committed other offences or is of bad character, the case falls outside the statute, and the accused may be cross-examined with regard to the matter disclosed by him. The accused may also be cross-examined with regard to past offences, previous convictions, and bad character whenever they have been properly made the subject of the prosecution's evidence in-chief. The crucial time for determining whether the questions "tend to show" other offences or bad character is the moment at which it is sought to put them. If the jury have already been made aware of the questionable nature of the accused's past, the questions may be put although the case does not come within s. 1 (f) (i), (ii), or (iii). If the jury has not up to then been made aware of the accused's questionable past, the questions are only permissible if the case does come within these provisions.

The authority for the last paragraph is the view of the majority of the House of Lords in *Jones* v. *Director of Public*

Prosecutions[14]. Jones was charged with the murder of a girl guide. When first interrogated by the police, he set up an alibi to the effect that he was with relations at the time. This alibi could of course have been corroborated by the relations, but they did not corroborate it, and, at the trial, Jones set up an alibi to the effect that he was with a prostitute when the girl guide was murdered. It was obviously expedient for Jones to account for the change in his alibi, and he did so in the course of his evidence in-chief by saying that he had been in trouble before; he said that this accounted for his reluctance to give an alibi which could not be corroborated. He also deposed to a conversation which he had had with his wife on returning home on the night of the murder. He said that she had recriminated with him for going with a prostitute. This evidence was strikingly similar to that which Jones had given at an earlier trial for the rape of another girl guide. On that occasion he had set up a similar alibi and deposed to a similar conversation with his wife. He was cross-examined with regard to these similarities on the footing that it was an extraordinary coincidence that he should have an identical alibi for the two occasions on which he had been in trouble. The cross-examination was held to have been proper by the House of Lords and by the majority on the ground that, at the time it was administered, the jury knew that Jones had been in trouble and the question did not "tend to show" bad character.

In *R.* v. *Chitson*[15], the accused was charged with unlawful intercourse with B, a girl of fourteen. In her evidence in-chief, B said that Chitson had told her that he had done the same thing with H, another young girl. This evidence was relevant because it related to the means by which the accused was alleged to have encouraged B. It was not clear whether H was sixteen, in which case no offence would have been committed on her. The Court of Criminal Appeal upheld the propriety of the cross-examination of Chitson with regard to H and, in the light of the view of the majority of the House of Lords in Jones's case, it may be taken that the cross-examination was proper, whatever the age of H may have been, because the jury had already been made aware of the allegation concerning H.

---

[14] [1962] A.C. 635; [1962] 1 All E.R. 569, H.L.
[15] [1909] 2 K.B. 945.

"Charged"

The word "charged" in s. 1 (f) means "charged in court". Therefore it was held in *Stirland* v. *Director of Public Prosecutions*[16] that, even when the accused had given evidence of character by saying that he had never been "charged" before, the trial judge ought not to have allowed the prosecution to cross-examine the accused about an occasion on which he was suspected of dishonesty, i.e. "charged" by a former employer.

Acquittals

In *Maxwell* v. *Director of Public Prosecutions*[17], a doctor was charged with manslaughter in consequence of an illegal operation. He gave evidence of good character and was cross-examined about a previous charge at assizes which had resulted in an acquittal. His appeal to the House of Lords was allowed because the cross-examination was improper. This is an important decision on the structure of s. 1 (f). Maxwell had thrown his shield away, accordingly it might appear that questions about charges in court were permissible, whatever the result of the charge may have been. But it was held that the question must be relevant either to the issue of the accused's guilt, or else to his credit as a witness. The acquittal was irrelevant to guilt, because the accused must be assumed to have been innocent of the offence charged and it was equally irrelevant to credit for the same reason.

Discretion

Another respect in which the right to cross-examine is qualified is that of judicial discretion. Although the accused has thrown away his shield, and although the cross-examination would be relevant, the judge may disallow it if he thinks it would be unduly prejudicial.

Section 1(f) (i)

Section 1(f) (i) permits cross-examination about previous convictions and other offences when they may be proved in-chief. There are very few cases in which the accused's previous convictions may be proved in-chief, but, when this can be done, he may, if necessary, be cross-examined about them. Whenever evidence may be given in-chief of the details of the accused's offences, because it does more than show that he is

---

[16] [1944) A.C. 315; [1944] 2 All E.R. 13.

[17] [1935] A.C. 309.

the kind of man who would do the kind of thing charged, he may be cross-examined about them. The evidence will usually have been given in-chief by the prosecution, so the cross-examination will be proper without reference to s. 1 (f) (i).

Section 1 (f) (i) is confined to evidence tending to show that the accused has committed or been convicted of other offences. It does not permit cross-examination about a charge resulting in an acquittal, even if the charge is relevant to an issue raised by the defence. In *R.* v. *Cokar*[18], for instance, the accused, who was being tried for housebreaking, said that he did not know that it was no offence to break into a house in order to go to sleep. He was cross-examined about a previous charge and acquittal on the basis that he must have learnt this bit of law on that occasion and his conviction was quashed by the Court of Criminal Appeal because the cross-examination had infringed s. 1 (f).

Questions tending to show bad character are likewise inadmissible under s. 1(f)(i). They have to be justified under s. 1(f)(ii) or s. 1(f)(iii). Thus, on a charge of arson against a political agitator, it is improper to put to an accused who has not thrown his shield away questions suggesting that he has a disposition to resort to violence[19].

Section 1 (f) (ii)

It will be convenient to consider s. 1 (f) (ii) under two heads, cases in which the accused throws his shield away by putting his character in issue, and cases in which he throws his shield away by casting imputations on the character of the prosecutor or the witnesses for the prosecution.

(a) *Character.*—The accused gives evidence of character within the meaning of s. 1 (f) (ii) when, on a charge of theft by finding, he refers to his previous acts of honesty in returning lost property[20], or, when charged with speeding, says that he dislikes driving fast[1], or, if he says that he is a married man in regular employment[2]. The evidence of character may be given by the accused himself, or by his witnesses or it may be elicited from the witnesses for the prosecution. It covers evidence of

---

[18] [1960] 2 Q.B. 207.
[19] *Malindi* v. *R.*, [1967] 1 A.C. 439; [1966] 3 All E.R. 285.
[20] *R.* v. *Samuel* (1956), 40 Cr. App. Rep. 8.
[1] *R.* v. *Beecham,* [1921] 3 K.B. 464.
[2] *R.* v. *Coulman* (1927), 20 Cr. App. Rep. 106.

disposition as well as evidence tending to show that the accused has a good reputation[3]. In law the accused's character is indivisible. He cannot credit himself with a good character for chastity without running the risk of cross-examination concerning offences involving dishonesty[4].

"It is not implicit in an accusation of dishonesty that the accused is himself an honest man". Accordingly someone accused of stealing may, with impunity so far as his past is concerned, suggest to a Crown witness that others, not called, committed the crime[5].

(b) *Imputations.*—"Imputations" may be cast upon the prosecutor or his witnesses although it is not alleged that they committed a crime. In *R.* v. *Bishop*[6] a man over 21 charged with burglary sought to explain the presence of his fingerprints on articles in the room of the prosecutor, another man over 21, by the fact that they had had a consensual homosexual relationship, and it was held by the Court of Appeal that he had been properly cross-examined on his previous convictions for offences involving dishonesty.

Before the decision of the House of Lords in *Selvey* v. *Director of Public Prosecutions*[7] the authorities on the construction of the second half of s. 1 (f) (ii) were difficult to reconcile on one very important point. There were two schools of thought on the question whether the accused lost his shield if the imputations made on the character of the prosecutor or his witnesses were necessary for the proper development of the defence as distinct from a mere attack on the witnesses' credit. It is for practical purposes impossible to raise certain defences without making imputations on the character of witnesses for the prosecution. Examples of such defences are self defence, an allegation that the crime was committed by a prosecution witness and an allegation that money said to have been handed over in response to blackmail was in fact paid as "hush" money in respect of indecent overtures made to the accused by the prosecutor. An intermediate view was that, in such cases, the discretion to disallow cross-examination should, as a general rule, be exercised by the judge.

---

[3] *R.* v. *Dunkley,* [1927] 1 K.B. 323.
[4] *R.* v. *Winfield,* [1939] 4 All E.R. 164.
[5] *R.* v. *Lee,* [1976] 1 All E.R. 570.
[6] [1974] 2 All E.R. 1206.
[7] [1970] A.C. 304; [1968] 2 All E.R. 497.

Selvey was charged with buggery. Indecent photographs were found in his room, and there was medical evidence that the prosecutor had been sexually assaulted by someone on the day in question. Selvey's defence was that the prosecutor had told him that he had already "been on the bed" with a man for a pound and that he would do the same for him for a pound. According to Selvey it was annoyance at the rejection of this offer which had caused the prosecutor to dump the photographs on him. These were plainly imputations on the character of the prosecutor, and, equally plainly, they were essential for the development of the defence which Selvey was running. Nonetheless the trial judge allowed him to be cross-examined on his previous convictions for homosexual offences and he was convicted. Selvey's appeal against conviction was dismissed by the Court of Appeal and House of Lords.

Lord DILHORNE said that the cases establish the following propositions:

> 1. The words of the statute must be given their natural ordinary meaning;
>
> 2. The section permits cross-examination of the accused as to character both when imputations on the character of the prosecutor and his witnesses are cast to show their unreliability as witnesses independently of the evidence given by them and also when the casting of such imputations is necessary to enable the accused to establish his defence;
>
> 3. In rape cases the accused can allege consent without placing himself in peril of cross-examination;
>
> 4. If what is said amounts in reality to no more than a denial of the charge, expressed, it may be, in emphatic language, it should not be regarded as coming within the section[8].

The existence of a judicial discretion to prohibit cross-examination permitted by s. 1 (f) (ii) was recognised after full argument, but the existence of a general rule that it should be exercised in favour of the accused when the imputations were necessary for the proper development of his defence was denied.

The authorities before Selvey's case made it plain that the defence of consent to a charge of rape, even if accompanied by allegations of gross indecency on the part of the prosecutrix,

---

[8] [1970] A.C. 304, at p. 339.

did not deprive the accused of his shield[9]. It was suggested in the House of Lords that rape must, for this purpose, be regarded as *sui generis*, or, alternatively, that, as absence of consent is an essential ingredient of the charge, the accused must be allowed to allege consent with impunity.

The judge should always warn the accused when he is running the risk of cross-examination under s. 1 (f) (ii) and counsel for the prosecution must always apply to the judge for leave to cross-examine when he thinks that the case comes within the subsection. Furthermore, the judge must direct the jury that the cross-examination merely goes to the accused's credit and not to the probability of his guilt[10].

R. v. *Butterwasser*, discussed on p. 269, *ante*, serves as a reminder that, if the accused does not go into the witness box, his past record cannot be proved merely because the conduct of his defence has cast imputations on the character of the prosecutor or his witnesses.

Section 1 (f) (iii)

The test for determining whether one of two accused has "given evidence" against the other is the tendency of his testimony to undermine the other's defence. Accordingly if two people are jointly charged with stealing an article in circumstances in which the theft must have been effected by one or other or both of them, the mere denial of one that he had anything to do with taking the article will expose him to cross-examination under s. 1 (f) (iii)[11]. On the other hand it was held in *R.* v. *Bruce*[12] that, where one of several co-defendants to a charge of robbery swore that there had been a plan between them to commit the crime though he had withdrawn from it, another had not given evidence against him when he denied that there had been a plan because he also denied that there had been any robbery.

An accused against whom evidence has been given by his co-accused has a right to cross-examine him under s. 1 (f) (iii); the court has no discretion to prevent him because, so far as he is concerned, the co-accused is a witness for the prosecution[13].

---

[9] *R.* v. *Turner,* [1944] K.B. 463; [1944] 1 All E.R. 599.

[10] *R.* v. *Vickers,* [1972] Crim. L.R. 101; *R.* v. *Inder* (1977), 67 Cr. App. Rep. 143.

[11] *R.* v. *Davis,* [1975] 1 All E.R. 233.

[12] [1975] 3 All E.R. 277.

[13] *Murdoch* v. *Taylor,* [1965] A.C. 574; [1965] 1 All E.R. 406.

Even when not incriminated by his co-accused, an accused is entitled to cross-examine him, but the co-accused would then be protected by the main part of s. 1 (f).

It has been held that, when a case does not come within s. 1 (f) (iii), an accused who has cast imputations on a Crown witness can, at the discretion of the court, be cross-examined by a co-accused under s. 1 (f) (ii), and that, likewise at the discretion of the court, the prosecution may cross-examine under s. 1 (f) (iii) in a case falling within that subsection[14].

Evidence in rebuttal

If the accused were to deny a previous conviction in cross-examination, it could be proved against him in rebuttal. When he gives or adduces evidence of good character, evidence of bad character may be given in rebuttal. If, in cross-examination to the issue, the accused were to deny previous misconduct of which no evidence in-chief had been given, it is possible that the judge would allow evidence in rebuttal to be given[15] but, if the cross-examination were merely as to credit, the accused's answers would be final[16].

---

[14] *R.* v. *Lovett,* [1973] 1 All E.R. 744.
[15] Article 27.
[16] Article 25.

CHAPTER 13

Convictions, Judgments and other Findings as Evidence of the Facts on which they were Based

ART. 81.—Convictions, findings of adultery and findings of paternity as evidence in subsequent civil proceedings

1. In any civil proceedings, the fact that a person has been convicted of an offence is admissible in evidence for the purpose of proving that he committed that offence, and he must be taken to have done so unless the contrary is proved[1].

2. In any civil proceedings, (a) the fact that a person has been found guilty of adultery in any matrimonial proceedings, and (b) the fact that a person has been adjudged to be the father of a child in affiliation proceedings is admissible in evidence for the purpose of proving that he committed the adultery or was the father of the child, and he must be taken to have committed the adultery or to be the father of the child unless the contrary is proved[2].

3. In an action for libel or slander in which the question whether a person did or did not commit an offence is relevant, proof that a person stands convicted of that offence is conclusive evidence that he committed it[3].

---

[1] Civil Evidence Act 1968, s. 11.

[2] *Ibid.*, s. 12.

[3] *Ibid.*, s. 13.

4. Acquittals of crime and judgments in civil proceedings other than matrimonial and affiliation proceedings are inadmissible in subsequent civil proceedings as evidence of the innocence of the accused or of the facts on which the judgment was based.

Explanation: The question with which we are concerned in this chapter must be distinguished from two matters discussed in Chapter 11. It was pointed out in that chapter that a judgment is conclusive, so far as all persons are concerned, with regard to the state of affairs it actually establishes; the fact, for example, that A is a convict or that B is divorced. In Chapter 11 we also showed how a judgment in civil proceedings may operate as an estoppel between the parties to it, and those claiming under them. Provided certain conditions are fulfilled, the parties and those in privity with them cannot deny the facts on which the judgment was based in subsequent proceedings in which they are acting in the same capacity. The question with which we are now concerned is whether a judgment is evidence of the facts on which it was founded in proceedings between different parties.

Suppose A has obtained a decree of divorce from his wife B involving a finding of her adultery with C. If Mrs. C were to start divorce proceedings against Mr. C on the ground of his adultery with B, could the decree in the previous case of A v. B and C be produced as evidence of C's adultery with B? Suppose that A has been convicted of forging a bill of exchange, is the conviction admissible as evidence of the forgery in proceedings between B and C, subsequent parties to the bill? If A has been convicted of reckless driving or driving without due care and attention, is the conviction admissible evidence of negligence in proceedings brought against A by someone injured in the accident in consequence of which A was convicted?

The decision of the Court of Appeal in *Hollington* v. *F. Hewthorn & Co. Ltd.*[4] answered each of the above questions in the negative. The plaintiff claimed damages from the defendant for injuries arising out of a motor accident on the footing that they were vicariously liable for the negligence of one of their drivers. The driver's conviction for careless driving on the occasion of the accident was tendered as evidence of neg-

---

[4] [1943] K.B. 587; [1943] 2 All E.R. 35.

ligence, but it was rejected by the trial judge, and his decision was affirmed by the Court of Appeal. The main reason for the decision was that the conviction was only evidence of the opinion of the criminal court that the driver was guilty and, as such, it was irrelevant in the subsequent civil proceedings. The conviction was tendered as the equivalent of an assertion by the criminal court of its opinion that the accused was guilty. The reception of the conviction as evidence of negligence would therefore have amounted to the reception of hearsay evidence of opinion. The Court of Appeal expressly stated that a divorce decree was not evidence in subsequent proceedings between different parties of the facts on which it was founded, and they affirmed the view that a conviction for forgery of a bill of exchange would not be admissible as evidence of the forgery in subsequent proceedings on the bill.

Sections 11 and 12 of the Civil Evidence Act 1968 have reversed the effect of *Hollington* v. *F. Hewthorn & Co., Ltd.* on each of the three questions we have so far considered, but there are important vestigial remains applicable to civil cases of what was, before the Act of 1968, the general rule that in proceedings in which one or both of the parties are different, previous judgments and findings are inadmissible as evidence of the facts on which they were based.

(1) *Convictions*

Some examples of the effect of s. 11 of the Civil Evidence Act 1968, abstracted in the article, are that proof of the defendant's conviction of careless driving places the burden of disproving want of care on him in a running down action, proof of a husband's conviction of incest places on him the burden of disproving that incest in subsequent divorce proceedings[5], and, on a claim against an insurance company in respect of a robbery, the company bears the burden of disproving the occurrence of the robbery if someone is shown to have been convicted of that offence. Although the point has not been finally decided, the standard of proof may safely be taken to be that appropriate in all civil cases, proof on a preponderance of probability.

It is an open question whether s. 11 has any further effect than that of placing the burden of disproving the facts upon which the conviction was based on the party denying the

[5] *Taylor* v. *Taylor,* [1970] 2 All E.R. 609.

existence of those facts. Is it incumbent on the defendant in a running down action who has been convicted of careless driving to do more than adduce evidence which, were it not for the conviction, would satisfy the judge that there was no want of care, or must he satisfy the judge that the conviction was wrong by, for instance, explaining why he pleaded guilty, or pointing to fresh evidence or showing that evidence on which the conviction was procured was unreliable? BUCKLEY, L.J. takes the former view, while Lord DENNING takes the latter; but they agree that it is not proper for the judge to ask himself whether he would, had he been a juror, have found the accused guilty on the evidence on which he was in fact convicted[6].

The conviction must be that of a court in the United Kingdom or a Court Martial. Convictions of foreign or Commonwealth tribunals continue to be inadmissible as evidence of the facts on which they were based.

The conviction must also be a "subsisting conviction"; this includes a conviction which is subject to a pending appeal[7], but it does not include a "spent conviction" within the meaning of the Rehabilitation of Offenders Act 1974, although the point is hardly likely to arise in practice owing to the length of time before a conviction becomes spent. In any event the judge has power to admit evidence of a spent conviction under s. 7 (3) of the Act if justice cannot be done otherwise.

(2) *Findings of adultery and paternity*

The effect of s. 12 of the Civil Evidence Act 1968, abstracted in clause 2 of the article, is that, if, in divorce proceedings brought by a husband against his wife, adultery were proved, production of the decree, in subsequent proceedings brought against the co-respondent by his wife, would place on him the burden of disproving that adultery on the balance of probability[8].

A finding of paternity in affiliation proceedings will likewise suffice to establish the respondent's adultery with the mother in divorce proceedings brought by his wife, unless he disproves the adultery (presumably on the balance of probability).

---

[6] *J. W. Stupple* v. *Royal Insurance Co. Ltd.*, [1971] 1 Q.B. 50; [1970] 3 All E.R. 230.

[7] *Re Raphael, Raphael* v. *d'Antin*, [1973] 3 All E.R. 19.

[8] *Sutton* v. *Sutton*, [1969] 3 All E.R. 1348.

Section 12 (5) of the Civil Evidence Act defines "matrimonial proceedings" as "any matrimonial cause in the High Court or a County Court in England and Wales or in the High Court in Northern Ireland, any consistorial action in Scotland, or any appeal arising out of any such cause or action". The effect is that findings of adultery in a Magistrates' Court are excluded. If a husband is found guilty of adultery by such a Court, the finding is inadmissible evidence of his adultery in divorce proceedings in which he is a co-respondent; the finding would likewise be inadmissible as evidence of adultery in support of a plea of justification in a libel action brought by the husband against someone who had referred to him as an adulterer.

(3) *Defamation actions*

Dissatisfaction with the effect of the decision in *Hollington* v. *F. Hewthorn & Co., Ltd.* reached its climax when it was held that a conviction of robbery was inadmissible in support of a plea of justification of a libel alleging that the plaintiff had been guilty of the robbery[9]. It was thought that it would not be enough, in such a case to place the burden of disproving his guilt on the plaintiff because convicted criminals might still be prone to seek to establish their innocence by seeking to have their cases retried whenever there was an opportunity of suing for defamation. Hence the somewhat draconian provisions of s. 13 of the Civil Evidence Act which are abstracted in clause 3 of the article. A spent conviction may be pleaded in justification of a libel or slander, but the plea is liable to be defeated by proof of malice[10].

(4) *Other judgments and findings*

Examples of the effect of the vestigial remains of what is sometimes spoken of as the rule in *Hollington* v. *Hewthorn & Co. Ltd.* have already been mentioned, but there are others. In addition to the cases of a conviction by a foreign court and a magisterial finding of adultery, the following may be cited. A judgment in a civil action between A and B is no evidence of the facts on which it was based in subsequent civil proceedings between B and C. Accordingly, if 20 passengers were injured on a bus and each of them brought separate actions, which for some reason were not consolidated, against the driver, the fact

---

[9] *Goody* v. *Odhams Press Ltd.*, [1967] 1 Q.B. 333; [1966] 3 All E.R. 369.

[10] Rehabilitation of Offenders Act 1974, s. 8.

that he had been found negligent in 19 of those actions would be inadmissible as evidence of negligence in the twentieth. An acquittal is inadmissible as evidence of the innocence of the person acquitted when that fact is relevant in subsequent civil proceedings. Accordingly, if A is acquitted on a charge of murder, and he later sues B for libel in referring to him as a murderer, A cannot rely on his acquittal as evidence of his innocence in answer to B's plea of justification. The verdict of a Coroner's jury is no evidence of the cause of death to which it refers or of any other fact which it finds to have existed[11]. Accordingly, if A is found to have committed suicide while of unsound mind, this finding is inadmissible evidence of A's state of mind in proceedings against an insurance company which alleges that A committed suicide when sane.

ART. 82.—Convictions of persons other than the accused in criminal cases

In a criminal case the conviction of someone other than the accused is inadmissible as evidence of the facts on which it was based.

Explanation:—The rule in *Hollington* v. *Hewthorn & Co. Ltd.* applies to criminal proceedings and, in relation to such proceedings, it has not been in any way abrogated by statute. There are, however, relatively few situations in which the facts on which the conviction of someone other than the accused was founded could be relevant. One example is provided by *Taylor* v. *Wilson*[12]. In that case the licensee of a public house was charged with suffering betting to take place on licensed premises. It was held that a bookmaker's conviction for betting with people resorting to the premises was inadmissible as evidence against the licensee that betting took place there. Further examples are the inadmissibility of the conviction of the thief of certain goods as evidence that those goods were stolen in subsequent proceedings against another person for handling them[13]; the inadmissibility of the conviction of a

---

[11] *Bird* v. *Keep*, [1918] 2 K.B. 692.
[12] (1911), 76 J.P. 69.
[13] *R.* v. *Turner* (1832), 1 Mood. C.C. 347.

woman of being a prostitute as evidence that she was a prostitute in subsequent proceedings against a man for living on her earnings[14]; and the inadmissibility of the conviction of the principal offender as evidence that he was guilty of the offence in proceedings under s. 4 of the Criminal Law Act 1967, for impeding his apprehension.

A fortiori previous findings of civil courts are inadmissible as evidence of the facts on which they were based in subsequent criminal proceedings.

[14] *R.* v. *Hassan,* [1970] 1 Q.B. 423; [1970] 1 All E.R. 745.

CHAPTER 14

Extrinsic Evidence of the Terms of a Document

ART 83.—The exclusiveness and conclusiveness of a document as to its terms

The general rule is that a document is both exclusive and conclusive as evidence of its terms. This means that extrinsic evidence is generally inadmissible (1) to prove the contents of a document, (2) to add to, vary or contradict the terms of a document and (3) to prove the meaning intended by the author of the document.

Explanation: In this chapter, "extrinsic evidence" means any evidence outside the document itself; it includes other documentary evidence as well as oral evidence. The general rule is that, once a transaction has been embodied in a document, the court must refer to the document and nothing else. This means that evidence that might otherwise be considered relevant is excluded, and it is customary to state the rule in its three aspects as an exclusionary rule of evidence, allowing for exceptions in each instance.

(1) *The exclusiveness of a document*

The rule that only the document is evidence of its terms is simply another way of stating the rule, discussed in Article 62, that the contents of a private document can usually only be proved by production of the original. Exceptions to the rule under which secondary evidence may be given of the contents of a document were mentioned in the same article. The general rule does not prevent the reception of extrinsic evidence to connect together two documents when one refers to another; nor does it prevent proof of a fact, such as the relationship of landlord and tenant, established by the document[1]; nor does it

1 *R.* v. *Holy Trinity, Kingston-upon-Hull* (1827), 7 B. & C. 611.

prevent one of the parties to a transaction from adducing evidence that the transaction was in reality an oral one, and that the document was a mere receipt.

In *Allen* v. *Pink*[2], the plaintiff bought a horse from the defendant who handed him a receipt for the price. It was held that the plaintiff might nonetheless prove that the defendant orally warranted that the animal was fit. Whether the writing is to be treated as a receipt or memorandum or whether it will be held to be, not a memorandum of a contract, but itself a contractual document, depends on the intention of the parties. In the absence of direct evidence on this point from one or both of the parties, their intention must be ascertained from the inferences which a reasonable man would draw from the surrounding circumstances.

(2) *Conclusiveness of a document as to its terms*

The rule that extrinsic evidence is inadmissible to add to, vary or contradict the terms of a document likewise depends on the intention of the parties. In *Angell* v. *Duke*[3] the defendant agreed in writing to let a house to the plaintiff together with the furniture therein. The plaintiff tendered evidence that, before the execution of the writing, the defendant had orally agreed to send in additional furniture. It was held that the evidence was inadmissible, because the plaintiff had chosen to execute the writing without making the alleged oral agreement part of it. Additional terms can be proved if it is clear that the transaction between the parties was intended to be partly oral and partly in writing, but, in the case of leases and tenancy agreements, there is a presumption that the writing is intended to be all embracing.

In *Re Sutro (L.) & Co. & Heilbut, Symons & Co.*[4], a written contract provided for the sale of rubber which was to be shipped to New York. It was held that one of the parties could not adduce evidence to show that the agreement was made subject to a common practice of carrying the goods part of the way by rail for to do so would have allowed a variation of the writing. There is no objection to proof of a subsequent variation of a written agreement, provided that variation complies with the ordinary law of contract, i.e. is under seal or

[2] (1838), M. & W. 140.
[3] (1875), L.R. 10 Q.B. 174.
[4] [1917] 2 K.B. 348.

supported by consideration, etc. The rule that extrinsic evidence is inadmissible to add to, vary or contradict the terms of a document is confined to evidence relating to matters occurring before, or at the time of, the execution of the document.

Henderson v. *Arthur*[5] is an example of an attempt to contradict the terms of a written agreement by extrinsic evidence. A lease provided for the payment of rent in advance, and the lessee was not allowed to give evidence of a prior undertaking by the lessor to accept rent in arrears.

Exceptions.—The following are the principal exceptions to the rule that extrinsic evidence is inadmissible to add to, vary or contradict the terms of a document.

(a) *Validity or effectiveness.*—Extrinsic evidence is admissible to show that a written contract or other transaction embodied in a document is void for mistake[6] or illegality[7] or to show the nature of the consideration[8]. The transaction may also be shown to have been voidable for fraudulent or innocent misrepresentation[9], and for this purpose, extrinsic evidence will always be received.

Extrinsic evidence is admissible to show that a deed or written contract, unconditional on its face, was delivered as an escrow or signed subject to a condition precedent as to its effectiveness. In *Pym* v. *Campbell*[10], the defendants agreed in writing to buy an invention from the plaintiff. It was stipulated orally that the transaction was conditional on the approval of the invention by the defendants' engineer. Extrinsic evidence was received concerning this stipulation and the fact that the invention had not been approved by the defendants' engineer.

(b) *Real nature of transaction.*—Extrinsic evidence is admissible to prove the real nature of any transaction. Thus, a will may appear to confer an absolute beneficial interest on a particular person, but this does not prevent the establishment of a secret trust by means of extrinsic evidence.

(c) *Capacity of signatories.*—If someone signs a document as

---

[5] [1907] 1 K.B. 10.
[6] *Henkle* v. *Royal Exchange Assurance Co.* (1749), 1 Ves. Sen. 317.
[7] *Collins* v. *Blantern* (1767), 2 Wils. 347.
[8] *Turner* v. *Forwood,* [1951] 1 All E.R. 746.
[9] *Dobell* v. *Stevens* (1825), 3 B. & C. 623.
[10] (1856), 6 E. & B. 370.

"owner" or "proprietor", extrinsic evidence has been held to be inadmissible to show that he was acting as agent for an undisclosed principal[11]. Such descriptions can only apply to one person, and the extrinsic evidence would inevitably contradict the document. Extrinsic evidence of agency has been received in the case of such other forms of signature as "charterer"[12], "tenant"[13] and "landlord"[14].

(d) *Collateral undertaking.*—We have seen that extrinsic evidence is only excluded when the parties intended, or must be taken to have intended, that the document should embody the entire transaction between them. In many cases the intention will be presumed, but it is always open to one of the parties to seek to establish that the transaction was intended to be partly oral and partly in writing. One way of doing this is for one of the parties to show that, when signing the document, he made it plain that he would not do so unless an oral undertaking was given by the other party. In *De Lassalle* v. *Guildford*[15], the plaintiff made it plain to his landlord, the defendant, that he would not execute a lease unless the defendant gave a warranty concerning the healthy conditions of the drains. The defendant gave the required warranty verbally, and the plaintiff executed the lease. The lease did not refer to the drains, but it was held that this fact did not prevent the plaintiff from adducing evidence concerning the warranty. This case is distinguishable from *Angell* v. *Duke*[16] because, in that case, the tenant was unable to adduce any evidence suggesting that he signed the agreement in consideration, not merely of the written terms, but also of the oral undertaking alleged by him.

(e) *Usage*

"In all contracts as to the subject-matter of which known usages prevail, parties are bound to proceed with the tacit assumption of these usages; they commonly reduce into writing the special particulars of their agreement but omit to specify these known usages, which are included, however, as

---

[11] *Humble* v. *Hunter* (1848), 12 Q.B. 310; *Formby Bros.* v. *Formby* (1910), 102 L.T. 116.

[12] *Drughorn (Fred), Ltd.* v. *Rederiaktiebolaget Trans-Atlantic,* [1919] A.C. 203.

[13] *Danziger* v. *Thompson,* [1944] K.B. 654; [1944] 2 All E.R. 151.

[14] *Epps* v. *Rothnie,* [1945] K.B. 562.

[15] [1901] 2 K.B. 215.

[16] P. 292, *ante*.

of course, by mutual understanding: evidence therefore of such incidents is receivable. The contract in truth is partly express and in writing; partly implied or understood and unwritten."[17]

The rule that extrinsic evidence is inadmissible to add to, vary or contradict the terms of a document is frequently called "the parole evidence rule". Its abolition is tentatively recommended in the Law Commission's Working Paper No. 70 on the ground that it has come to be eroded by exceptions.

(3) *Conclusiveness of document as to meaning of words used*

The general rule is that extrinsic evidence is not admissible to show what the words used in a document were intended to mean. The words must be construed in their ordinary meaning or, where there is one, their legal meaning. Extrinsic evidence is always admissible to prove the existence of persons and things to which the word used might apply. If someone leaves everything by will to his "child" for instance, evidence must be admissible to show that he had a child; but, once it appears that there are in existence or property to which the words used by the testator are capable of applying, extrinsic evidence is generally inadmissible to vary the ordinary or legal meaning of those words as applied to such persons and property.

In *Higgins* v. *Dawson*[18], the question was whether any portion of the legacies left by a testator was payable out of two sums due to his estate from mortgagors. He had bequeathed these sums to named persons, giving those persons "all the residue and remainder" of the sums after "payment of my debts, funeral and testamentary expenses". On the literal meaning of the words used, no portion of the legacies was payable out of the sums due from the mortgagors to the testator, provided the residuary estate was adequate to meet the legacies. There was, however, cogent evidence that the testator intended the mortgage debts to be liable for part of the legacies because, when he made his will, there was, to his knowledge, insufficient residue to meet the legacies. Nevertheless, it was held that extrinsic evidence of intention was inadmissible, because the language used by the testator clearly meant that the residue of the sums due on mortgage was to be calculated without deducting anything in respect of the legacies.

[17] COLERIDGE, J., in *Brown* v. *Byrne* (1854), 3 E. & B. 703.
[18] [1902] A.C. 1.

Striking examples of what may be termed the "plain meaning" rule are provided by cases in which there is a person who was known to a testator who precisely fits the description of a legatee given by the testator in his will although there are strong reasons for supposing that some other person was intended. For example, in *Del Mare* v. *Robello*[19] a gift to the children of the testator's two sisters, Reyne and Estrella, was taken literally although, some 28 years before the will was made, Reyne had become a nun and adopted the name in religion of Maria Hieronyma and the testator had a third sister Rebecca who had children; evidence that she was intended was excluded.

Nevertheless, it is open to question whether the rule is an absolutely rigid one. Perhaps there is simply a very strong presumption that people mean what they say in their considered written documents[20]. In most of the cases, the evidence in favour of a different meaning, as distinct from the grounds for suspecting that the author did not mean what he said, has consisted of somewhat vague declarations.

Exceptions.—There are two groups of exceptions to the general rule prohibiting evidence of the intended meaning of the author of a document. These concern the admissibility of extrinsic evidence to aid in the translation of the document, and the admissibility of such evidence to resolve uncertainties which still exist after the words of the document in their ordinary or legal meaning have been applied to the case.

(a) *Translation.*—If a document is written in a foreign language, evidence of the meaning of the words used is of course admissible; but the same is also true when the author has used a cipher or special language of his own. For example, in *Goblet* v. *Beechey*[1] the judge admitted extrinsic evidence of the intention of a sculptor when making a bequest in the following terms:

"All the marble in the yard, the tools in the shop, bankers, mod tools and carving."

On similar principles, evidence is admissible to show that the author of a document was accustomed to attach a special

---

[19] (1792), 3 Bro. C.C. 446.

[20] *National Society for the Prevention of Cruelty to Children* v. *Scottish National Society for the Prevention of Cruelty to Children,* [1915] A.C. 207.

[1] (1831), 2 Russ. & M. 624.

meaning, accorded by a particular local custom, to the words used by him. In *Smith* v. *Wilson*[2], "a thousand rabbits" was held to mean "1,200 rabbits."

> "Then we must suppose that the parties to this deed used the word 'thousand' with reference to the subject-matter according to the meaning which it received in that part of the country. I cannot say, then, that evidence to show what was the acceptation of the term 'thousand' with reference to this subject-matter ought not to have been received at all."[3]

In the case of documents of some antiquity, extrinsic evidence is admissible to show what was the contemporary meaning of the words used. In *Shore* v. *Wilson*[4], a question arose concerning the effect of a deed conferring benefits on "poor and godly preachers of Christ's holy Gospel". In their commonly accepted meaning, these words would have been too vague to be effective but evidence was admitted to show that, in 1704, when the deed was executed, there existed a religious sect by whom the phrase was used, and of which the lady who executed the deed was a member.

(b) *Uncertainty.*—Extrinsic evidence of intention is admissible whenever there is a misdescription so that, literally construed, the words used apply to nothing. In *Doe d. Hiscocks* v. *Hiscocks*[5], land was devised to "John Hiscocks, the eldest son of John Hiscocks." John Hiscocks had two sons, Simon, the eldest, and John, his second son who, however, was his eldest son by a second marriage. It was held that this fact, and a number of other circumstances, pointing to an intention that the second son should benefit, were admissible in evidence.

When extrinsic evidence is admissible in cases of misdescription, it may consist of testimony concerning the author's relations with other people, his habits of speech and the names by which he referred to persons and things. It may not consist of the author's declarations of his intentions concerning the effect of the document, and evidence of this nature was excluded in *Doe d. Hiscocks* v. *Hiscocks*.

In the very special case of an equivocation, however, these declarations are admissible in addition to the other kinds of

---

[2] (1832), 3 B. & Ad. 728.
[3] Lord TENTERDEN, C.J.
[4] (1842), 9 Cl. & Fin. 355.
[5] (1839), 5 M. & W. 363.

extrinsic evidence. There is an equivocation when the words used are equally applicable to two persons or things. In *Doe d. Gord* v. *Needs*[6], land was devised to "George Gord, the son of Gord". Extrinsic evidence showed that there were two persons answering that description, and extrinsic evidence was admitted of the testator's declarations of intention, indicating which of the two he meant to benefit.

The reason for the general exclusion of the testator's declarations of intention in aid of the construction of his will was presumably the unreliable nature of the evidence; it is hearsay, and it is arguable that it has been rendered admissible in all cases by s.2 (1) of the Civil Evidence Act 1968, set out on p. 132. Conversely it is arguable, on a very literal construction of s. 2 (1), that the testator's declarations of intention have ceased to be admissible in aid of the interpretation of his will even in cases of equivocation. The subsection allows statements to be proved "as evidence of any fact stated therein of which direct oral evidence by [the maker] would be admissible", and, ex hypothesi, deceased testators cannot give direct oral evidence of the intentions they entertained when making their wills. It would be a great pity if the courts were to adopt such a pedantic construction of the statute, for it would mean that statements by deceased testators concerning the contents of their wills would be inadmissible, whereas they were certainly admissible before the Act under a common law exception to the rule against hearsay[7]. Assuming the pedantic construction is not adopted, an argument that the Act has rendered the testator's declarations of intention admissible in aid of interpretation in all cases can only be resisted by an argument that the general inadmissibility of the testator's declarations of intention and their exceptional reception in cases of equivocation are independent rules of evidence and not merely instances of the hearsay rule and an exception to it; it could then be urged that the Civil Evidence Act 1968 was not intended to affect them.

An equivocation is an ambiguity in the strict sense of that word, but all uncertainties and misdescriptions are sometimes called "ambiguities". It is also sometimes said that extrinsic evidence is only admissible to resolve a latent, but not a patent ambiguity, but the authorities are against this view[8].

---

[6] (1836), 2 M. & W. 129.

[7] *Sugden* v. *Lord St. Leonards* (1876), 1 P.D. 154.

[8] *Colpoys* v. *Colpoys* (1822), Jac. 451.

Proposals for reform

The 19th report of the Law Reform Committee recommends that extrinsic evidence should be admissible for the purpose of—(a) establishing the special meaning or significance which the testator was accustomed to attach to any word, name or expression used in the will, or (b) of establishing, as well as resolving, an ambiguity in a will. The effect of the adoption of this recommendation would be, so far as (a) is concerned, to overrule old cases such as *Doe d. Chichester* v. *Oxenden*[9] where "my estate of Ashton" was held to comprise no more than lands locally situated at Ashton in spite of the fact that the testator and his steward had repeatedly spoken of "the Ashton estate" as including other lands; the effect of the second part of the recommendation would be to overrule *Higgins* v. *Dawson*[10]. The majority of the Committee was in favour of continuing the present prohibition on the admissibility of the testator's declarations of intention save in the exceptional case of an equivocation as defined above.

---

[9] (1810), 3 Taunt. 147.
[10] *Supra.*

PART III

Miscellaneous

CHAPTER 15

Evidence in civil and criminal cases, judicial discretion and the 11th report of the Criminal Law Revision Committee

At different points in this book, attention has been drawn to the fact that a particular rule applies in civil cases only or in criminal cases only, and to the existence of a judicial discretion to exclude certain items of evidence. In this chapter we collect together the principal differences between civil and criminal cases so far as the law of evidence is concerned, and discuss generally the judicial discretion to exclude evidence. The chapter concludes with a brief account of the controversial 11th report of the Criminal Law Revision Committee mentioned in the introduction.

Evidence in civil and criminal cases

The general rule is that the law of evidence is the same in civil and criminal cases. The following list indicates the principal points at which it differs.

(1) The standard of proof demanded of the prosecution in a criminal case is higher than that demanded of either party to civil litigation.

(2) The accused is not a compellable witness in a criminal case; either party to civil litigation is compellable at the instance of the other although it is of course rare in practice for plaintiffs to call defendants as their witnesses and vice versa.

(3) Special rules govern the competence and compellability of the accused's spouse in a criminal case; the spouses of the parties to civil litigation are always compellable witnesses.

(4) The accused may make an unsworn statement in a criminal case; there is no counterpart to this right in a civil case.

(5) A child who, though not appreciating the nature of an oath, understands the duty of telling the truth, can give

unsworn evidence in a criminal case; in civil cases, the evidence of children must be sworn.

(6) The rules concerning corroboration differ according to whether the case is civil or criminal. The only civil case in which corroboration is required as a matter of law is that of affiliation, for the rest there are more or less strict rules of practice in the cases of matrimonial causes and claims against the estates of deceased persons, nothing like the rigorous requirements of the warning in certain criminal cases.

(7) There is no issue estoppel, estoppel by conduct or deed in a criminal case.

(8) The rules governing the reception of evidence of character differ according to whether the case is civil or criminal.

(9) The rules concerning the admissibility of witnesses' previous statements and hearsay differ according to whether the case is civil or criminal. In civil cases these matters are now governed by the general provisions of the Civil Evidence Acts of 1968 and 1972, while the common law, modified by a number of particular statutes, applies in criminal cases. In criminal cases there are special rules governing the admissibility of confessions.

(10) The rules with regard to a witness's privilege differ according to whether the case is civil or criminal. The privileges with regard to marital communications, questions concerning marital intercourse and the production of title deeds now only apply to criminal cases.

(11) In criminal cases the conviction of someone other than the accused is inadmissible as evidence of the facts on which it was based, whereas, in civil cases, convictions, findings of adultery and findings of paternity are admissible as evidence of the facts on which they were based.

Some of these differences are difficult to justify, but others are attributable to the necessity of protecting the accused. The accused needed a great deal of protection in former times when he could not give evidence or, in the case of felony, be fully represented by counsel in the sense that a closing speech might be made on his behalf. It is open to question whether he needs quite so much protection nowadays, although the dislike of obliging people to criminate themselves which lies at the root of the accused's right not to give evidence, and the fear of arousing undue prejudice in the minds of the jurors or magistrates, which lies at the root of the exclusion of similar fact evidence and rules governing the admissibility of evidence of character, is undoubtedly a serious one.

In practice the rules of evidence are applied more strictly in criminal than in civil cases. On the other hand, the judicial discretion to exclude evidence is exercised far more frequently in criminal cases. Indeed it is arguable that, "when it comes to the forensic crunch" at a civil trial, there is no exclusionary discretion[1].

Judicial discretion

(1) *Criminal cases*.—The speeches in the House of Lords in *R.* v. *Sang*[2] must be the starting point of any discussion of such a discretion in a criminal case. The actual decision, confirming the decisions of the trial judge and Court of Appeal, was that there is no discretion to exclude evidence procured by police entrapment because, as a matter of substantive law, such entrapment is no defence. But the case was argued on a broader basis and the following question was certified by the Court of Appeal for consideration by the House of Lords:

> "Does a trial judge have a discretion to refuse to allow evidence – being evidence other than evidence of admissions – to be given in any circumstances in which such evidence is relevant and of more than minimal probative value?"

The answer of the House of Lords was:

> "(1) A trial judge at a criminal trial has always a discretion to refuse to admit evidence if in his opinion its prejudicial effect outweighs its probative value. (2) Save with regard to admissions and confessions and generally with regard to evidence obtained from the accused after the commission of the offence, he has no discretion to refuse to admit relevant admissible evidence on the ground that it was obtained by improper or unfair means. The court is not concerned with how it was obtained."

The general tenor of the speeches was that there is but one basis of the exclusionary discretion in a criminal case, the paramount necessity of ensuring a fair trial for the accused.

---

[1] See *per* Lord SIMON OF GLAISDALE in *D.* v. *N.S.P.C.C.*, [1978] A.C. 171, at p. 239.

[2] [1979] 2 All E.R. 1222.

The following propositions seem to be reasonably clear:

(a) There is a discrection to exclude similar fact evidence[3], cross-examination under the Criminal Evidence Act 1898[4] and statements in the presence of the parties[5] when their prejudicial propensity outweighs their probative value; and

(b) there is a discretion to exclude confessions which, though voluntary, were obtained either in breach of the Judges' Rules or in circumstances in which the accused has been unfairly made to incriminate himself;[6] and

(c) by way of extension of the discretion with regard to confessions, the judge has power to exclude an accountant's books obtained in consequence of a statment that he would not be prosecuted if he produced them[7], or the results of a medical examination of a consenting accused who had, however, not been warned that they might be put in evidence against him[8].

It is reasonably clear that the judge has a discretion to exclude evidence obtained in consequence of an illegal search when the accused's consent to it was obtained by a trick. For no obvious reason it is less clear that there is a discretion to exclude evidence obtained in consequence of an illegal search to which there was no consent of any kind as in *Jeffery* v. *Black*[9].

(2) *Civil cases.*—There is no doubt that the judge exercises a considerable persuasive power at a civil trial to procure the exclusion of legally admissible evidence if he thinks that it ought not to be tendered or elicited. In *D.* v. *N.S.P.C.C.*[10], however, the House of Lords was evenly divided upon the question whether, when his moral persuasive powers have been exhausted, the judge has power to direct a witness that he need not answer certain questions, such as those addressed to a priest about the confessional, or to a doctor concerning his patients. Outside the realm of privilege, the question of the existence of an exclusionary discretion at a civil trial seems never to have been fully discussed judicially.

---

[3] P. 266, *supra*.
[4] P. 281, *supra*.
[5] P. 147, *supra*.
[6] P. 167, *supra*.
[7] *R.* v. *Barker,* [1941] 2 K.B. 381; [1941] 3 All E.R. 33.
[8] *R.* v. *Payne,* p. 234, *supra*.
[9] [1978] Q.B. 490; [1978] 1 All E.R. 555.
[10] [1978] A.C. 171.

(3) *Exclusionary nature of the discretion.*—Whether the case is a civil or criminal one, the discretion of the judge is almost wholly an exclusionary discretion. He may exclude evidence which is legally admissible, but, at common law, he may not, at discretion, admit evidence which is legally inadmissible[11]. Under the Civil Evidence Act 1968, however, and R.S.C. Ord. 38, r. 29 the court has power to admit evidence in spite of non-compliance with the conditions of admissibility prescribed by the Act. This is an inclusionary discretion and must be regarded as an isolated instance.

The 11th report of the Criminal Law Revision Committee

Many of the proposals of the 11th report of the Criminal Law Revision Committee came in for severe criticism, and none of them has been adopted. The following is no more than a brief summary of the principal suggestions and major criticisms. Some of them will no doubt come up for further discussion when the report of the Royal Commission on Criminal Procedure is published.

1. Two recommendations would tend to restrict the reliance by a suspect or the accused on what has come to be known as "the right to silence"[12]. They are first that the court or jury should have power to draw such inferences as appear proper from the accused's failure, when interrogated by a police officer, to mention any fact relied on by him at his trial which he might reasonably be expected to have mentioned; the second is that the court or jury should have power to draw proper inferences from the accused's failure to give evidence. No doubt common sense suggests that a man's omission to mention before his trial the fact that he only entered the house he is charged with having burgled for the sake of warmth and sleep indicates that the defence is probably bogus, and this may in its turn prompt the conclusion that there is no defence; but critics think that the Committee's first proposal would place too much power in the hands of police and operate unfairly against the inadequate or inarticulate suspect. The accused's failure to answer a *prima facie* case made against him in court certainly suggests that there is no answer, but there may have been other reasons for his not testifying, the fact, for example, that he feared cross-examination on his compromising, though

---

[11] *Myers* v. *Director of Public Prosecutions,* [1965] A.C. 1001, at p. 1024; [1964] 2 All E.R. 881, at p. 893.

[12] P. 100, *ante*.

innocent, association with the prosecutrix in a sexual case.

2. It is suggested that a confession should only be inadmissible if made in consequence of oppressive treatment of the accused or of a threat or inducement of a sort likely to render the confession unreliable[13]. No doubt there is an element of unreality about some of the decisions according to which confessions have been held not to have been made voluntarily, but the critics consider that the proposal might lead to minor, and thence to major, police improprieties.

3. After proposing the statutory formulation of the rule concerning similar fact evidence like that contained in Articles 75 and 76, the Committee suggests that the sphere of admissibility of such evidence should be enlarged by a provision under which, in cases in which the *actus reus* of the crime charged is admitted, evidence of the improper conduct of the accused should be admissible as tending to prove *mens rea* on the occasion under investigation although it is only relevant because it tends to show a disposition to commit the kind of offence charged. In such a case it is also proposed that previous convictions of similar offences should be admissible even though no evidence is adduced concerning the facts on which they were based. The proposal does not lack logical support because a greater strain is placed on the court's credulity when an accused with previous convictions for fraud admits that he obtained property in consequence of a false statement, but says that he had no intent to defraud, than is the case when someone with such convictions denies that he made the statement at all; but the critics are opposed to the extension of the ambit of admissibility of evidence of this nature on account of its prejudicial tendencies.

4. A modification, favourable to the accused, of s. 1 (f) of the Criminal Evidence Act 1898[14] is proposed. It relates to cases in which the nature or conduct of the defence is such as to cast imputations on the character of the prosecutor or witnesses for the prosecution. The effect of the proposal would be that the accused would only lose his shield if the main purpose of casting the imputations was to discredit the prosecutor or his witnesses and not directly to further the defence of the accused. If the proposal were adopted, *Selvey* v. *Director of Public Prosecutions*[15] would be overruled; some members of the

[13] Article 46.
[14] Article 80.
[15] P. 281, *ante*.

Committee favoured the total repeal of that part of s. 1 (f) which deals with imputations.

5. Another proposal favourable to the accused is that in all cases in which the common law or statute casts a burden on him, that burden should be the burden of adducing evidence and not the burden of proof[16]. The adoption of this proposal would mean, among other things, that the ultimate burden of disproving insanity or diminished responsibility would be borne by the prosecution while *R.* v. *Edwards*[17] would be overruled.

6. It is proposed that the accused's spouse should be a competent witness for the prosecution in all cases though only compellable on charges of violence by the accused against him or her or a member of the household under sixteen, or of a sexual offence committed by the accused against such a person[18]. There has not been much significant criticism of this recommendation, and its adoption, together with that of some subsidiary proposals would greatly simplify the law.

7. This would also be the effect of adopting the proposals to abolish the privileges concerning marital communications and marital intercourse, mentioned in Articles 30 and 31.

8. Another non-controversial recommendation is that the evidence of witnesses beneath the age of fourteen should always be unsworn, but subject to penalties for wilful falsity and admissible if the witness is possessed of sufficient intelligence to justify the reception of the evidence and understands the importance of telling the truth in the particular case.

9. Substantial changes in the law relating to corroboration are proposed. It is suggested that, subject to minor amendments, the statutory requirement of corroboration should continue in the case of perjury; corroboration by evidence implicating the accused in a material particular would also be required in the case of the complainant's evidence on a sexual charge when he or she is under fourteen. In other sexual cases it will be necessary to warn the jury of the need for special caution where there is no corroboration of the complainant's testimony. Apart from the above cases, there would be no requirements of corroboration or of a warning of the dangers of convicting in its absence except that a warning of the need

---

[16] Articles 5–6.

[17] P. 33, *ante*.

[18] See now *Hoskyn* v. *Metropolitan Police Commissioner*, [1978] 2 All E.R. 136.

for special caution would have to be given in cases of disputed identification. The critics deplore the suggestion that the requirement of a corroboration warning should be abolished in the case of accomplices, and we shall see in the next chapter that the problem of identification evidence has been dealt with more fully by the courts.

10. It is suggested that s. 11 of the Civil Evidence Act 1968 should be made applicable to criminal cases[19].

11. It is also suggested that the provisions of Part 1 of the 1968 Act concerning hearsay should, subject to necessary modifications, be applied to criminal cases[20]. This is not the place for a detailed consideration of the proposal, but two criticisms may be mentioned. In the first place it is said that it would be wrong to apply s. 3 of the 1968 Act, under which contradictory statements of a witness may be treated as evidence of the facts stated[1], to a criminal case, on account of the danger that the statement may have been taken, in the case of a Crown witness, by an over-enthusiastic police officer, and, in the case of a defence witness, by an over-enthusiastic solicitor. Secondly it is said that it would be wrong to allow the extrajudicial statement of one of two co-accused to be admissible evidence against the other, especially when the maker of the statement does not testify. This is on account of the dangerous tendency of one of two suspects to "cut the other's throat".

12. Finally it is suggested that the provisions of the Civil Evidence Act 1972, relating to opinion evidence, should be applied to criminal cases; there has been no violent objection to this proposal.

---

[19] Articles 81–2.

[20] Articles 39–41.

[1] P. 89, *ante*.

CHAPTER 16

Proof of frequently recurring Facts

Opinions may well differ with regard to the number of facts which should be included in a chapter of this sort. We will deal with evidence of identity, proof of foreign law, proof of birth, age, marriage, legitimacy and death, proof of judgments and convictions, and proof of the existence of a custom. Proof of handwriting was dealt with in Article 59, proof of bankers' books was discussed on pp. 210–11, and proof of a vast number of public documents was mentioned in Article 63.

Identity

Identity, like any other fact, may be proved by direct or circumstantial evidence. Typical examples of the use of circumstantial evidence to establish identity are provided by evidence of fingerprints and other physical resemblances. Nothing further need be said with regard to circumstantial evidence of identity, but the courts have approved of certain precautionary practices to be taken with regard to direct evidence of identification at a criminal trial, and something must be said of these.

At first sight it might seem that there could not be better evidence of the identification of the accused than the direct statement of a witness in court that the accused is "the man"; but the witness is all too apt to think that the police must have got hold of the right man, with the result that he may be prepared to swear positively to a fact of which he is by no means certain. It has therefore been held that it is undesirable for the police to do nothing about the question of identification until the accused is brought before the court. An identification parade should first have been held, the suspect being placed together with a number of other people, and the witness being left to point him out if he can. The Court of Appeal may quash a conviction, if the police have attempted to point the accused out beforehand to someone who is then asked to identify him.

Great precautions must be taken in the use of photographs.

> "It is one thing for a police officer, who is doubtful upon the question who shall be arrested, to show a photograph to another person in order to obtain information or a clue upon that matter; it is another thing for a police officer dealing with witnesses who are afterwards to be called as identifying witnesses to show to those persons photographs of those whom they are about to be asked to identify beforehand. The fair thing is . . . to show a series of photographs, and to see if the person who is expected to give information can pick out the prospective defendant."[1]

Even when these precautions have been taken, it is desirable to guard against informing the jury that the witness's identification of the accused before trial had been made possible by means of a photograph in the possession of the police. Otherwise the jury would assume that the accused had a criminal record.

If the identifying witness is uncertain at the trial whether the accused is the person he or she picked out at the parade, it has been held that a police officer who was present may swear that the accused was identified by the witness at the parade[2]. It is difficult to see why this decision does not infringe the rule against hearsay because the pointing out of the accused by the identifying witness is the equivalent of his statement "That is the man I saw commit the crime."

Concern about convictions in cases in which it subsequently appeared that the accused had been wrongly identified led to the appointment of a committee under the chairmanship of Lord DEVLIN. Its report, published in 1976, recommended that, as a general rule, there should not be a conviction in a case in which the evidence of identification was visual, even if there were more than one identifying witness. The general rule was to be subject to exceptions in special circumstances to be worked out in practice. One example would be a case in which the identifying witness was familiar with the accused.

In *R.* v. *Turnbull and others*[3] the Court of Appeal laid down guide-lines of a less drastic nature. The Court was opposed to the proposed general rule subject to exceptions, but said that

---

[1]Lord HEWART, C.J., in *R.* v. *Dwyer,* [1925] 2 K.B. 799, at p. 802.
[2]*R.* v. *Osbourne and Virtue,* [1973] Q.B 678; [1973] 1 All E.R. 649.
[3][1977] Q.B. 244; [1976] 3 All E.R. 549.

the judge should direct an acquittal if he considered that the evidence of visual identification was of poor quality. If the case is left to the jury, there must be a warning of the special need for caution before convicting on visual identification alone. Furthermore, the judge must explain the reason for the need of such caution and direct the jury to examine the circumstances closely. The jury should be reminded that a mistaken witness can be convincing, and that a false alibi only supports the identification evidence if they are satisfied that it was advanced in order to deceive them and for no other reason.

Foreign law

Foreign law is a question of fact, and it must normally be proved by an expert witness. There is a good deal of case law on what constitutes a suitable qualification. There is no doubt that a judge or practitioner in the courts of the country whose law has to be proved is suitably qualified; but, from time to time, the English courts have been less exacting in their requirements. The reader in Roman Dutch law at the Council of Legal Education has, for example, been held qualified to testify to the provisions of Roman Dutch law[4]; but, in *Bristow* v. *Sequeville*[5], it was held that a jurisconsult, adviser to the Prussian embassy in England, who had taken a law degree at Leipzig (part of a territory governed by the Code Napoleon), was not qualified to testify concerning the provisions of the Code. It is almost certain that this decision goes too far, and s. 4 (1) of the Civil Evidence Act 1972 puts the matter beyond doubt in civil proceedings by declaring that the evidence may be given by a suitably qualified person irrespective of whether he has acted or is entitled to act as legal practitioner in the foreign country concerned.

In a strictly limited number of cases, expert evidence of foreign law is unnecessary. Very exceptionally, judicial notice may be taken of a provision of foreign law as a notorious fact: that roulette is legal in Monte Carlo[6], for example. Judicial notice may also be taken of the common law of Northern Ireland, and, in the House of Lords, judicial notice will be taken of the provisions of Scots law. In maintenance proceedings, judicial notice must be taken of the law of all parts of the United Kingdom on the subject of maintenance[7].

---

[4]*Brailey* v. *Rhodesia Consolidated, Ltd.*, [1910] 2 Ch. 95.
[5](1850), 5 Exch. 275.
[6]*Saxby* v. *Fulton*, [1909] 2 K.B. 208.
[7]Maintenance Orders Act 1950, s. 22 (2).

The Evidence (Colonial Statutes) Act 1907 provides for the reception in evidence by all courts of the United Kingdom of the statutes and ordinances of any British Possession; if printed by the Government Printer of the Possession, no proof of their having been passed by the legislature is necessary. When such a statute is before the English courts, they are often prepared to construe its provisions without the assistance of expert evidence. A "British Possession" includes any part of Her Majesty's Dominions apart from the United Kingdom.

An English judge may even construe a foreign statute himself if the statute has been properly put in evidence as part of the foreign law by an expert; but he should be slow to do so where the expert's evidence is uncontradicted[8].

Under s. 4 (2) of the Civil Evidence Act 1972, findings in reported cases concerning the law of a foreign country are admissible evidence of that fact in civil proceedings.

Birth

There are three ways in which the fact and date of a person's birth may be proved. When considering them, and when considering the ways of proving marriage, legitimacy and death, the student should bear in mind that it is often necessary to prove these matters long after they have occurred.

The first, and most usual, method of proving birth is the production of a birth certificate. This is evidence of the facts stated, under the exception to the hearsay rule relating to statements in public documents discussed in article 43. It is only necessary to produce the certificate to the court, no proof of the original entry or the accuracy of the copy is required. The court will, however, require some evidence identifying the person whose birth is in question with the person whose birth is certified. Unless the matter is disputed, only slight *prima facie* evidence is required, and it may take the form of a statement by a witness that the two persons are identical. Certificates of baptism may be received in cases in which the birth was not registered because it took place before compulsory registration.

The second method by which birth may be proved is under three exceptions to the hearsay rule, discussed in Articles 48–50, now only applicable to criminal cases, relating to the declarations of deceased persons against interest, in the course of duty or with regard to pedigree. Two of them, declarations

[8]*Sharif* v. *Azad,* [1967] 1 Q.B. 605; [1966] 3 All E.R. 785, at p. 788.

against interest and in the course of duty, may be proved as evidence of the facts stated in all proceedings, while the third, declarations of pedigree, can only be proved on genealogical issues. In civil cases, the fact and date of birth may be proved under the Civil Evidence Act 1968 by any relevant statements or records or by evidence of reputation.

A third method of proving birth is by means of the evidence of someone who was present when it took place.

Age

One of the most frequently quoted examples of the broad effect of the rule against hearsay is that it prevents a person from giving evidence of his own age, as his information on the subject must necessarily be derived from what other people have told him. There are, however, four well-recognised ways in which age may be proved.

In the first place, proof of the date of a person's birth is a means of proving his age. Accordingly age can be proved by production of a birth certificate coupled with evidence of identity.

Secondly, age may be proved in criminal cases by means of the three types of declaration of deceased persons referred to in Articles 48–50. In civil cases age may be proved by relevant statements and records admissible under the Civil Evidence Act 1968.

Thirdly, age may be proved by someone who was present at the birth of the person whose age is in question.

Finally, in certain specified proceedings, age may be proved by inference from a person's appearance[9].

Marriage

There are four ways of establishing a valid marriage, and, in the case of marriages celebrated outside England and Wales, there may be a complicating factor, on account of the necessity of establishing that the ceremony constituted a valid marriage according to the law of the place of celebration.

In the first place, reliance may be placed on the presumption of a marriage ceremony from the cohabitation and repute of the parties discussed on p. 55.

The remaining three ways of establishing a marriage ceremony are the same as those discussed in connection with

---

[9]Children and Young Persons Act 1933, s. 99; Criminal Justice Act 1948, s. 80 (3); Magistrates' Courts Act 1952, s. 126 (5); Sexual Offences Act 1956, s. 12 (3), 15 (5) and 28 (5).

proof of birth. A marriage certificate may be produced, and evidence of identity given; the evidence will usually be that of one of the parties when available. In criminal cases, reliance may be placed on the declarations of deceased persons against interest, in the course of duty and, on genealogical issues, declarations as to pedigree; in civil cases reliance may be placed on statements, records and evidence of reputation by virtue of the Civil Evidence Act 1968. Evidence of the due celebration of the ceremony may be given by someone who was present at it. The court will require production of the certificate wherever this is possible.

Foreign Ceremony

If the ceremony took place in England or Wales, the certificate is evidence of the marriage to which it relates; but, in other cases, the general rule is that some evidence of formal validity under the local law must be given. This is just as true of an Irish marriage as of one celebrated in a wholly foreign country[10].

There are, however, a number of exceptions to the general rule, and proof of foreign law is unnecessary when one of them applies. The chief of these exceptions relate to marriages celebrated in Scotland and Northern Ireland, marriages celebrated in countries to which the Evidence (Foreign, Dominion and Colonial Documents) Act 1933 has been applied by order in council and marriages celebrated under the Foreign Marriage Act 1892. In the first two cases proof is by certificate, and in the third it is only necessary to show that the requirements of the statute which relates to the marriage of British subjects abroad were complied with. The Act of 1933 provides for the recognition of foreign certificates of birth, death and marriage in England. It has been applied to quite a large number of countries abroad and in the Commonwealth. In an uncontested case a foreign marriage certificate will probably be accepted as evidence of a valid foreign marriage under the Civil Evidence Act 1968[11], and, in matrimonial proceedings in which the validity of the marriage is not disputed it may be proved by the evidence of one of the parties and the production of a foreign marriage certificate or similar document, or of a certified entry in a foreign register[12].

---

[10] *Todd* v. *Todd*, [1961] 2 All E.R. 881.

[11] *Henaff* v. *Henaff*, [1966] 1 W.L.R. 598.

[12] Matrimonial Causes Rules 1977, r. 40.

Legitimacy

A person's legitimacy may be established by reliance on the presumption of legitimacy discussed in Article 13. Alternatively, reliance may be placed in a criminal case on one of the three declarations by deceased persons mentioned in Articles 48–50; and in a civil case reliance may be placed on statements, records and evidence of pedigree under the Civil Evidence Act 1968. Finally, a declaration of legitimacy constitutes a judgment *in rem* and is binding on all the world on principles discussed on p. 237.

Death

There are six ways in which death may be established.

In the first place, reliance may be placed on the presumption of death discussed in Article 15.

Secondly, quite apart from any question of the application of the presumption, death may be proved by inference from the fact that someone has been unheard of for a long time. The circumstances in which the inference will be warranted will vary enormously, relevant considerations being the age and state of health of the person in question, when he was last heard of, the circumstances in which he disappeared and the inquiries that were made.

Thirdly, death may be proved by someone who was present at its occurrence.

Fourthly, death may be proved by someone who has identified the corpse.

Fifthly, death may be proved by production of the death certificate coupled with evidence of identity.

Sixthly, death may be proved in a criminal case by any of the three declarations of deceased persons mentioned in Articles 48–50, and in civil cases under the appropriate sections of the Civil Evidence Act 1968.

Judgments and convictions

(1) *Civil cases.*—A judgment of the House of Lords may be proved by production of the journal of the House. Judgments of the Court of Appeal and High Court are proved by production of an office copy. Judgments of the County Court and Magistrates' Court are proved by production of certified extracts from the Courts' books. Foreign or colonial judgments may be proved by production of an examined copy or, more usually, by a copy sealed with the seal of the foreign court under s. 7 of the Evidence Act 1851.

In all the above cases, production of the relevant document will usually be sufficient to establish its authenticity because judicial notice will be taken of the seal or certificate attached to the document, but, in the absence of an admission, oral evidence will be required to identify the parties to the judgment with the persons whose rights the court is considering or those through whom such persons claim.

(2) *Criminal cases.*—A conviction on indictment may be proved under a number of statutory provisions. A certified copy of the relevant parts of the court's record is admissible under three of these[13]. The certification is by the clerk to the court, but evidence of identity is necessary, and is usually provided by someone who was present in court at the time of the conviction.

Another method of proving convictions on indictment is provided for by s. 39 of the Criminal Justice Act 1948. The conviction may be proved by means of fingerprints or palm-prints. There must be a certificate of conviction by or on behalf of the Commissioner of Metropolitan Police exhibiting a copy of the fingerprints or palm-prints of the person convicted. A second certificate is signed by or on behalf of the governor of the prison or remand centre where the person in question was detained; this too exhibits fingerprints or palm-prints taken while the person was detained. Finally there is a third certificate signed by or on behalf of the Commissioner of Metropolitan Police stating that the two sets of fingerprints are identical.

A conviction after a summary trial may be proved by a certified copy together with evidence of identity. Section 39 of the Criminal Justice Act 1948 also applies to summary cases.

Under s. 101 (1) of the Road Traffic Act 1972, the indorsement of a licence is *prima facie* evidence of a conviction for the relevant traffic offence.

Custom

The existence of a custom may be proved in four ways. First, direct evidence may be given by a witness of his personal knowledge of the custom's existence. Secondly, a witness may testify to particular instances in which the custom has been exercised. Thirdly, evidence may be given of a comparable custom in similar localities or trades. Finally, reliance may be

---

[13]Evidence Act 1851, s. 13; Criminal Procedure Act 1865, s. 6; Prevention of Crimes Act 1871, s. 18.

placed on the exception to the rule against hearsay relating to statements by deceased persons concerning public rights discussed in Article 51. This exception is preserved, in so far as it involves second hand hearsay, by s. 9 of the Civil Evidence Act 1968.

INDEX

F